The
Serious
Investor's TAX
SURVIVAL
GUIDE

Ted Tesser MS, CPA

 Traders' Library • Ellicott City, Maryland

This publication is designed to provide accurate and authoritative information in regard to the subject matter covered. It is sold with the understanding that the publisher is not engaged in rendering legal, accounting, or other professional service. If legal advice or other expert assistance is required, the services of a competent professional person should be sought. *From a Declaration of Principles jointly adopted by a Committee of the American Bar Association and a Committee of Publishers.*

ISBN 1–883272–00–9

This Book Is Dedicated
To Murray B. Tesser.

Acknowledgements

I want to extend my appreciation to Charles Morrow for technically reviewing the transcript, and for his assistance in researching this material. Additionally, I would like to thank Mark Press, Esq., for his input in the sections on retirement and estate planning. I also want to thank A. Dennis and B. Liby for their assistance in the typing of this manuscript. These people have been instrumental in the completion of this book.

A special acknowledgement to my family, Mrs. Dorothy Tesser, Dr. Larry Tesser and Mrs. Nettie Wool, for their continual support. Without them this book never would have been written.

Also, I'd like to acknowledge the memory of Hyman Wool, Herbert Wool, and Arthur Wool.

Thanks to Jeff Freiert, Jeff Whinston, Justin Sterling, Rolling Thunder, Dr.Gerald Herman, Dr. John Graham, Marion McGarry, Tom Bunzel, Bob Goodman, and my publishers at Traders' Library for the unique role they each played in the production of this book.

Special Thanks to my wife and "True Companion" Jane Davis Tesser for her overall support and editorial assistance. She has been an integral part of this project as well as my life.

Table of Contents

Table of Contents

Chapter Four
Tax Facts
Concepts Investors Need to Know 33

Chapter Five
Tax Classification
The Three Baskets of Income 43

Chapter Six
Expenses Allowable as Deductions 55

Table of Contents

Chapter Ten
Playing For Keeps With the IRS 151

Chapter Eleven
Retirement Plans 173

Chapter Twelve
Transferring Your Wealth
to Future Generations 197

List of Exhibits

Chapter 10

Chapter 11

Chapter 12

Chapter 1

Investment Taxation
Who Cares?

Story of Phantom Gain on a Losing Investment

A client was referred to me last tax season by a colleague to analyze a rather extensive investment portfolio. The portfolio consisted of a combination of standard investments, including stocks, bonds, mutual funds. Some of these investments needed to be analyzed for their tax status. Several of the items in the portfolio were new to the investment scene in 1990 and I had not anticipated that they would present a problem. Upon further examination, however, I discovered that they did.

The investments I am referring to were put warrants on the Nikkei, the Japanese stock index similar to the U.S. OEX or Dow Jones Industrial Average. These put warrants had been purchased for Madam X by her investment advisor, who had, in fact, made a very good call from a pure investment point of view.

The puts which were purchased in June, 1990, for approximately $10,000, had virtually doubled in price by year end, and were worth $19,500 on December 31. (As you recall, the second half of 1990 was a disaster in the foreign and domestic markets due to the Iraqi war.) So here we had a "very good investment," a doubler in terms of price in just six months. The investment advisor, however, failed to do one very important piece of research before these puts were purchased – that was to consult with a tax advisor as to the taxability of these new trading vehicles.

You see, the Internal Revenue Code has very strict classifications of investments, and some of these have no apparent logic to them. The I.R.C. considers put warrants on the Nikkei to be "regulated futures contracts" subject to being "marked to market" at year end. In other words, whether or not the investor sells the puts by year end or still has them in the portfolio, there is no difference from a tax standpoint. The put warrants must be treated as if they were sold on December 31, and a gain or loss is taken on the tax return for that year based on the closing price at year end.

Now getting back to Madam X, who, as I said before, had a $9,500 profit in the put warrants on December 31, 1990. The advisor believed that the market was going down further in 1991, and Madam X held onto the puts, as they did not expire until early 1992. As it turns out this was not a very good call by the investment advisor. The Persian Gulf War was over shortly, and in January 1991 the domestic and foreign markets took off. This poor investment decision was compounded greatly by his lack of tax planning.

By the time I reviewed the portfolio in March of 1991, the Dec. 31st gain of $9,500 had completely evaporated. In fact, the $10,000 investment was now worth only $4,500 – i.e., they now had a **loss** of $5,500. Aside from my feelings about position management which would have precluded me from watching a $9,500 profit turn into a $5,500 loss, the loss was actually exacerbated by the tax consequences.

I was forced to recognize the $9,500 gain on Madam X's 1990 tax return even though no gain was actually realized. The 40% tax (federal, state, and city) had to be paid on this phantom gain and the result was an additional $3,800 tax liability. At this point, they sold the put warrants for $4,500 to cover the additional tax. Thus, the total loss, including taxes, was virtually the entire investment.

There will, of course, be a capital carryforward loss of $15,000 which can be used to offset future gains; and $3000 of it can be deducted straight out on the 1991 tax return. But, this is small consolation to my client compared to the immediate loss of cash flow and capital.

Calculation or Loss

Value of Puts at Year–End:	$19,500
Purchase Price of Puts:	−10,000
Gain Recognized for Taxes:	9,500
28% Federal+ 12% State & City:	x 40%
Tax Liability for 1990:	3,800

Investment Taxation: Who Cares?

Puts Sold for in April 1991:	4,500
Tax paid on Phantom Gain:	–3,800
Remainder of Original Investment:	700
New Tax Basis of investment:	$19,500
Puts Sold for in April 1991:	–4,500
Amount of Loss for tax Purposes	
(Subject to Annual Limitation):	$15,000

This situation might have been avoided through tax planning. They could have offset the gain by selling another investment in the portfolio at a loss that year, or they could have simply invested in another instrument instead of Nikkei put warrants (which would not have to have been marked to market at year end). Oddly enough, although they are basically the same type of investment, puts on the FTSE 100, the British stock index, were not required to be marked to market and reported at year end. These would have had similar movements as Nikkei puts but much different tax consequences.

Tax Consequences–The Final Investment Filter

The moral of this story is that good investment planning can never be separated from good tax planning. They are one and the same, especially in light of recent tax law changes on investments, and some of the recent hybrid investments now being offered. It is important that you find a tax advisor who is knowledgeable in investment planning and investment taxation, and that you use him or her as a final filter for screening all your investments.

This book will help you understand the basic structure of the current tax law with regard to investment taxation. I will give you a brief but effective methodology to use in evaluating your investments from a "total return" perspective, that is, one which integrates good tax planning with good investment planning. I call this interdisciplinary approach to tax and financial planning Total Return Investment Planning (TRIP), and it should be an integral part of your investment approach. It is a synthesis which introduces the concept of Total Return on your money **After Taxation** as the major factor in evaluating your overall investment yield.

In this day of the 4 1/2 % interest bearing savings account and the 4% Treasury Bill, we'd all better use whatever resources are available to us to maximize our return on capital. The government has radically changed the Tax Code with the passage of the Tax

Reform Act of 1986 and subsequent technical changes to it. No area was affected more than that of investments.

As Will Rogers used to say, "I'm not as concerned about the return **on** my money as I am about the return **of** my money," and preinvestment–tax analysis can be a major factor in effecting a positive outcome in this regard. With this in mind, let's proceed now with some basic tax knowledge, an historical perspective of where this tax law fits in, and ultimately what we can do, as both investors and taxpayers, to maximize our investment return while minimizing our tax liability.

Chapter 2

Tax Simplification
An Investor's Worst Nightmare

The Rug Gets Pulled Out From Under Us

What if you opened up a savings account with an initial deposit of $5,000 which you were going to use for your child's college tuition in the fall? In fact, you put it into a time deposit account for a 90–day period which paid a higher rate of return than the regular day of deposit/day of withdrawal account. Come August 30th you go to the bank to get your money and the teller says, "I'm sorry, Mr. Jones, there's been a change in bank procedure and you'll have to speak to a Vice President. Have a seat, and he'll be with you shortly."

After several uncomfortable moments, the V.P. motions you to his desk and tells you that the teller is correct. There's been a change in bank procedure, and all 90–day time deposits have been converted into **annual** time deposit accounts. You will have to wait until next summer to withdraw your money or suffer a substantial premature withdrawal penalty.

You are flabbergasted and reply, "But I never authorized such a conversion. I was never given the opportunity to get my money out before this took place."

The Vice President very politely replies, "I'm sorry, but we did post notification in all our branches that this change had taken place."

"HAD taken place?" you scream, "Why wasn't I advised of this before it was done so that I could have withdrawn my money? You can't change the rules AFTER my money is already deposited!"

"I'm sorry, Mr. Jones, it is within our rights to change bank policy at any time. It's written in our charter."

You give it one last try but somehow sense that you have very little chance of winning this discussion. "You've never done anything like this before and I've been banking here for 25 years. This isn't fair."

"You may be right, Mr. Jones, it might not be fair, but you know something? It works."

A far–fetched story? Couldn't happen here in America, you say? The government would never let anyone get away with it. They would have had to let people know ahead of time so that they could get their money out BEFORE the change. You think so? Well, guess again. Not only did the government allow it, they DID it to many, many investors. I'll relate to you how they did it and the effect this has had, and is still having, on investors and on the economy as a whole.

But, first of all, I want to make one very important point. There has been an historical precedent established here which has had a particularly negative effect on the individual investor. The government, for the first time in history, has taken several investment vehicles, such as real estate and other passive activities which I will discuss later on, and has said to the investor, "I know we told you that if you invested in certain areas you would have substantial future tax benefits, but we changed our mind. And not only does this apply to investments you make from now on, it also applies to all such investments which you might have made in the past under the old tax law. There is NO GRANDFATHERING of prior investments to the old tax laws under which they may have been purchased."

An example of grandfathering of past investments which **was** allowed is the case of an investment called the "Private Activity Bond." These bonds are issued by a state or locality and are sold to the public to raise money for specific projects which benefit the private sector, such as a new garbage dump for industry. In the past, all interest earned on these by the investor was 100% tax free on the federal tax return. With the change in the 1986 tax law, the interest on this investment is now subject to taxation as an Alternative Minimum Tax item. However, and here is the big difference, anyone holding these bonds from **before** the 1986 Tax Reform Act is **not** subject to this tax. Anyone who purchases them after 1986 **is** taxed.

Compare this to what has been done to the person who invested in a piece of real estate pre-tax reform. He or she is now subject to all sorts of additional taxation, regardless of what the law stated when it was purchased. The government has essentially taken a basically non-liquid investment made it even less liquid. Consequently, its value has been reduced significantly. This is just part of the investment changes which have come about with tax simplification. We will discuss the real estate issue further and the effects it has had on the overall economy. But first, let's talk about the 1986 Reform Act's more basic changes to investment taxation, the government's purpose for tax reform, and indeed how the government perpetrated what I believe has now become the crime of the century against the average investor.

How Many Oxymorons Does it Take to Change the Tax Law?

What is Simplification, Anyway?

Has anyone you know ever had "jumbo shrimp?" Has anyone you know ever dealt with so called "government intelligence?" Well, how about "tax simplification?" I believe this concept is truly an oxymoron, or a phrase which inherently contradicts itself. In this age of over-governmentalization, no attempt by the government to "simplify" anything, let alone the complex tax law, ever really gets accomplished.

But, the idea was a catchy one. The concept of one tax rate, 15%, and no deductions. All you do then is to multiply your income by 15% to come up with your tax liability. Fair, in fact, very fair. Tax simplification **and** tax reduction!

All taxpayers will now be created equal. No more write–offs for the very shrewd, no more favoritism for those with tax preferences, no more benefits for those who can afford to hire high priced tax accountants or attorneys. This was great! It was so damn SIMPLE.

Well, that was before the politicians got a hold of it.

Unfortunately for tax reformers, there are very few tax accountants or economists elected to Congress. And, in fact, most legislation is passed only after numerous compromises and changes. Different Congressmen have different vested interests, and there is a great deal of pork barrelling, or, "I'll vote for your section if you vote for mine." The tax bill was no exception.

By the time it made it through Congress, the basic objective had been compromised to the point where the phrase "tax simplification" was just a bad joke. I know some very competent tax practitioners who are still sorting out some of the more obscure points of the new tax law.

As we are taught in school, taxes are needed to support government budgets. The government is elected by the people to run society. They have our proxy to raise funds necessary to support social programs appropriate for the common good. As Justice Oliver Wendell Holmes, Jr. once said, "Taxes are what we pay for civilized society".[1] Thus, tax laws are changed and amended to meet the changing budgetary needs of the government.

The Logic Behind all This and the Reality of its Outcome

President Reagan was a proponent of supply–side economics. A theory that the notion of increasing taxes to increase government revenue is totally inaccurate, and, in fact, unworkable. Very simply put, supply–siders assert that in order to RAISE revenue, a government has to CUT taxes. This will ostensibly put more money into investors' hands which would, in turn, ultimately create more taxable wealth. In other words, a smaller tax percentage multiplied times a much larger income base will yield more money than a greater tax rate multiplied times a smaller income base.

Also, with more investing being done by taxpayers, the government should be able to tax the income on one more level. Thus, the government can tax income when the corporation earns it, through corporate taxation, and then it can tax the same money again when the corporation pays it out in shareholder dividends through personal income taxation.

This seems to be a workable theory if, and only if, the second purpose for governmental taxation is carefully executed. Historically, the government has guided society's growth in terms of favored industries and sectors deemed necessary at that time.

A good example of this was the recent federal allowance in the mid–1980s of a direct tax credit for the purchase of energy conservation items, such as storm windows. This was motivated by the fuel shortages of the 1970s and the need to conserve energy. It was a direct attempt by the federal government to stimulate this country's energy conservation industry. By giving the taxpayer a break for purchasing items such as storm windows, or a more efficient furnace, they were helping these manufacturers attract new business.

Another example of this was the recent allowance of "investment tax credit" for the purchase af new machinery for the production and generation of business. This was in response to the recession of the early 1980s and demonstrated the government's desire to stimulate overall business growth, which it did. By the way, both of these credits are, for the most part, history, as neither one is included in the new Tax Act. This has been a major problem for the economy and probably a contributing cause of the current recession.

Chapter 3

Changes for the Investor
Now You See It,
Now You Don't

The Investor: Life After Tax Reform

There are many aspects of the 1986 Tax Reform Act and subsequent technical corrections, in fact, which appear to discourage taxpayer investment in business. This seems incongruous, and indeed, inconsistent with the first purpose, which was to generate more government revenue through a supply–side taxation policy. Before we get into what we as taxpayers and investors can do to work within the new tax law, let's discuss some of the specific changes to which I refer.

The Vanishing Act and the Rabbit Appears From the Hat

From the Long–Term Capital Gain Exclusion to All Gains Taxed as Ordinary:

The most basic and significant tax break taken away from the individual investor was the elimination of the 60% exclusion on long–term capital gains. *Long–term* was defined as either six months or a year depending on which year's tax law was in effect at the time. This provision translated into a maximum tax on long–term capital gains of 20%.* Obviously, with this provision in effect, people were

---

*Longterm Capital Gain

x40%	(taxable after 60% exclusion)
x50%	(maximum tax rate)
20%	(of Long–Term Capital Gain Payable as Tax)

encouraged to invest in capital items (stocks and bonds) and to hold on to these investments for at least the required period to qualify them for long–term capital gain treatment.

This tax break was completely eliminated from the Code with the 1986 Tax Reform Act. Although there still remains a distinction between short– and long–term capital gains on the tax return, it is meaningless because they both are currently taxed at the ordinary rate which, as of this writing, is 28%, maximum. For those of you who are not familiar with exactly how this once worked, I'd like to provide you with an example of the government's first sleight of hand toward the investor.

In Exhibits 3A and 3B we see the Schedule D form for reporting capital gains and losses before the change in the tax law, and in Exhibits 3C and 3D we see it after tax reform. For the purpose of illustration, we will use the case of Mr. and Mrs. N. Vestor, who have $200,000 of long–term capital gains from sales of stocks.

In the case of the pre-tax reform return, Exhibit 3A, the initial entry is to line 9A, Part 2, of the front of the Schedule D, the section for long–term capital gains. This is also the initial entry on the post-tax reform return, Exhibit 3C, line 8A, Part 2, of the front of the Schedule D. On both forms, the entry is carried down the page to the bottom line and to the backs of the forms (Exhibits 3B and 3D, lines 18 and 17 respectively).

Now here's where the magic begins. You see line 20 on the old form, Exhibit 3B? That was the place where you backed out 60% of your long–term capital gains. If you look on Exhibit 3D for the comparable line, you won't find it. Now you see it, now you don't.

Looking to Exhibits 3E and 3F respectively, you will see the difference in amounts being carried to the front of the tax return for the calculation of taxable income. For the sale of the same securities in 1991 as you had in 1986, you are now required to pay tax on an extra $120,000 of income!

You don't have to be a CPA to figure out that at even a reduced maximum tax rate for capital gains of 28% in 1991 verses the 50% rate in 1986, you would be required to pay an additional $16,000 in taxes on that same gain. Who said anything about lower taxes?

As I pointed out before, and as you can readily see in these examples, although there is no longer a tax break for long–term gains, there is still a distinction in the way the gain is reported. This is because there is always the possibility of lowering the long–term capital gains rate, and hence, the government wants to maintain the

12

distinction. Don't worry, I doubt that they will allow you to go back and reduce the tax on long–term gains you have already reported, but some people would like you to believe that possibility exists.

Although there is much talk about reducing long–term capital gains, it is my belief that, a long–term capital gain rate reduction like 15% or so will have trouble getting through Congress. The reason for this is that Congressmen feel that this provision appears to favor the well–to–do, which stigmatizes the whole idea.

And, just a footnote to this change: although they took away the concept of a short–term and long–term "capital gain," the limitation of a "capital loss" still remains intact. Investment gains are now taxed at ordinary rates, dollar for dollar, however, investment **losses** are still limited to a maximum $3,000 per taxpayer per annum. So, although the term *capital gain* is virtually meaningless in light of its tax effect, the term *capital loss* is still quite significant.

The Dividend Exclusion Versus Double Taxation

The second change, the $200 per taxpayer, $400 per married couple, dividend exclusion part of the tax law for many years also has disappeared. This gave the investor some break from double taxation where dividends are taxed on the corporate income level and again on the personal income level to the individual receiving the dividend.

For those of you who missed this trick, we once again look to Exhibits 3E and 3F, lines 9 and 8 respectively. Notice on line 9b, on the pre-tax reform return, Exhibit 3E, there is a space for the $400 per couple exclusion. As you observe on line 8a, Exhibit 3F, however, it is gone. No more $400 exclusion. Now you see it, now you don't.

Fully Deductible Investment Interest and the Appearance of Form 4952:

Another change to the law of significant concern to the investor is the elimination of the investment interest expense deduction beyond investment income. In the good old days, when all interest was created equal and was fully deductible, any interest associated with the cost of investing was deductible up to the amount of investment income plus an additional $10,000 beyond this. Basically, this is margin interest or the cost of borrowing money from your broker to invest in securities, sell securities short, or invest in any other similar investment vehicle, such as the purchase of mutual funds on margin, where allowed.

13

With the advent of tax simplification, it became even simpler. The margin interest expense deduction is now limited to the amount of income you make by investing only. It appears that the government considers investing a hobby if you're not successful at it! There was a very complicated formula in phasing out this deduction over five years, but after 1990 it became strictly limited to this amount, and not one penny more.

I reference now Exhibit 3G, the pre-tax reform Schedule A, Form for Itemized Deductions. As you can see, line 13 is for the deduction of interest which you paid, not including credit card, charge account, or home mortgage interest. Notice that the amount you put down on this line is carried directly to the total deductions on line 26. Contrast this, however, with line 11 on Exhibit 3H, the post-tax reform Schedule A, Form for Itemized Deductions.

Here we see that the people who brought you the Tax Reform Act of 1986 did not only perform disappearing acts but, in fact, made new and amazing things suddenly appear before your very eyes. One of these new items was the revised limitation on investment interest expense and the convoluted method of calculating your deductible amount. Notice where it says "attach Form 4952 if required." Well I have news for you. If you have investment interest, Form 4952 **is** required unless **all** of the following apply: 1) your only investment income was from interest or dividends; 2) you have no other deductible expenses connected with the production of interest or dividends; 3) your investment interest expense is not more than your investment income; **and** 4) you have no carryovers of investment interest expense from the prior year. Haven't you heard about tax simplification yet?

Let's now look at Exhibit 3I, Form 4952. Line 1 is for the total amount of margin interest or other investment interest you paid in 1991. This was the figure which went directly to your Schedule A deductions on the pre-tax reform tax return. Line 2 is for your carryforward of any margin interest which was disallowed from last year, and line 3 is the total of the two.

Line 4 is where the fun begins, as we now must enter our total investment income earned this year. Net investment income is defined as the excess, if any, of investment income over investment expenses. You must include income (not derived in the ordinary course of a trade or business) from interest, dividends, annuities, royalties, and net gain from the disposition of property held for investment. Investment expenses are your allowable deductions,

14

other than interest expense, directly connected with the production of this investment income.

And now for the good news, you have to net the two figures to arrive at your deductible margin interest. But, if you have investment expenses that were **dis**allowed as miscellaneous itemized deductions on Schedule A, you do **not** have to deduct them from income!

Other Fully Deductible Investment Expenses Versus the 2% and 3% Exclusions:

This, however, leads us to another very damaging blow to the investor. The next surprise of the 1986 Tax Reform Act was the introduction of the 2% floor (of adjusted gross income) which was subtracted from Schedule A, Itemized Deductions, before they are allowed as deductions. This sounds very complicated, but what this all means is that before you get to deduct any investment expenses as itemized deductions, you have to give up an amount equal to the first 2% of your income.

As unfair as it may be, you may not deduct **directly from your capital gain** the cost of items such as investment advisory fees, custodial fees, a portion of computer hardware and any related investment software, investment publications, tax or investment fees, bank custodial fees, and any other investment related expense. What the government has done with investment interest expense is to give with one hand and take away with the other. The deduction they allow here for other investment expense reduces allowable investment interest. It accomplishes this by first reducing the investment income before the calculation of allowable investment interest based upon this income.

Looking once again at Exhibit 3G, pre-tax reform Schedule A, Itemized Deductions, line 22, miscellaneous deductions, we see here under the category "Other" that there is a dollar for dollar deduction for the types of miscellaneous investment expenses to which I refer above. Compare this to Exhibit 3H, post-tax reform, Schedule A, Itemized Deductions, line 20. It is also categorized as "Other Miscellaneous Expenses" and **reported** dollar for dollar. But, here's where the similarity ends.

We now have lines 22 and 23 in the area of miscellaneous deductions. These lines require that you enter your adjusted gross income and 2% of adjusted gross income respectively. Line 24 is the total amount of miscellaneous deductions allowable as itemized deductions on Schedule A. This line is a net figure from which the

2% of adjusted gross income has been subtracted from any reported investment expenses.

As you will observe, there is one more change on this form, and that is line 26 on exhibit 3H. If the amount of adjusted gross income is more than $100,000, there is yet another worksheet which you must complete in order to determine how much more of your deductions will be eliminated. This additional exclusion can go as high as another 3% of adjusted gross income above $100,000.

As Joseph Gelband, in his very fine *Barron's* article of August 12, 1991 states, "Suppose you, as an investor with $150,000 (including salary and income from securities investing) of adjusted gross income, have spent $5,000 (on investment expenses, such as the ones discussed above).

First they are deductible only from your adjusted gross income, which means you must itemize your deductions and forgo the standard deduction in order to get them onto your tax return at all. You will list these $5,000 of investment-related costs as miscellaneous expenses on Schedule A. Now that they're on the return, you confront the next hurdle: you may deduct only the portion of those expenses in excess of 2% of your adjusted gross income. With $150,000 of AGI, the $3,000 haircut leaves you a mere $2,000 deduction for your $5,000 of actual costs. And if the use of the standard deduction ($5,700 on a joint return this year) is preferable in your particular circumstances, your investment expenses are of no help whatsoever.

The latest blow was delivered by the Revenue Reconciliation Act of 1990, effective in 1991, which slashed your net itemized deductions (except for medical and investment interest expenses and casualty and theft losses) by 3% of the excess of your AGI over $100,000 (or over $50,000 if you're married and file a separate tax return) so that your already pre-shrunk $2,000 deduction (the remains of your actual $5,000 costs of earning your fully taxed investment income) may hardly be worth discussing.

Another feature of our tax system that confirms your second-class citizenship as an investor is the limitation on the deduction for 'investment interest,' which in most cases is the monthly interest charged by your broker in a margin account. Let's say you paid $10,000 of margin interest, and that you have $10,500 of dividends, interest, and net capital gains for the year. Your investment expenses, as in our example, amounted to $5,000, which was reduced to $2,000 after the 2% limit. The ceiling of your deduction for the margin interest is set by your 'net investment income,' i.e., $10,500 investment income less the $2,000 (reduced) investment expenses of $8,500. So you get a deduction for $8,500 of your $10,000 margin interest cost (you may carry the unused $1,500 balance forward to next year's tax return), which you may take as an itemized deduction.

Did you spot the sleight of hand? After grudgingly allowing you a token deduction (at least before the 1990 cut) for your investment expenses, they took it back by applying it to decrease your deduction for margin interest."*

Whatever Happened to the Investment Tax Credit?

One of the tax breaks which was **not** renewed, and one which I consider to be a most significant change, was the one I mentioned earlier, "Investment Tax credit." When this was in effect up through 1986, it allowed the investor to deduct up to 10% of the cost of most new income producing machinery from his or her TAX LIABILITY. Not from income to be taxed, as most deductions are, but directly from the tax due. Because of the way this was treated (as a credit), it turned out to be a much greater tax break than 10% of the cost of the machine. At the old maximum income tax rate of 50%, the tax break turned out to be as much as 20% against income. And, in fact, investments in certain areas, such as historic restorations, were given as much as a 15% or 25% tax credit which thereby translated to a 30% to 50% deduction from income.

For example, if you invested in a real estate partnership, and the partnership needed to purchase a new machine for processing invoices, they could buy one. And you, as a partner, would get to write off your share of 10% of its cost immediately **against your tax liability**. If this machine cost the partnership $11,000, the partners would immediately take $1,100 off their combined tax bill. This was in addition to the normal deduction for annual depreciation expense of the item which could be deducted from income before the tax calculation that year (although the amount taken as investment credit reduced the total amount deducted over the life of the asset as depreciation).

---

*Reprinted by permission of *Barron's*, ©1991, Dow Jones & Company, Inc. All Rights Reserved Worldwide.

Adequate Depreciation on Investment Property and the Increased Life of Business Assets:

This leads me to another area which was drastically changed, the depreciation calculation itself. The time periods for the depreciation of most business assets were expanded for tax purposes with the advent of the 1986 Tax Reform Act. This meant that the actual amount of expense you could deduct for depreciation each year was decreased. In the above example of the billing machine, let's assume that under the new tax law the life of the machine was changed for tax purposes from   five to ten years, the depreciation expense deduction would be cut in half for each of those years.

Fully Excludable Tax–Exempt Bond Interest and the Private Activity Bond:

Let me mention once again another area which I touched upon previously, the creation by the government of the "Private Activity Bond." This was an expansion of taxation to cover certain previously exempted municipal bonds by the Alternative Minimum Tax. At this point I want to reference you to Exhibit 3J, Form 6251, the Alternative Minimum Tax for Individuals. Looking at line 6B, we see the interest which was generated from these bonds, and previously exempt, is now being taxed on all private activity, municipal bonds issued after August 7, 1986.

Full Deduction for Charitable Donations on Stock and the Birth of the AMT Addback:

As long as we are in this area of the AMT form, I want to refer to line 6A. Another category which was created by the Tax Reform Act was the addback for appreciated property which was donated by the taxpayer as a charitable contribution. What they are referring to here is quite significant to many investors who previously had donated stocks and/or bonds, or any other investment to a charitable organization. The taxpayer is now being taxed on the difference between what he paid for these items and what the items were worth at the time of the contributions. This effectively eliminates a good deal of tax benefit derived from donating these items to charitable organizations. In fact, in certain cases the tax payer would do just as well to sell the item first, recognize the gain, and then donate the cash to the charity.

Childrens' Tax Rates on Investment Income and the "Kiddie Tax":

One more significant creation of the Tax Reform Act was that of the "kiddie tax." This change required that any investment income over $1,000 which was earned by a child under the age of 14 would be taxed at the same rate as the parents' income. This provision somewhat negated the value of shifting assets which generated investment income to children under the age of 14. Many of my clients had used this vehicle as a major component of their tax planning. I will address this area in further detail at a later point when I discuss the techniques which I use to somewhat neutralize this provision, the gifting of low income, high appreciation property to children under 14 years of age.

Tax–Free Transfer of Investments Between Generations and the Creation of the Generation Skipping Transfer Tax:

The generation skipping transfer tax was yet another blow to taxpayers and investors who wanted to maximize the sheltering of wealth and its passage from one generation to the next. What this tax did was to place an additional surcharge, beyond an initial exclusion, on all previously tax free transfers beyond the first generation. In other words, if your father gifted stocks to your son, he was now required to pay a surcharge on all such transfers beyond the excluded amount. The exclusion is a one time $1,000,000 amount, and I will discuss this further in another chapter. I'm just mentioning it here as part of an overall summary of changes which have affected investors the most.

Birth of the PIG and the PAL:

In this context, I will briefly touch upon one more area, and a very significant one, affecting the investor. This area is the virtual elimination of the Passive Activity Loss as a deduction against ordinary income. Passive activities cover such investments as rental properties, nonworking partnership interests, and any other activity whereby the investor invests money and does not actively participate in the business. This is a very broad area and one which is quite significant. I will address this further in my discussion of "Tax Classification–The Three Baskets of Income," and the introduction of PIGS (Passive Income Generators) and PALS (Passive Activity Losses).

SCHEDULE D (Form 1040) Department of the Treasury Internal Revenue Service (O)	**Capital Gains and Losses** **and Reconciliation of Forms 1099-B** ▶ Attach to Form 1040. ▶ See Instructions for Schedule D (Form 1040). For Paperwork Reduction Act Notice, see Form 1040 Instructions.	OMB No. 1545-0074 **1986** Attachment Sequence No. 12

Name(s) as shown on Form 1040 MR. & MRS N. VESTOR

Your social security number 123 45 6789

1 Report here, the total sales of stocks, bonds, etc., reported for 1986 by your broker to you on Form(s) 1099-B or an equivalent substitute statement(s) . . . . | 1 | 400 000

If this amount differs from the total of lines 2b and 9b, column (d), attach a statement explaining the difference. See the instructions for line 1, Schedule D (Form 1040) for examples.

Part I Short-term Capital Gains and Losses—Assets Held Six Months or Less

(a) Description of property (Example, 100 shares 7% preferred of "Z" Co.)	(b) Date acquired (Mo., day, yr.)	(c) Date sold (Mo., day, yr.)	(d) Sales price (see instructions)	(e) Cost or other basis (see instructions)	(f) LOSS If (e) is more than (d), subtract (d) from (e)	(g) GAIN If (d) is more than (e), subtract (e) from (d)
2a Form 1099-B Transactions (Sales of Stocks, Bonds, etc.):						
2b Total (add column (d)) . . . . ▶						
2c Other Transactions:						

3 Short-term gain from sale or exchange of a principal residence from Form 2119, lines 6 or 12	3	
4 Short-term gain from installment sales from Form 6252, lines 22 or 30	4	
5 Net short-term gain or (loss) from partnerships, S corporations, and fiduciaries .	5	
6 Short-term capital loss carryover from years beginning after 1969	6	
7 Add all of the transactions on lines 2a and 2c and lines 3 through 6 in columns (f) and (g) . . .	7 (	)
8 Net short-term gain or (loss), combine columns (f) and (g) of line 7	8	

Part II Long-term Capital Gains and Losses—Assets Held More Than Six Months

9a Form 1099-B Transactions (Sales of Stocks, Bonds, etc.):						
STOCKS			400,000	200,000		200,000
9b Total (add column (d)) . . . . ▶						
9c Other Transactions:						

10 Long-term gain from sale or exchange of a principal residence from Form 2119, lines 6, 8, or 12	10		
11 Long-term gain from installment sales from Form 6252, lines 22 or 30	11		
12 Net long-term gain or (loss) from partnerships, S corporations, and fiduciaries .	12		
13 Capital gain distributions	13		
14 Enter gain from Form 4797, lines 6 or 8	14		
15 Long-term capital loss carryover from years beginning after 1969	15		
16 Add all of the transactions on lines 9a and 9c and lines 10 through 15 in columns (f) and (g)	16 (	)	200,000
17 Net long-term gain or (loss), combine columns (f) and (g) of line 16		17	200,000

Schedule D (Form 1040) 1986

Exhibit 3A

Schedule D (Form 1040) 1986   Attachment Sequence No. **12**   Page **2**

Note: *If you have capital loss carryovers from years beginning before 1970, do not complete Parts III or IV. See Form 4798 instead.*

Name(s) as shown on Form 1040 (Do not enter name and social security number if shown on other side.)

N . VESTOR

Your social security number

123 45 6789

Part III	**Summary of Parts I and II**

18	Combine lines 8 and 17, and enter the net gain or (loss) here	18	*200,000*
	Note: *If line 18 is a loss, skip lines 19 through 21 and complete lines 22 and 23. If line 18 is a gain, complete lines 19 through 21 and skip lines 22 and 23.*		
19	If line 18 shows a gain, enter the smaller of line 17 or line 18. Enter zero if there is a loss or no entry on line 17 . . . . **19** *200,000*		
20	Enter 60% of line 19	20	*120,000*
	If line 20 is more than zero, you may be liable for the alternative minimum tax. See Form 6251.		
21	Subtract line 20 from line 18. Enter here and on Form 1040, line 13	21	*80,000*
22	If line 18 shows a loss, enter one of the following amounts:		
a	If line 8 is zero or a net gain, enter 50% of line 18;		
b	If line 17 is zero or a net gain, enter line 18; or		
c	If line 8 and line 17 are net losses, enter amount on line 8 added to 50% of the amount on line 17 . .	22	
23	Enter here and as a loss on Form 1040, line 13, the smallest of:		
a	The amount on line 22;		
b	$3,000 ($1,500 if married and filing a separate return); or		
c	Taxable income, as adjusted (see instructions)	23	

Part IV	**Computation of Post-1969 Capital Loss Carryovers From 1986 to 1987**
	(Complete this part if the loss on line 22 is more than the loss on line 23)

24	Enter loss shown on line 8; if none, enter zero and skip lines 25 through 28, then go to line 29	24	
25	Enter gain shown on line 17. If that line is blank or shows a loss, enter zero	25	
26	Subtract line 25 from line 24 .	26	
27	Enter smaller of line 23 or line 26	27	
28	Subtract line 27 from line 26. This is your short-term capital loss carryover from 1986 to 1987 . . .	28	
29	Subtract line 27 from line 23. (Note: If you skipped lines 25 through 28, enter amount from line 23.)	29	
30	Enter loss from line 17; if none, enter zero and skip lines 31 through 34	30	
31	Enter gain shown on line 8. If that line is blank or shows a loss, enter zero	31	
32	Subtract line 31 from line 30 .	32	
33	Multiply amount on line 29 by 2	33	
34	Subtract line 33 from line 32. This is your long-term capital loss carryover from 1986 to 1987 . . .	34	

Part V	**Complete This Part Only if You Elect Out of the Installment Method and Report a Note or Other Obligation at Less Than Full Face Value**

Check here if you elect out of the installment method . . . . ▶ ☐

Enter the face amount of the note or other obligation. ▶ ....

Enter the percentage of valuation of the note or other obligation. ▶ ....

Part VI	**Reconciliation of Forms 1099-B For Bartering Transactions**	Amount of bartering from Form 1099-B or equivalent statement
	Complete this part if you received one or more Form(s) 1099-B or an equivalent substitute statement(s) reporting bartering income. Enter the amount on the line that indicates the form or schedule you used to report the bartering income.	

35	Form 1040, line 22	35	
36	Schedule C (Form 1040)	36	
37	Schedule D (Form 1040)	37	
38	Schedule E (Form 1040)	38	
39	Schedule F (Form 1040)	39	
40	Other (identify) (if not taxable, indicate reason—attach additional sheets if necessary) ▶		
	....	40	
41	Total (add lines 35 through 40)	41	

Note: *The amount on line 41 should be the same as the total bartering on all Forms 1099-B or equivalent statements received.*

°U.S. GOVERNMENT PRINTING OFFICE: 1986-493-090

Exhibit 3B

SCHEDULE D	**Capital Gains and Losses**	OMB No. 1545-0074
(Form 1040)	(And Reconciliation of Forms 1099-B for Bartering Transactions)	19**91**
Department of the Treasury	▶ Attach to Form 1040.　　▶ See Instructions for Schedule D (Form 1040).	Attachment
Internal Revenue Service (5)	▶ For more space to list transactions for lines 1a and 8a, get Schedule D-1 (Form 1040).	Sequence No. **12A**

Name(s) shown on Form 1040 **MR. & MRS. N. VESTOR**　　　　Your social security number **123 45 6789**

Caution: *Add the following amounts reported to you for 1991 on Forms 1099-B and 1099-S (or on substitute statements): (a) proceeds from transactions involving stocks, bonds, and other securities, and (b) gross proceeds from real estate transactions not reported on another form or schedule. If this total does not equal the total of lines 1c and 8c, column (d), attach a statement explaining the difference.*

Part I   Short-Term Capital Gains and Losses—Assets Held One Year or Less

(a) Description of property (Example, 100 shares 7% preferred of "Z" Co.)	(b) Date acquired (Mo., day, yr.)	(c) Date sold (Mo., day, yr.)	(d) Sales price (see instructions)	(e) Cost or other basis (see instructions)	(f) LOSS If (e) is more than (d), subtract (d) from (e)	(g) GAIN If (d) is more than (e), subtract (e) from (d)
1a Stocks, Bonds, Other Securities, and Real Estate. Include Form 1099-B and 1099-S Transactions. See instructions.						

1b Amounts from Schedule D-1, line 1b (attach Schedule D-1)		
1c Total of All Sales Price Amounts. Add column (d) of lines 1a and 1b . . ▶	**1c**	

1d Other Transactions (Do NOT include real estate transactions from Forms 1099-S on this line. Report them on line 1a.)

2 Short-term gain from sale or exchange of your home from Form 2119, line 10 or 14c	**2**		
3 Short-term gain from installment sales from Form 6252, line 22 or 30	**3**		
4 Net short-term gain or (loss) from partnerships, S corporations, and fiduciaries .	**4**		
5 Short-term capital loss carryover from 1990 Schedule D, line 29	**5**		
6 Add lines 1a, 1b, 1d, and 2 through 5, in columns (f) and (g).	**6**	( )	
7 Net short-term capital gain or (loss). Combine columns (f) and (g) of line 6		**7**	

Part II   Long-Term Capital Gains and Losses—Assets Held More Than One Year

8a Stocks, Bonds, Other Securities, and Real Estate. Include Form 1099-B and 1099-S Transactions. See instructions.

(a)	(b)	(c)	(d)	(e)	(f)	(g)
STOCKS			400,000	200,000		200,000

8b Amounts from Schedule D-1, line 8b (attach Schedule D-1)			
8c Total of All Sales Price Amounts. Add column (d) of lines 8a and 8b . . ▶	**8c**	400,000	

8d Other Transactions (Do NOT include real estate transactions from Forms 1099-S on this line. Report them on line 8a.)

9 Long-term gain from sale or exchange of your home from Form 2119, line 10 or 14c	**9**		
10 Long-term gain from installment sales from Form 6252, line 22 or 30	**10**		
11 Net long-term gain or (loss) from partnerships, S corporations, and fiduciaries .	**11**		
12 Capital gain distributions	**12**		
13 Gain from Form 4797, line 7 or 9	**13**		
14 Long-term capital loss carryover from 1990 Schedule D, line 36.	**14**		
15 Add lines 8a, 8b, 8d, and 9 through 14, in columns (f) and (g)	**15**	( )	200,000
16 Net long-term capital gain or (loss). Combine columns (f) and (g) of line 15		**16**	200,000

For Paperwork Reduction Act Notice, see Form 1040 instructions.　　Cat. No. 11338H　　Schedule D (Form 1040) 1991

Exhibit 3C

Schedule D (Form 1040) 1991 | Attachment Sequence No. **12A** | Page **2**

Name(s) shown on Form 1040. (Do not enter name and social security number if shown on other side.) — *MR & MRS N. VESTOR*

Your social security number — *123 45 6789*

Part III — Summary of Parts I and II

17 Combine lines 7 and 16 and enter the net gain or (loss) here. If the result is a gain, also enter the gain on Form 1040, line 13. **(Note:** *If both lines 16 and 17 are gains, see Part IV below.)* . . . . . . | **17** | *200,000*

18 If line 17 is a (loss), enter here and as a (loss) on Form 1040, line 13, the **smaller** of:

a The (loss) on line 17; **or**

b ($3,000) or, if married filing a separate return, ($1,500) . . . . | **18** |( )

Note: *When figuring whether line 18a or 18b is **smaller**, treat both numbers as positive.*
Complete Part V if the loss on line 17 is more than the loss on line 18, OR if Form 1040, line 37, is zero.

Part IV — Tax Computation Using Maximum Capital Gains Rate

USE THIS PART TO FIGURE YOUR TAX ONLY IF BOTH LINES 16 AND 17 ARE GAINS, AND:

You checked filing status box:	AND	Form 1040, line 37, is over:	You checked filing status box:	AND	Form 1040, line 37, is over:
1		$49,300	3		$41,075
2 or 5		$82,150	4		$70,450

19 Enter the amount from Form 1040, line 37 . . . . | **19** |

20 Enter the **smaller** of line 16 or line 17. . . . . | **20** |

21 Subtract line 20 from line 19 . . . . | **21** |

22 Enter: **a** $20,350 if you checked filing status box 1; **b** $34,000 if you checked filing status box 2 or 5; **c** $17,000 if you checked filing status box 3; or **d** $27,300 if you checked filing status box 4 . . . | **22** |

23 Enter the **greater** of line 21 or line 22. . . . . | **23** |

24 Subtract line 23 from line 19 . . . . | **24** |

25 Figure the tax on the amount on line 23. Use the Tax Table or Tax Rate Schedules, whichever applies | **25** |

26 Multiply line 24 by 28% (.28) . . . . | **26** |

27 Add lines 25 and 26. Enter here and on Form 1040, line 38, and check the box for Schedule D . | **27** |

Part V — Capital Loss Carryovers from 1991 to 1992

Section A.—Carryover Limit

28 Enter the amount from Form 1040, line 35. If a loss, enclose the amount in parentheses . . . . | **28** |

29 Enter the loss from line 18 as a positive amount . . . . | **29** |

30 Combine lines 28 and 29. If zero or less, enter -0-. . . . . | **30** |

31 Enter the **smaller** of line 29 or line 30 . . . . | **31** |

Section B.—Short-Term Capital Loss Carryover to 1992 (Complete this section only if there is a loss on both lines 7 and 18.)

32 Enter the loss from line 7 as a positive amount . . . . | **32** |

33 Enter the gain, if any, from line 16. . . . . | **33** |

34 Enter the amount from line 31 . . . . | **34** |

35 Add lines 33 and 34 . . . . | **35** |

36 **Short-term capital loss carryover to 1992.** Subtract line 35 from line 32. If zero or less, enter -0-. . | **36** |

Section C.—Long-Term Capital Loss Carryover to 1992 (Complete this section only if there is a loss on both lines 16 and 18.)

37 Enter the loss from line 16 as a positive amount . . . . | **37** |

38 Enter the gain, if any, from line 7 . . . . . . | **38** |

39 Enter the amount from line 31 . . . . | **39** |

40 Enter the amount, if any, from line 32. . . | **40** |

41 Subtract line 40 from line 39. If zero or less, enter -0- . . | **41** |

42 Add lines 38 and 41 . . . . | **42** |

43 **Long-term capital loss carryover to 1992.** Subtract line 42 from line 37. If zero or less, enter -0- . | **43** |

Part VI — Election Not To Use the Installment Method (Complete this part only if you elect out of the installment method and report a note or other obligation at less than full face value.)

44 Check here if you elect out of the installment method . . . . ▶ ☐

45 Enter the face amount of the note or other obligation. . . . . . . ▶ ....

46 Enter the percentage of valuation of the note or other obligation . . . . ▶ .... %

Part VII — Reconciliation of Forms 1099-B for Bartering Transactions (Complete this part if you received one or more Forms 1099-B or substitute statements reporting bartering income.)

Amount of bartering income from Form 1099-B or substitute statement reported on form or schedule

47 Form 1040, line 22 . . . . | **47** |

48 Schedule C, D, E, or F (Form 1040) (specify) ▶ .... | **48** |

49 Other form or schedule (identify) (if nontaxable, indicate reason—attach additional sheets if necessary):
.... | **49** |

50 **Total.** Add lines 47 through 49. This amount should be the same as the total bartering income on all Forms 1099-B and substitute statements received for bartering transactions . . . . . . | **50** |

Exhibit 3D

Form **1040**	Department of the Treasury—Internal Revenue Service **U.S. Individual Income Tax Return** 1986 (O)		

For the year January 1-December 31, 1986, or other tax year beginning , 1986, ending , 19   OMB No. 1545-0074

Use IRS label. Otherwise, please print or type.

Your first name and initial (if joint return, also give spouse's name and initial) Last name — MR. & MRS. N. VESTOR

Your social security number — 123 45 6789

Present home address (number and street or rural route) — 401 KAY STREET

Spouse's social security number — 987 65 4321

City, town or post office, state, and ZIP code — If this address is different from the one shown on your 1985 return, check here ▶

Presidential Election Campaign — Do you want $1 to go to this fund? Yes / No. If joint return, does your spouse want $1 to go to this fund? Yes / No. Note: Checking "Yes" will not change your tax or reduce your refund.

Filing Status — Check only one box.
1 Single
2 ☒ Married filing joint return (even if only one had income)
3 Married filing separate return. Enter spouse's social security no. above and full name here.
4 Head of household (with qualifying person).
5 Qualifying widow(er) with dependent child (year spouse died ▶ 19).

Exemptions
6a ☐ Yourself 65 or over Blind
b ☐ Spouse 65 or over Blind
c First names of your dependent children who lived with you
...
f Total number of exemptions claimed (also complete line 36)

Income
7 Wages, salaries, tips, etc. — 7
8 Interest income — 8
9a Dividends , 9b Exclusion
9c Subtract line 9b from line 9a — 9c
10 Taxable refunds — 10
11 Alimony received — 11
12 Business income or (loss) — 12
13 Capital gain or (loss) (attach Schedule D) — 13   80 000
14 40% of capital gain distributions — 14
15 Other gains or (losses) — 15
16 Fully taxable pensions — 16
17a Other pensions and annuities — b 17b
18 Rents, royalties, partnerships — 18
19 Farm income or (loss) — 19
20a Unemployment compensation — b 20b
21a Social security benefits — b 21b
22 Other income — 22
23 Add the amounts shown... total income ▶ 23

Adjustments to Income
24 Moving expenses
25 Employee business expenses
26 IRA deduction
27 Keogh retirement plan
28 Penalty on early withdrawal
29 Alimony paid
30 Deduction for a married couple when both work
31 Add lines 24 through 30. total adjustments ▶ 31

Adjusted Gross Income
32 Subtract line 31 from line 23. adjusted gross income — 32

Exhibit 3E

Form **1040**	Department of the Treasury—Internal Revenue Service **U.S. Individual Income Tax Return** 19**91** (5)		OMB No. 1545-0074

For the year Jan.–Dec. 31, 1991, or other tax year beginning , 1991, ending , 19

Label
(See instructions on page 11.)
Use the IRS label. Otherwise, please print or type.

Your first name and initial: MR. N.   Last name: VESTOR

If a joint return, spouse's first name and initial: MRS. N.   Last name: VESTOR

Home address (number and street). (If you have a P.O. box, see page 11.): 401 KAY STREET   Apt. no.

City, town or post office, state, and ZIP code. (If you have a foreign address, see page 11.)

Your social security number: 123 45 6789

Spouse's social security number: 987 65 4321

For Privacy Act and Paperwork Reduction Act Notice, see instructions.

Presidential Election Campaign (See page 11.)

Do you want $1 to go to this fund? — Yes ☐ No ☐

If joint return, does your spouse want $1 to go to this fund? — Yes ☐ No ☐

Note: Checking "Yes" will not change your tax or reduce your refund.

Filing Status

Check only one box.

1 ☐ Single
2 ☐ Married filing joint return (even if only one had income)
3 ☐ Married filing separate return. Enter spouse's social security no. above and full name here. ▶
4 ☐ Head of household (with qualifying person). (See page 12.) If the qualifying person is a child but not your dependent, enter this child's name here. ▶
5 ☐ Qualifying widow(er) with dependent child (year spouse died ▶ 19). (See page 12.)

Exemptions
(See page 12.)

6a ☐ Yourself. If your parent (or someone else) can claim you as a dependent on his or her tax return, do not check box 6a. But be sure to check the box on line 33b on page 2 .
b ☐ Spouse
c Dependents:

(1) Name (first, initial, and last name)	(2) Check if under age 1	(3) If age 1 or older, dependent's social security number	(4) Dependent's relationship to you	(5) No. of months lived in your home in 1991

If more than six dependents, see page 13.

No. of boxes checked on 6a and 6b
No. of your children on 6c who:
• lived with you
• didn't live with you due to divorce or separation (see page 14)
No. of other dependents on 6c
Add numbers entered on lines above ▶

d If your child didn't live with you but is claimed as your dependent under a pre-1985 agreement, check here ▶ ☐
e Total number of exemptions claimed .

Income

Attach Copy B of your Forms W-2, W-2G, and 1099-R here.

If you did not get a W-2, see page 10.

Attach check or money order on top of any Forms W-2, W-2G, or 1099-R.

7	Wages, salaries, tips, etc. (attach Form(s) W-2)	7
8a	Taxable interest income (also attach Schedule B if over $400) .	8a
b	Tax-exempt interest income (see page 16). DON'T include on line 8a 8b	
9	Dividend income (also attach Schedule B if over $400)	9
10	Taxable refunds of state and local income taxes, if any, from worksheet on page 16 . . .	10
11	Alimony received	11
12	Business income or (loss) (attach Schedule C)	12
13	Capital gain or (loss) (attach Schedule D)	13 200,000
14	Capital gain distributions not reported on line 13 (see page 17). . .	14
15	Other gains or (losses) (attach Form 4797)	15
16a	Total IRA distributions . 16a 16b Taxable amount (see page 17)	16b
17a	Total pensions and annuities 17a 17b Taxable amount (see page 17)	17b
18	Rents, royalties, partnerships, estates, trusts, etc. (attach Schedule E) . .	18
19	Farm income or (loss) (attach Schedule F)	19
20	Unemployment compensation (insurance) (see page 18)	20
21a	Social security benefits. 21a 21b Taxable amount (see page 18)	21b
22	Other income (list type and amount—see page 19)	22
23	Add the amounts shown in the far right column for lines 7 through 22. This is your total income ▶	23

Adjustments to Income
(See page 19.)

24a	Your IRA deduction, from applicable worksheet on page 20 or 21 24a	
b	Spouse's IRA deduction, from applicable worksheet on page 20 or 21 24b	
25	One-half of self-employment tax (see page 21) . . . 25	
26	Self-employed health insurance deduction, from worksheet on page 22 26	
27	Keogh retirement plan and self-employed SEP deduction 27	
28	Penalty on early withdrawal of savings 28	
29	Alimony paid. Recipient's SSN ▶ 29	
30	Add lines 24a through 29. These are your total adjustments . . . . . . ▶	30

Adjusted Gross Income

31 Subtract line 30 from line 23. This is your adjusted gross income. If this amount is less than $21,250 and a child lived with you, see page 45 to find out if you can claim the "Earned Income Credit" on line 56. . . . . ▶ | 31 |

Cat. No. 11320B

Exhibit 3F

			OMB No. 1545-0074
SCHEDULES A&B (Form 1040) Department of the Treasury Internal Revenue Service (O)	**Schedule A—Itemized Deductions** (Schedule B is on back) ▶ Attach to Form 1040. ▶ See Instructions for Schedules A and B (Form 1040).		19**86** Attachment Sequence No. **07**

Name(s) as shown on Form 1040 | Your social security number

Medical and Dental Expenses
(Do not include expenses reimbursed or paid by others.)
(See Instructions on page 19.)

1 Prescription medicines and drugs; and insulin **1**
2 a Doctors, dentists, nurses, hospitals, insurance premiums you paid for medical and dental care, etc. **2a**
b Transportation and lodging **2b**
c Other (list—include hearing aids, dentures, eyeglasses, etc.) ▶ **2c**
3 Add lines 1 through 2c, and enter the total here **3**
4 Multiply the amount on Form 1040, line 33, by 5% (.05) . . . **4**
5 Subtract line 4 from line 3. If zero or less, enter -0-. **Total** medical and dental . ▶ **5**

Taxes You Paid
(See Instructions on page 20.)

6 State and local income taxes **6**
7 Real estate taxes **7**
8 a General sales tax (see sales tax tables in instruction booklet) **8a**
b General sales tax on motor vehicles **8b**
9 Other taxes (list—include personal property taxes) ▶ **9**
10 Add the amounts on lines 6 through 9. Enter the total here. **Total** taxes . . ▶ **10**

Interest You Paid
(See Instructions on page 20.)

11 a Home mortgage interest paid to financial institutions (report deductible points on line 13) **11a**
b Home mortgage interest you paid to individuals (show that person's name and address) ▶ **11b**
12 Total credit card and charge account interest you paid **12**
13 Other interest you paid (list payee's name and amount) ▶ **13**
14 Add the amounts on lines 11a through 13. Enter the total here. **Total** interest . ▶ **14**

Contributions You Made
(See Instructions on page 21.)

15 a Cash contributions. (If you gave $3,000 or more to any one organization, report those contributions on line 15b.) . . . **15a**
b Cash contributions totaling $3,000 or more to any one organization. (Show to whom you gave and how much you gave.) ▶ **15b**
16 Other than cash. (You must attach Form 8283 if over $500.) . . **16**
17 Carryover from prior year **17**
18 Add the amounts on lines 15a through 17. Enter the total here. **Total** contributions . ▶ **18**

Casualty and Theft Losses

19 Total casualty or theft loss(es). (You must attach Form 4684 or similar statement.) (See page 21 of Instructions.) . . . . ▶ **19**

Miscellaneous Deductions
(See Instructions on page 22.)

20 Union and professional dues **20**
21 Tax return preparation fee **21**
22 Other (list type and amount) ▶ **22**
23 Add the amounts on lines 20 through 22. Enter the total here. **Total** miscellaneous . ▶ **23**

Summary of Itemized Deductions
(See Instructions on page 22.)

24 Add the amounts on lines 5, 10, 14, 18, 19, and 23. Enter your answer here. . . . **24**
25 If you checked Form 1040 { Filing Status box 2 or 5, enter $3,670 / Filing Status box 1 or 4, enter $2,480 / Filing Status box 3, enter $1,835 } **25**
26 Subtract line 25 from line 24. Enter your answer here and on Form 1040, line 34a. (If line 25 is more than line 24, see the Instructions for line 26 on page 22.) . . . ▶ **26**

For Paperwork Reduction Act Notice, see Form 1040 Instructions. Schedule A (Form 1040) 1986

Exhibit 3G

SCHEDULES A&B
(Form 1040)

Department of the Treasury
Internal Revenue Service   (5)

Schedule A—Itemized Deductions

(Schedule B is on back)

▶ Attach to Form 1040. ▶ See Instructions for Schedules A and B (Form 1040).

OMB No. 1545-0074

1991

Attachment
Sequence No. 07

Name(s) shown on Form 1040

Your social security number

Medical and Dental Expenses		Caution: *Do not include expenses reimbursed or paid by others.*		
	1	Medical and dental expenses. (See page 38.)	1	
	2	Enter amount from Form 1040, line 32	2	
	3	Multiply line 2 above by 7.5% (.075)	3	
	4	Subtract line 3 from line 1. Enter the result. If less than zero, enter -0- ▶		4
Taxes You Paid (See page 38.)	5	State and local income taxes	5	
	6	Real estate taxes	6	
	7	Other taxes. (List—include personal property taxes.) ▶	7	
	8	Add lines 5 through 7. Enter the total ▶		8
Interest You Paid (See page 39.) **Note:** Personal interest is no longer deductible.	9a	Home mortgage interest and points reported to you on Form 1098	9a	
	b	Home mortgage interest not reported to you on Form 1098. (If paid to an individual, show that person's name and address.) ▶	9b	
	10	Points not reported to you on Form 1098. (See instructions for special rules.)	10	
	11	Investment interest (attach Form 4952 if required). (See page 40.)	11	
	12	Add lines 9a through 11. Enter the total ▶		12
Gifts to Charity (See page 40.)		Caution: *If you made a charitable contribution and received a benefit in return, see page 40.*		
	13	Contributions by cash or check	13	
	14	Other than cash or check. (You **MUST** attach Form 8283 if over $500.)	14	
	15	Carryover from prior year	15	
	16	Add lines 13 through 15. Enter the total ▶		16
Casualty and Theft Losses	17	Casualty or theft loss(es) (attach Form 4684). (See page 40.) ▶		17
Moving Expenses	18	Moving expenses (attach Form 3903 or 3903F). (See page 41.) ▶		18
Job Expenses and Most Other Miscellaneous Deductions (See page 41 for expenses to deduct here.)	19	Unreimbursed employee expenses—job travel, union dues, job education, etc. (You **MUST** attach Form 2106 if required. See instructions.) ▶	19	
	20	Other expenses (investment, tax preparation, safe deposit box, etc.). List type and amount ▶	20	
	21	Add lines 19 and 20	21	
	22	Enter amount from Form 1040, line 32	22	
	23	Multiply line 22 above by 2% (.02)	23	
	24	Subtract line 23 from line 21. Enter the result. If less than zero, enter -0- ▶		24
Other Miscellaneous Deductions	25	Other (from list on page 41 of instructions). List type and amount ▶		25
Total Itemized Deductions	26	• If the amount on Form 1040, line 32, is $100,000 or less ($50,000 or less if married filing separately), add lines 4, 8, 12, 16, 17, 18, 24, and 25. Enter the total here. • If the amount on Form 1040, line 32, is more than $100,000 (more than $50,000 if married filing separately), see page 42 for the amount to enter. ▶		26
		Caution: *Be sure to enter on Form 1040, line 34, the **LARGER** of the amount on line 26 above or your standard deduction.*		

For Paperwork Reduction Act Notice, see Form 1040 instructions.   Cat. No. 11330X   Schedule A (Form 1040) 1991

Exhibit 3H

Form **4952**	**Investment Interest Expense Deduction**	OMB No. 1545-0191
Department of the Treasury Internal Revenue Service	▶ Attach to your tax return.	19**91** Attachment Sequence No. **72**
Name(s) shown on return		Identifying number

1	Investment interest expense paid or accrued in 1991. See instructions	1
2	Disallowed investment interest expense from 1990 Form 4952, line 23	2
3	Total investment interest expense. Add lines 1 and 2	3
4	**Net investment income.** See instructions	4
5	**Disallowed investment interest expense to be carried forward to 1992.** Subtract line 4 from line 3. If zero or less, enter -0-	5
6	**Investment interest expense deduction.** Enter the smaller of line 3 or line 4. See instructions	6

General Instructions

Paperwork Reduction Act Notice

We ask for the information on this form to carry out the Internal Revenue laws of the United States. You are required to give us the information. We need it to ensure that you are complying with these laws and to allow us to figure and collect the right amount of tax.

The time needed to complete and file this form will vary depending on individual circumstances. The estimated average time is:

Recordkeeping . . . . . . 13 min.
Learning about the law or the form . . . . . 14 min.
Preparing the form . . . . . 11 min.
Copying, assembling, and sending the form to the IRS . 10 min.

If you have comments concerning the accuracy of these time estimates or suggestions for making this form more simple, we would be happy to hear from you. You can write to both the IRS and the Office of Management and Budget at the addresses listed in the instructions for the tax return with which this form is filed.

Purpose of Form

Interest expense paid by an individual, estate, or a trust on a loan that is allocable to property held for investment (defined on page 2), may not be fully deductible in the current year. Form 4952 is used to figure the amount of investment interest expense deductible for the current year and the amount, if any, to carry forward to future years.

For more details, get **Pub. 550,** Investment Income and Expenses.

Who Must File

If you are an individual, estate, or a trust, and you claim a deduction for investment interest expense, you must complete and attach Form 4952 to your tax return, unless **all** of the following apply:

● Your only investment income was from interest or dividends,

● You have no other deductible expenses connected with the production of interest or dividends,

● Your investment interest expense is not more than your investment income, and

● You have no carryovers of investment interest expense from 1990.

Allocation of Interest Expense Under Temporary Regulations Section 1.163-8T

If you paid or accrued interest on a loan and you used the proceeds of the loan for more than one purpose, you may have to allocate the interest paid. This is necessary because of the different rules that apply to investment interest, personal interest, trade or business interest, home mortgage interest, and passive activity interest. See Pub. 550.

Specific Instructions

Line 1—Investment Interest Expense

Enter the investment interest paid or accrued during the tax year, regardless of when the indebtedness was incurred. Include interest paid or accrued on a loan (or part of a loan) that is allocable to property held for investment.

Be sure to include investment interest expense reported to you on Schedule

K-1 from a partnership or an S corporation. Include amortization of bond premium on taxable bonds purchased after October 22, 1986, but before January 1, 1988, unless you elected to offset amortizable bond premium against the interest payments on the bond. A taxable bond is a bond on which the interest is includible in gross income.

Investment interest expense does not include the following:

● Home mortgage interest;

● Interest expense that is properly allocable to a passive activity (see **Passive Activities** below);

● Any interest expense that is capitalized, such as construction interest subject to section 263A; or

● Interest expense related to tax-exempt interest income under section 265.

Passive Activities

Investment interest expense does not include any interest expense that is taken into account in determining your income or loss from a passive activity. However, interest expense that is properly allocable to portfolio income is investment interest expense and is not taken into account when determining your income or loss from a passive activity. Portfolio income includes income (not derived in the ordinary course of a trade or business) from interest, dividends, annuities, royalties, and net gain from the disposition of property held for investment. See the instructions for Schedule E (Form 1040) for the definition of passive activity.

Line 4—Net Investment Income

Net investment income is the excess, if any, of investment income over investment expenses (see page 2). Include investment income and

Cat. No. 13177Y

Form **4952** (1991)

Exhibit 3I

Form **6251**	**Alternative Minimum Tax—Individuals**	OMB No. 1545-0227
Department of the Treasury Internal Revenue Service	▶ **See separate instructions.** ▶ **Attach to Form 1040 or Form 1040NR. Estates and trusts, use Form 8656.**	**1991** Attachment Sequence No. **32**

Name(s) shown on Form 1040 | Your social security number

1	Enter the amount from Form 1040, line 35. (If Form 1040, line 35 is less than zero, enter as a negative amount.)	**1**	
2	Net operating loss deduction, if any, from Form 1040, line 22. (Enter as a positive amount.)	**2**	
3	Overall itemized deductions limitation (see instructions)	**3**	( )
4	Combine lines 1, 2, and 3	**4**	
5	**Adjustments:** (See instructions before completing.)		
a	Standard deduction, if any, from Form 1040, line 34	**5a**	
b	Medical and dental expenses. (Enter the smaller of the amount from Schedule A (Form 1040), line 4 or 2½% of Form 1040, line 32.)	**5b**	
c	Miscellaneous itemized deductions from Schedule A (Form 1040), line 24	**5c**	
d	Taxes from Schedule A (Form 1040), line 8	**5d**	
e	Refund of taxes	**5e**	( )
f	Certain home mortgage interest	**5f**	
g	Investment interest expense	**5g**	
h	Depreciation of tangible property placed in service after 1986	**5h**	
i	Circulation and research and experimental expenditures paid or incurred after 1986	**5i**	
j	Mining exploration and development costs paid or incurred after 1986	**5j**	
k	Long-term contracts entered into after 2/28/86	**5k**	
l	Pollution control facilities placed in service after 1986	**5l**	
m	Installment sales of certain property	**5m**	
n	Adjusted gain or loss and incentive stock options	**5n**	
o	Certain loss limitations	**5o**	
p	Tax shelter farm loss	**5p**	
q	Passive activity loss	**5q**	
r	Beneficiaries of estates and trusts	**5r**	
s	Combine lines 5a through 5r	**5s**	
6	**Tax preference items:** (See instructions before completing.)		
a	Appreciated property charitable deduction	**6a**	
b	Tax-exempt interest from private activity bonds issued after 8/7/86	**6b**	
c	Depletion	**6c**	
d	Accelerated depreciation of real property placed in service before 1987	**6d**	
e	Accelerated depreciation of leased personal property placed in service before 1987	**6e**	
f	Amortization of certified pollution control facilities placed in service before 1987	**6f**	
g	Intangible drilling costs	**6g**	
h	Add lines 6a through 6g	**6h**	
7	Combine lines 4, 5s, and 6h	**7**	
8	Energy preference adjustment for certain taxpayers. (Do not enter more than 40% of line 7.) See instructions	**8**	
9	Subtract line 8 from line 7	**9**	
10	Alternative tax net operating loss deduction. See instructions for limitations	**10**	
11	**Alternative minimum taxable income.** Subtract line 10 from line 9. If married filing separately, see instructions	**11**	
12	Enter: $40,000 ($20,000 if married filing separately; $30,000 if single or head of household)	**12**	
13	Enter: $150,000 ($75,000 if married filing separately; $112,500 if single or head of household)	**13**	
14	Subtract line 13 from line 11. If zero or less, enter -0- here and on line 15 and go to line 16	**14**	
15	Multiply line 14 by 25% (.25)	**15**	
16	**Exemption.** Subtract line 15 from line 12. If zero or less, enter -0-. If completing this form for a child under age 14, see instructions for amount to enter	**16**	
17	Subtract line 16 from line 11. If zero or less, enter -0- here and on line 22 and skip lines 18 through 21	**17**	
18	Multiply line 17 by 24% (.24)	**18**	
19	Alternative minimum tax foreign tax credit. See instructions	**19**	
20	Tentative minimum tax. Subtract line 19 from line 18	**20**	
21	Enter your tax from Form 1040, line 38, minus any foreign tax credit on Form 1040, line 43. If an amount is entered on line 39 of Form 1040, see instructions	**21**	
22	**Alternative minimum tax.** Subtract line 21 from line 20. If zero or less, enter -0-. Enter this amount on Form 1040, line 48. If completing this form for a child under age 14, see instructions for amount to enter	**22**	

For Paperwork Reduction Act Notice, see separate instructions.   Cat. No. 13600G   Form **6251** (1991)

Exhibit 3J

29

Summary of Major Changes Affecting the Investor as a Result of The Tax Reform Act

Pre Tax Reform Act	Post Tax Reform Act
1) 60% exclusion on Long–Term Capital Gains.	1) Long–Term Capital Gains taxed as ordinary income (28% Maximum).
2) First $400 of dividends earned tax free for married taxpayers.	2) All dividend income taxed, with no exclusions.
3) Margin and investment interest expense deductible up to $10,000 beyond investment income.	3) Margin and investment interest deduction limited to amount of investment income for any one year.
4) All expenses associated with the cost of producing investment income fully deductible.	4) Only amounts exceeding 2% floor (of Adjusted Gross Income) are deductible (additional 3% exclusion with income above $100,000).
5) An investment tax credit of 10% of the cost of most business-related assets.	5) Investment tax credit provision not renewed for business-related assets.
6) Depreciation periods of three to five years for most business-related assets.	6) Depreciable lives of most business assets extended and yearly expense reduced.
7) Municipal bond interest fully exempt from federal taxation.	7) Certain types of municipal bond interest now taxable.
8) Full value deduction for charitable contribution of stocks, bonds, and other appreciated property.	8) Tax on amount of appreciation of stocks, bonds, and other appreciated property.
9) Investment income of children taxed at child's tax rates.	9) "Kiddie tax" imposed on investment income of children under 14.

10) Gift tax exclusion includes tax free transfers to/from all generations.

10) Generation Skipping Transfer Tax imposed on transfers of wealth from second generation giftors.

11) Losses generated from passive activities are fully deductible.

11) Passive Activity Losses fully deductible only against passive income.

Conclusion: The Effect of Tax Simplification and Where Do We Go From Here?

If you take, for example, the taxpayer N. Vestor who had a $200,000 long–term capital gain in both 1986 and 1991 and expand on his situation, you will become fully aware of the impact of this tax bill. Let us add these other items to his tax situation: N. Vestor had investment interest expenses of $10,000, other investment expenses of $20,000, dividends of $12,000, a rental building, which he owns and manages with a net $35,000 loss, an oil and gas partnership which generated a $10,000 tax loss, and $15,000 in charitable contributions of stocks with a basis appreciation of 200%. The results are somewhat startling for anyone who thought we had a tax rate cut. His tax would have **increased** by approximately $10,000 (30%) from 1986 to 1991 on the same set of taxable items. In addition, the fees for preparation of his tax return, based on man hours spent, would have probably **tripled**! So much for tax simplification, so much for tax reduction, and so much for any benefit at all to the individual investor.

Now, let's also analyze what these tax law changes have had on the economy as a whole. For reasons which seem obvious to me, they have discouraged individual investment in long–term growth stocks, in real estate, and in business in general, small business particularly. The Tax Reform Act has made real estate a very unfavorable investment from a tax point of view, has made taking gains on stocks and bonds very expensive, and has made investing in a business you do not actively participate in a more treacherous investment.

Is it any wonder that the real estate market has become a disaster, and that people who have spent their life's savings to own a house are having to take **losses** on an investment which they **can't** deduct? That is, assuming that they can sell their property at all. And, at this point, I am convinced that the only reason the stock market hasn't followed suit is that no one can get any yield by putting their money elsewhere.

And, for that matter, it should come as no surprise at all that our economy is stuck in the worst recession since the early 1970s– recession which has taken the government five successive interest rate cuts (to this point) to try to break up. It is my position that there would have been a much better way to stimulate the economy, which would have been more effective, ultimately less inflationary, and more beneficial to the average taxpayer. That method would have been to have given the investor back some of the tax advantages which were taken away with the last major tax bill.

Anyway, with that being said, let us now move on to the next several sections of this book. These chapters deal with how to best approach the law as it now exists and how to develop strategies which will serve us in the present circumstances, as well as, hopefully, in the future. With a solid tax background, the **average** investor can dramatically improve his rate of return, and the **good** investor can become a **double winner**!

Chapter 4

Tax Facts
Concepts Investors
Need to Know

Selling Off the Family Jewels

Several years ago I was hired as an advisor by a wealthy family. In fact, they were fourth and fifth generation heirs to a man who was one of the pioneer industrial entrepreneurs of the 19th century. Their finances had been handled by a family office which was staffed by some very competent, but non–investment/tax–oriented accountants. This staff handled all their financial needs other than investment advice, which was provided by another, very competent group of professionals. The arrangement had always provided them with the expertise they needed to keep their wealth, and, in fact, to add to it, throughout the years.

Most of the family members depended on this office to provide them with all financial services, and a good deal of non–financial ones as well. These services included the securing of mortgages for their houses, the selection and procurement of insurance for their autos, life, and for their home. And, in earlier days, the office had even provided such services as the arrangement of travel accommodations and the walking of family dogs during short vacations. In other words, over the years, this family had come to depend on the office to provide them with the most basic of financial and non–financial services.

I had taken on the assignment of heading up and reorganizing their tax department when the manager retired after being with the firm for over 25 years. This was quite a task in and of itself and one which was soon to be made even more challenging by the Tax Reform Act of 1986!

I started in May of 1986, about the time that many of the provisions of the Tax Reform Act had been introduced into Congress but only a handful of which had been approved. At that time, I had no idea of the magnitude of the Act, nor of its potential implications regarding the new position I had just accepted.

Jewels

In reviewing the portfolios of my new clients, it soon became clear to me that the new tax law would indeed affect their holdings, and that they should be made aware of this fact. Some had invested in real estate over the years, both in limited partnerships as well as in single rental units. In addition, there were investments in passive activities which generated losses which would be disallowed and, quite frankly, some of these transactions should have been structured quite differently from a tax point of view. I noted that a good deal of money was being put into smaller, growth–oriented stocks, such as computer stocks, drug company stocks, and other NASDAQ equities.

Also, there was a good deal of investment through venture capital funds. The president of this office would find an under–financed, high potential company and would set up a family partnership to infuse large sums of money into the company. This was done in order to acquire the stock at a low cost, and hopefully put the company back on its feet. At this point they would either sell the stock at a much higher price or hold on to it in anticipation of additional profits, added value, and future dividends.

The first potential problem with these types of investments was that the nature of the investments themselves were generally more aggressive than they should have been. This was a family who had sufficient funds to get them through the rest of their lives and who simply wanted to keep pace with the economy. They were not concerned with generating a great deal of additional wealth, but rather in keeping up with inflation, protecting themselves in case of recession, or, for that matter, protecting themselves from any unforeseen economic event. Some of the investment advisors, however, were not particularly in tune with these needs and the smaller, low capitalized, high risk companies in which they invested were not the best alternatives.

Secondly, under the old tax law where, as we know, capital gains were only taxed at a maximum 20% on their return, it made more sense to take these risks. That is because, as we will see, it made sense through the concept of "total return investment planning." However, with the maximum tax rate on long–term capital gains going up to 28% in the near future, it did not make sense for these people to be risking as much of their capital under these circumstances.

A third problem with the nature of these investments was that many of them were in passive activities, such as real estate, oil and gas partnerships, and other non–working partnership interests. Prior to 1986 this made good sense. Even with a low rate of return on these investments, they served a very useful purpose and were of tremendous value to them for several reasons: the investments generated larger paper losses than actual cash losses through such processes as depreciation and depletion of assets. This meant that each year they were able to write off a portion of the original investment as an expense against income.

If, as in many cases, you had excess expenses over income for the first several years, you were then able to write off these losses, dollar for dollar against all types of other income. This no longer was allowed after 1986. The new tax law phased out, over five years, the offset of passive losses against non–passive income. (Although it is generally thought of as a five year phase out, by the fifth year there was no deduction allowed.) We will discuss this in further detail in my next section, "The Three Baskets of Income."

There were also some investments in municipals which were either entirely or partially tax free, and investments in U.S. Treasuries which were 100% state tax free. The problem with this was that some of the family members who had been investing in these tax–free vehicles lived in tax–free states, or low tax bracket states. Therefore, the benefit of these investments was not being fully reaped. In other words, at times, the trade–off of a lower yielding product for the tax–free status on state income tax returns may not have been worth it.

Another problem with this was the alternative minimum tax as it applied to Private Activity Bonds. Some of these bonds would now be taxed under the alternative minimum tax calculation even though they were not taxable previously. The reason this made a significant difference was the change in regular tax rate versus alternative minimum tax rate.

Under the old tax system there was a maximum tax rate of 50%, and an alternative minimum tax of 20%. With the change in tax laws, the new maximum rate was 31% and the new alternative minimum tax rate was 21% (24% in 1991). Because of this, AMT items become much more significant.

The way this works is that the government has you calculate your tax in two ways. First you are taxed at the regular tax at a rate of say 31%, and then you calculate your tax at the alternative minimum tax rate of 21%. The difference, however, is that although the minimum tax rate is lower, it encompasses a much broader base of income. Therefore, at times a tax calculated at the 21% rate can be higher than a smaller income base calculated at the 31% rate. The government then looks at the larger of these taxes and this becomes your tax liability.

Let's look at an example of this and how the change in tax law affects your ordinary tax liability versus your alternative minimum tax liability. As you see, the change in tax laws narrowed the gap between the two tax rates. The difference between the 50% regular tax rate and the 20% alternative minimum tax rate was 30%. You had to have an awful lot more income, taxed at 20%, to have a higher tax than what would be calculated at the regular rate of 50%.

However, the difference between the 31% maximum tax rate under the new law and the 21% alternative minimum tax rate was much smaller. Therefore, you did not have to have as big an increase in alternative minimum taxable income to fall into this category.

Let's look at our old friends Mr. and Mrs. N. Vestor. One year they had the following situation with regard to income and deductions: they had $500,000 of ordinary income, $250,000 of municipal bond income associated with private activities, and $100,000 of charitable contributions of assets purchased for $10,000. For the purposes of this illustration we will disregard all other income and expense deductions, as well as exemptions.

Under the old tax rates of 50% maximum and 20% AMT, the liability would be calculated as follows:

Ordinary Tax Calculation:

Ordinary Income	$500,000
Private Activity Municipals	250,000*
Charitable Contributions	(100,000)
Taxable Income	$400,000
Tax Rate	x .50^2
Ordinary Tax	$200,000

* Fully non–taxable

Alternative Minimum Tax Calculation:

Taxable Income	$400,000
Private Activity Bonds	250,000
Appreciation on Charitable Contribution Property	90,000
AMT Income	$740,000
AMT Exemption	(40,000)
AMT Income Net of Exemption	$700,000
Tax Rate	X .20
Alternative Minimum Tax	$140,000

Larger of the Tax Liabilities:

Ordinary Tax Liability	$200,000

As you can see, the larger of the two liabilities is the ordinary tax liability of $200,000. In fact, this amount was $60,000 more than the alternative minimum tax liability of $140,000. There is a lot of room for additional alternative minimum tax items to be added before the alternative minimum tax liability will catch up to and surpass the ordinary tax liability under the old tax rates.

Under the new tax rates of 31% maximum and 21% alternative minimum tax, the liability for the same set of income and expense items would be calculated as follows:

Ordinary Tax Calculation:

Ordinary Income	$500,000
Private Activity Municipals	250,000*
Charitable Contributions	(100,000)
Taxable Income	$400,000
Tax Rate	X .31^3
Ordinary Tax	$124,000

* Fully non–taxable

Alternative Minimum Tax Calculation:

Taxable Income	$400,000
Private Activity Bonds	250,000
Appreciation on Charitable Contribution Property	90,000
AMT Income	$740,000
AMT Exemption	(40,000)
AMT Income Net of Exemption	$700,000
Tax Rate	X .21
Alternative Minimum Tax	$147,000

Larger of the Tax Liabilities:

Alternative Minimum Tax Liability	$147,000

In this case, under the new tax law, the larger of the two liabilities due the federal government is the alternative minimum tax liability of $147,000. In fact, this was $23,000 more than the ordinary tax liability of $124,000. As you can see, you do not have much room to determine for which tax rate you will be liable. Although, under the new tax laws, and under AMT liability, Mr. and Mrs. N. Vestor will be subject to less tax in this situation, items such as private activity municipal bonds and other alternative minimum tax items become much more significant. The Tax Reform Act did lower tax rates on earned income, but not on investment income.

The Dections and Expenses

Another area which needed to be examined immediately was that of charitable contributions. Most of the family members were community–minded individuals who made a habit of regularly contributing to their favorite charities. This was being done without regard to the nature of the gift and its original cost basis, appropriate under the old tax law. As we know, the rules were changed under the new tax law due to the restructuring of the alternative minimum tax. As a result, when an asset is gifted to a charity the difference between its cost and current market value is taxed under the AMT.

Now, whenever a donation was made, we had to first do a tax analysis to examine whether or not the alternative minimum tax would come into play, and if so, what implications the specific gift would have on this. If this was the case, we had to find the asset with the highest cost basis to be donated to the charity or we had to examine alternative methods of making this contribution.

It was often the practice of the family's investment advisors to margin investment accounts and to take maximum advantage of investment capital. As you recall, there was now a tighter limitation on the deduction of margin interest. If the individual, for example, had a bad year in the market, the investment interest expense deduction could be disallowed in that year. Therefore, we had to examine the amount of margining which was being done each year.

There also were several family members who traded stocks and commodities full time. They had offices down on Wall Street, computers, ticker tapes, and all sorts of expenses associated with their primary activity of trading stocks, options, and other commodities. Although they did not always make huge amounts of money through these activities, they were able to reap huge tax benefits by writing off 100% of all expenses associated with this endeavor. As you recall from my previous section, "Now You See It, Now You Don't," due to the 2% exclusion (of adjusted gross income), which in this case was very high, these expenses were soon to vanish.

Other Practices

Other practices which were to be affected by the new tax laws were the way in which wealth was being passed down and distributed from the older to the younger generations of the family. In the past family members generally passed down assets as they became elderly, and they did this in large gift amounts. Also, gifts were being made from grandparents to grandchildren without regard to the new generation skipping transfer tax. In addition, the gifts were being made regardless of the specific nature of the asset. The problem with this practice was threefold.

First of all, they were not taking full advantage of the $20,000 per year exemption, nor of the Unified Credit. The Unified Credit is a $600,000 lifetime credit against individual gifts of estates, and will be explained in further detail subsequently.

Secondly, there was a generation skipping transfer tax to be instituted in the near future and a very short–term $2,000,000 per grandchild exclusion which would be phased out. More on this allowance to be discussed in "Transferring Your Wealth To Future Generations."

The third aspect of this method of passing down wealth was that with the changes in tax law it was now necessary to look at the age of the person who was receiving the asset and the nature of that asset. Prior to the new tax law it did not matter if the asset was producing income in the present or producing income in the future. As you recall, we mentioned the advent of the "kiddie tax." What this meant is that if the receiver of the gift was under 14 years old they would be taxed on any unearned income over $1,000 at the same rate as the parent would be.

It made more sense, therefore, to only gift assets which did not produce current income to children under the age of 14. Instead, it made more sense to make gifts of potential growth–type assets, such as the small capitalization stocks which I discussed. Not only because these children were much younger and could afford to take more of a risk by holding onto these stocks for a longer period of time, but also that they could hold onto the stocks until after they reached 14 years of age. Hopefully by then the stocks would have increased in value, at which point they could be sold and the profits taxed once again at the child's lower tax rate.

Generally, these stocks did not pay dividends so that there would be no current income to be taxed at the higher parent's rate. It also made more sense now to hold onto the smaller capitalized stocks, which provided more growth potential and more capital gain potential until a future date for one other reason: since the long–term capital gain exclusion was now defunct we would either not want to sell the stock at all or to wait, perhaps, until a more favorable tax bill was passed providing for a lower tax on capital gains.

It had become increasingly clear to me that the investment advisory services were being rendered without adequate consideration of the new tax law being passed. This oversight would become significant in the next few years. These people had to find some other way, and it was my job to help them find it.

Now, let's take a look as I recap and summarize the practices which had to be changed under the new tax law and the reasons for the change. We will then examine some basic investment/tax concepts and then re–analyze the family portfolio from a tax point of view. In fact, we will devote an entire section of the book to analyzing the specific tax–related changes which were made to this portfolio and examine how you can structure your portfolio in the same taxwise manner.

Tax Analysis of a Poorly Structured Portfolio

Practice	Outcome and Effect
1. Investment in smaller, high risk, growth stocks and venture capital funds.	1. Increased risk for lower potential reward with increase in capital gains tax rate.
2. Investment in real estate and other passive activities generating losses.	2. Loss of deduction against other investment income less tax benefit of investment.
3. Investment in private activity bonds and other partially taxable municipals.	3. Loss of tax exempt status on future purchases and some prior holdings under newly revised alternative minimum tax.
4. Investment in U.S. Treasuries by those living in low tax bracket states.	4. Lower yielding investment as a tradeoff for less state tax benefit.

5. Charitable contributions being made with low cost basis, highly appreciated assets.

5. Loss of substantial part of deduction through revised alternative minimum tax calculation.

6. Investment accounts being margined.

6. Loss, or partial loss, of investment interest expense deduction.

7. Large miscellaneous expenses, relating to investments being taken as itemized deductions.

7. Disallowance of significant portion of these expenses due to 2% and 3% (of AGI) exclusions.

8. Gifts not always being made to younger family members on an annual basis.

8. Loss of $20,000 per couple, per year, per recipient, tax–free gift allowance.

9. High income producing gifts being made to children under the age of 14.

9. Children being taxed on investment income of over $1,000 at maximum parental tax rates due to new "kiddie tax."

10. Gifts being made from grandparents to grandchildren with the direct skip of the middle generation.

10. Such transfers would now be subject to "generation skipping transfer tax."

We will come back to this list in a short time and cover the changes made to the portfolio to effect a more beneficial tax treatment of these investments. It is necessary, however, to first spend some time learning a few elementary tax concepts. The next several chapters will discuss the broad concepts of what is considered income and what valid expenses are deductible from it.

Chapter 5

Tax Classification
The Three Baskets of Income

I don't want to get too involved with advanced tax concepts in this book as it is geared to the average investor who most likely has a fairly basic knowledge of taxation. However, it is necessary to introduce a few elementary tax concepts. I do this to build a structure within which we can work on planning our tax/investment strategy to reduce our tax liability. With this in mind, let's begin to look at a few tax definitions so that we may understand the rules before we play the game. All the discussions from here on in will address the cash basis, calendar year taxpayer, a category within which 99% of all individual taxpayers fall.[4]

Income Defined

For federal income tax purposes, any acquisition of wealth, except gifts and inheritances, is considered to be income unless it is specifically excluded by the Code (Code Sec.61). Fourteen specific types of income listed in this section of the IRS Code are:

(1) compensation for services, including fees, commissions, fringe benefits, and similar items;
(2) gross income from business;
(3) gains from dealings in property;
(4) interest;
(5) rents;

(6)   royalties;
(7)   dividends;
(8)   alimony and separate maintenance payments;
(9)   annuities;
(10) income from life insurance policies;
(11) pensions;
(12) income from discharge of debt;
(13) partner's share of partnership income; and
(14) income from an interest in an estate or trust.

"The Tax Court has, through its decisions, developed a concept of income which is quite different from the layman's concept. The Supreme Court has approved this definition: 'Income may be defined as the gain derived from capital, labor, or from both combined, provided it be understood to include profit gained through a sale or conversion of capital assets.' In addition, the Supreme Court has repeatedly held that Congress' broad definition of what constitutes gross income was intended to tax all gain unless specifically exempted."[5]

In addition to some specific exclusions which were mentioned by the Code, such as damage settlements in personal injury cases, the following three items are particularly relevant to investors, and are construed to **not** be income:

(1)   Return of Capital–Return of your original investment, such as the cost you have paid for shares of stock;
(2)   Gifts and Inheritances–Non–taxable to the recipient; and
(3)   Unrealized Appreciation–The value of the property which has increased, but has not been sold by the investor.

Some other relevant investment/tax principles and rulings are as follows: for a cash basis taxpayer, interest is taxed when it is **received**. For example, the interest on a two–year Certificate of Deposit which is credited to the account every quarter is taxable in the year that the interest is credited. The interest on a two–year Certificate of Deposit which gets the interest credited at the end of the two–year period is not taxable in the first year, but rather when the interest is received in the account.

Another good example of different tax treatments would be those involving different forms of U.S. government obligations: the one–year Treasury Bill, the three–year Treasury Note, and the ten–year Series EE type Treasury Bond. The Treasury issuances are an important subject as they are the standard to which most other investments are compared. In terms of rate of return, they are considered no–risk investments. For that reason, I use Treasuries as illustrations quite frequently.

The **Treasury Bill**, for example, that would be purchased in June of one year and redeemable in May of the following year would have the interest tacked on when the Bill is redeemed. Therefore, the interest would only be taxable in the year of redemption, the following tax year.

Typically how this works is that the investor would pay say $9,700 for a Bill that would be redeemed for $10,000. At redemption, $9,700 would be the non–taxable return of capital, and the $300 would be the interest earned and taxable in the year of redemption. A good tax strategy for an investor wanting to defer income from one year to the next would be to put some money into Treasury Bills which would become payable on or after January 2 of the following year.

Compare the prior tax treatment with that of the three–year **Treasury Note** which pays interest every six months. In this case, as I mentioned before, the interest is taxable as it is received. So, if the same taxpayer purchases a $10,000, three–year Treasury Note paying the same $300 per year, but paying $150 semiannually on June 30th and December 31st, the interest would be taxable in the year it was paid. An investor who wanted to accelerate income into the current year would opt for this type of government investment vehicle as opposed to the first.

Contrast this, again, with the ten–year **Series EE Treasury Bond**, which does not pay interest until the bond is redeemed at the end of the ten–year period. In this case, no interest income would have to be declared until the Bond matured. This type of investment might be appropriate as a gift to a four–year–old child who you would not want to have any income received and taxable until they turned fourteen years old. (Review my section on the "Kiddie tax.")

As long as we are on the subject of U.S. Treasuries, several more areas are worth discussing briefly. The first is that **all** interest from U.S. Bonds, Notes, or Bills issued after February 28, 1941 is taxable for **federal** purposes, but is exempt from **state** taxation in most states.

The second issue is in the handling of income as interest as opposed to capital gains. Although the method of treatment was much more significant prior to the Tax Reform Act due to the greater difference in tax rates for capital gains, it is still important now. The tax exempt status of the interest, but not the capital gain from sale of Treasuries on most state tax returns is one reason why. It is also important due to the limitations placed on capital losses and in the offset of losses against only capital gain income beyond the ($3,000) amount per couple, per year.

Capital Gain income is defined as the gain associated with the sale or disposition of a capital asset. A *capital asset* as defined by the Code (Section 1221) is any property which is held either as business or non–business property, **except**:

(1) Inventories;
(2) Other property held for sale in the normal course of a trade or business;
(3) An account receivable held in the ordinary course of a trade or business;
(4) Depreciable business property;
(5) Real property held in the taxpayer's business;
(6) A copyright (but not a patent); or
(7) A U.S. government publication held by the taxpayer who received it.

A taxpayer's household furnishings and personal property are capital assets to the extent that if you have a gain on the sale of these items it is a capital gain and taxed accordingly. If however, you have a loss, you would not be able to deduct it on your tax return. (For another case of the "Unlimited Gain/Limited Loss," see section to follow.)

Obviously, as investors, if you have a gain on the sale of a U.S. Treasury Bill, Note, or Bond, you have a gain, but what if the obligation is sold midway throughout its life? Isn't part of the gain attributable to the interest earned up until that point? The question is a rhetorical one, and the answer is yes. To illustrate this further, let's look at one of the prior scenarios we examined before. However, in this example, there is a capital gain, as well as interest, involved in the transaction.

In the case of the one–year, $10,000 Treasury Bill, purchased June 1, for $9,700, let us examine a sale of this item on November

30 of the same year for $9,900. Is the $200 difference between the cost and the sale price of the T–Bill interest or is it capital gain? Those of you who think the answer is interest are partially correct as are those of you who think it is capital gain. In truth, the proper way to handle this transaction is to split the $200 between both interest and capital gain.

In order to do this, we look at the amount which was to be paid as interest on the original T–Bill, and see that it was $300 for the year on a $9,700 investment, or that it paid 3.09% ($300/$9700). We are only looking at the percentage paid on the investment, and not at the **true yield**. For this calculation, it is appropriate because we are calculating interest paid. We then take the same percentage and multiply it by the investment and prorate it over the period of time it was held.

The calculation would be as follows:

$9,700 X .0309 X 6 months/12 months (1/2)= $150

In this example, it is easy as it is exactly one half a year. This amount, $150, becomes the accrued interest we received for holding this T–Bill for the six–month period. We would pick this amount up on our Schedule B, Part 1, Line 1, as interest income (see Exhibit 5B). However, we know that we also received an additional amount for the T–Bill, $50. This extra amount now becomes the capital gain associated with the sale of the T–Bill and will be reported on the Schedule D, Part 1, Line 1d, as other short term transactions (see Exhibit 5A).

To summarize our T–Bill Example:

Cost (Return of Capital):	$9,700	
Interest (6/1–11/30):	150	to Sch. B
Short–Term Capital Gain:	50	to Sch. D
Gross Proceeds Received:	$9,900	

Let us look for a minute at what conditions would have to be present for the holder of such a T–Bill to receive more money than he paid for the Bill, excluding the accrued interest portion. There is only one scenario that could take place in terms of interest rates, that being a decline in the short–term rates. In this case, a Treasury Bill which paid 3.09% for another six months would have been worth more now than upon issue if Treasury Bills at the time of the sale paid only 3.0%.

SCHEDULE D	**Capital Gains and Losses**	OMB No. 1545-0074
(Form 1040)	(And Reconciliation of Forms 1099-B for Bartering Transactions)	19**91**
Department of the Treasury Internal Revenue Service (5)	▶ Attach to Form 1040. ▶ See Instructions for Schedule D (Form 1040). ▶ For more space to list transactions for lines 1a and 8a, get Schedule D-1 (Form 1040).	Attachment Sequence No. **12A**

Name(s) shown on Form 1040	Your social security number
MR. & MRS. N. VESTOR	123 45 6789

Caution: *Add the following amounts reported to you for 1991 on Forms 1099-B and 1099-S (or on substitute statements): (a) proceeds from transactions involving stocks, bonds, and other securities, and (b) gross proceeds from real estate transactions not reported on another form or schedule. If this total does not equal the total of lines 1c and 8c, column (d), attach a statement explaining the difference.*

Part I   Short-Term Capital Gains and Losses—Assets Held One Year or Less

(a) Description of property (Example, 100 shares 7% preferred of "Z" Co.)	(b) Date acquired (Mo., day, yr.)	(c) Date sold (Mo., day, yr.)	(d) Sales price (see instructions)	(e) Cost or other basis (see instructions)	(f) LOSS If (e) is more than (d), subtract (d) from (e)	(g) GAIN If (d) is more than (e), subtract (e) from (d)
1a Stocks, Bonds, Other Securities, and Real Estate. Include Form 1099-B and 1099-S Transactions. See instructions.						
1b Amounts from Schedule D-1, line 1b (attach Schedule D-1)						
1c Total of All Sales Price Amounts. Add column (d) of lines 1a and 1b ▶ **1c**						

1d Other Transactions (Do NOT include real estate transactions from Forms 1099-S on this line. Report them on line 1a.)

(a)	(b)	(c)	(d)	(e)	(f)	(g)
TREAS. BILL	6/1	11/30	9750 *	9700		50

2 Short-term gain from sale or exchange of your home from Form 2119, line 10 or 14c	**2**		
3 Short-term gain from installment sales from Form 6252, line 22 or 30	**3**		
4 Net short-term gain or (loss) from partnerships, S corporations, and fiduciaries .	**4**		
5 Short-term capital loss carryover from 1990 Schedule D, line 29	**5**		
6 Add lines 1a, 1b, 1d, and 2 through 5, in columns (f) and (g).	**6**	(	)
7 Net short-term capital gain or (loss). Combine columns (f) and (g) of line 6	**7**	50	

Part II   Long-Term Capital Gains and Losses—Assets Held More Than One Year

8a Stocks, Bonds, Other Securities, and Real Estate. Include Form 1099-B and 1099-S Transactions. See instructions.

(a)	(b)	(c)	(d)	(e)	(f)	(g)
8b Amounts from Schedule D-1, line 8b (attach Schedule D-1)						
8c Total of All Sales Price Amounts. Add column (d) of lines 8a and 8b ▶ **8c**						

8d Other Transactions (Do NOT include real estate transactions from Forms 1099-S on this line. Report them on line 8a.)

(a)	(b)	(c)	(d)	(e)	(f)	(g)

9 Long-term gain from sale or exchange of your home from Form 2119, line 10 or 14c	**9**		
10 Long-term gain from installment sales from Form 6252, line 22 or 30	**10**		
11 Net long-term gain or (loss) from partnerships, S corporations, and fiduciaries .	**11**		
12 Capital gain distributions	**12**		
13 Gain from Form 4797, line 7 or 9	**13**		
14 Long-term capital loss carryover from 1990 Schedule D, line 36.	**14**		
15 Add lines 8a, 8b, 8d, and 9 through 14, in columns (f) and (g)	**15**	(	)
16 Net long-term capital gain or (loss). Combine columns (f) and (g) of line 15	**16**		

For Paperwork Reduction Act Notice, see Form 1040 instructions.   Cat. No. 11338H   Schedule D (Form 1040) 1991

* TOTAL RECEIVED WAS $9900, INCLUDING $150 INTEREST (SEE SCH B)

Exhibit 5A

Tax Classification: The Three Baskets of Income

Name(s) shown on Form 1040. (Do not enter name and social security number if shown on other side.)	Your social security number
MR. & MRS. N. VESTOR	123 45 6789

Schedule B—Interest and Dividend Income

Attachment Sequence No. **08**

Part I **Interest** **Income** (See pages 15 and 43.)	If you received more than $400 in taxable interest income, or you are claiming the exclusion of interest from series EE U.S. savings bonds issued after 1989 (see page 43), you must complete Part I. List ALL interest received in Part I. If you received more than $400 in taxable interest income, you must also complete Part III. If you received, as a nominee, interest that actually belongs to another person, or you received or paid accrued interest on securities transferred between interest payment dates, see page 43.

Interest Income		Amount
1 Interest income. (List name of payer—if any interest income is from seller-financed mortgages, see instructions and list this interest first.) ▶ .... INTEREST ON TREASURY BILL		150 —

Note: If you received a Form 1099-INT, Form 1099-OID, or substitute statement, from a brokerage firm, list the firm's name as the payer and enter the total interest shown on that form.

		1	
2 Add the amounts on line 1		**2**	150 —
3 Enter the excludable savings bond interest, if any, from Form 8815, line 14. Attach Form 8815 to Form 1040	**3**		
4 Subtract line 3 from line 2. Enter the result here and on Form 1040, line 8a . ▶		**4**	150 —

Part II **Dividend** **Income** (See pages 16 and 43.)	If you received more than $400 in gross dividends and/or other distributions on stock, you must complete Parts II and III. If you received, as a nominee, dividends that actually belong to another person, see page 43.

Dividend Income		Amount
5 Dividend income. (List name of payer—include on this line capital gain distributions, nontaxable distributions, etc.) ▶		

Note: If you received a Form 1099-DIV, or substitute statement, from a brokerage firm, list the firm's name as the payer and enter the total dividends shown on that form.

		5	
6 Add the amounts on line 5		**6**	
7 Capital gain distributions. Enter here and on Schedule D* .	**7**		
8 Nontaxable distributions. (See the inst. for Form 1040, line 9.).	**8**		
9 Add lines 7 and 8		**9**	
10 Subtract line 9 from line 6. Enter the result here and on Form 1040, line 9 . ▶		**10**	

*If you received capital gain distributions but do not need Schedule D to report any other gains or losses, see the instructions for Form 1040, lines 13 and 14.

		Yes	No
Part III **Foreign** **Accounts** **and** **Foreign** **Trusts** (See page 43.)	If you received more than $400 of interest or dividends, OR if you had a foreign account or were a grantor of, or a transferor to, a foreign trust, you must answer both questions in Part III.		
	11a At any time during 1991, did you have an interest in or a signature or other authority over a financial account in a foreign country (such as a bank account, securities account, or other financial account)? (See page 43 for exceptions and filing requirements for Form TD F 90-22.1.) . . .		X
	b If "Yes," enter the name of the foreign country ▶		
	12 Were you the grantor of, or transferor to, a foreign trust that existed during 1991, whether or not you have any beneficial interest in it? If "Yes," you may have to file Form 3520, 3520-A, or 926 .		X

For Paperwork Reduction Act Notice, see Form 1040 instructions.   Schedule B (Form 1040) 1991

Exhibit 5B

The same split between interest and capital gain would take place upon the sale during the holding period of any of the three Treasury items we have discussed. If, in fact, the converse took place and we received less than $9,850 ($9,700 + $150 interest) we would be able to recognize the loss to the extent of the limitation on capital losses (to be discussed later in this chapter). This situation probably would occur if the interest rates went up during the holding period, i.e. the T–Bill would be worth less at a 3.09% rate than a new T–Bill paying 3.20%.

The last issue involving Treasuries is that of the exclusion for U.S. Savings Bonds used for higher education. Anyone who redeems a qualified U.S. Savings Bond in a year during which he pays qualified higher education expenses may exclude from taxable income any amounts received providing that certain requirements are met. A qualified U.S. Savings bond is one which was issued after 1989 to an individual who had reached age 24 before the purchase of this bond. Qualified higher education expenses include tuition and fees required for attendance or enrollment at an eligible educational institution of either a taxpayer, his wife, or his dependent.

This amount, if excludable, is reported on form 8815, and is carried forward to Schedule B, Part 1, Line 3, as a subtraction from interest (see Exhibit 5C).

Earned and Passive Income Versus Investment Income

Prior to the Tax Reform Act of 1986, the classifications of income were as follows: there was earned income, on which social security tax was calculated and paid, and unearned income upon which it was not. There was also investment income, a specific type of unearned income, generated by capital gains and losses, which were taxed at a preferred rate, and interest and dividends which were taxed at ordinary rates. As we previously noted, the maximum rate of taxation on long–term capital gains was 20%.

The Tax Reform Act of 1986 regrouped income into three specific tax classifications. There is still earned income and still investment income which are now both taxed, for all intents and purposes, at the same ordinary tax rate. The maximum tax rate for capital gains for 1991, however, is limited to 28% as opposed to 31% for other types of income. Yet investment income is now subdivided

Tax Classification: The Three Baskets of Income

Form **8815**	**Exclusion of Interest From Series EE** **U.S. Savings Bonds Issued After 1989** (For Filers With Qualified Higher Education Expenses) ▶ Attach to Form 1040 or Form 1040A. ▶ See instructions on back.	OMB No. 1545-1173 **1991** Attachment Sequence No. **57**
Department of the Treasury Internal Revenue Service		

Caution: *If your filing status is married filing a separate return,* **do not** *file this form. You may not take the exclusion even if you paid qualified higher education expenses in 1991.*

Name(s) shown on return	Your social security number
MR. & MRS. N. VESTOR	123 45 6789

1 (a) Name of person (you, your spouse, or your dependent) who was enrolled at, or attended, an eligible educational institution

(b) Name and address of eligible educational institution

LITTLE N. VESTOR

If you need more space, attach a statement.

2 Enter the total qualified higher education expenses you paid in 1991 for the persons listed in column (a) of line 1. See the instructions to find out which expenses qualify . . . | **2**

3 Enter the total of any nontaxable educational benefits (such as nontaxable scholarship or fellowship grants) received for 1991 for the persons listed in column (a) of line 1. (See instructions.) | **3**

4 Subtract line 3 from line 2. (If the result is less than zero, enter -0-.) . . . . | **4**
Note: *If line 4 is zero, stop here; you* **may not** *take the exclusion.*

5 Enter the total proceeds (principal and interest) from all series EE U.S. savings bonds issued **after 1989** that you cashed **during 1991** . . . . | **5**

6 Enter the interest included on line 5. (See instructions.) . . . . | **6**
7 Compare the amounts on lines 4 and 5 above.
 ● If line 4 is **less than** line 5, divide line 4 by line 5. Enter the result as a decimal (to at least two places).
 ● If line 4 is **greater than or equal to** line 5, enter "1.00." | **7** ×.

8 Multiply line 6 by line 7 . . . . | **8**

9 Enter your modified adjusted gross income. (See instructions.) . . | **9**
Note: *If line 9 is $56,950 or more ($92,900 or more if married filing a joint return), stop here; you* **may not** *take the exclusion.*

10 ● If your filing status is **married filing a joint return,** enter $62,900. ● All others, enter $41,950. | **10**

11 Subtract line 10 from line 9. (If the result is zero or less, skip line 12, enter -0- on line 13, and go to line 14.) . . . . | **11**

12 ● If your filing status is **married filing a joint return,** divide line 11 by $30,000. Enter the result as a decimal (to at least two places). ● All others, divide line 11 by $15,000. Enter the result as a decimal (to at least two places). | **12** ×.

13 Multiply line 8 by line 12 . . . . | **13**
14 **Excludable savings bond interest.** Subtract line 13 from line 8. Enter the result here and on Schedule B (Form 1040), line 3, or Schedule 1 (Form 1040A), line 3, whichever applies . . ▶ | **14**

Paperwork Reduction Act Notice
We ask for the information on this form to carry out the Internal Revenue laws of the United States. You are required to give us the information. We need it to ensure that you are complying with these laws and to allow us to figure and collect the right amount of tax.

The time needed to complete and file this form will vary depending on individual circumstances. The estimated average time is: **Recordkeeping,** 53 min.; **Learning about the law or the form,** 11 min.; **Preparing the form,** 35 min.; and **Copying, assembling, and sending the form to the IRS,** 34 min.

If you have comments concerning the accuracy of these time estimates or suggestions for making this form more simple, we would be happy to hear from you. You can write to both the IRS and the Office of Management and Budget at the addresses listed in the instructions of the tax return with which this form is filed.

Cat. No. 10822S   Form **8815** (1991)

Exhibit 5C

more specifically into two further classifications: portfolio income and passive activity income.

The term **portfolio income** includes interest, dividends, royalties and annuities, as well as gain or loss from the disposition of income producing investment property not derived in the ordinary course of a trade or business (Code Section 469(e)(1)). Portfolio income is distinct and different from passive income.

Passive income, which was defined as a new category under the Tax Reform Act of 1986, is income derived from a "passive activity." A passive activity is one that involves the conduct of any trade or business in which the taxpayer does not materially participate (Code Section 469(c)(1)). Activities which are passive generally include partnerships in which the partner does not actively participate. All rental activities are considered passive regardless of whether or not the investor materially participates.

Distinguishing between the tax classification of income is not done for the purpose of the taxability of this income. It is basically all taxed at the same rate now except with regard to the 28% maximum tax rate on long–term gains. We separate the two because the type of activity determines the type of loss this activity may potentially generate. This determines how much of the loss can be deducted on your tax return.

Unlimited Gains/Limited Losses

When I was in grade school, I used to flip baseball cards with a friend named Bob. Whenever he won there was no problem. I would immediately fork over the cards I lost. When I won, however, Bob would always say "no fair, I'll give you half the cards today and half the cards tomorrow."

My friend, I believe, now works for the federal government, most likely for the Internal Revenue Service. I can't be sure of this, but that's what I heard at my last high school reunion. It makes sense though, when I think about the government's split personality regarding the taxation of capital gains, versus the allowance/disallowance of capital losses.

In the purchase and sale of stocks for instance, there exists a schism in government policy between the treatment of gains and losses. Although in the past the long–term capital gain rate was only 20%, the entire capital gain in any year was always taxed. If however, the taxpayer/investor had a losing year in the stock market, the story was quite different. He was only allowed to deduct his losses up to the point of his gains for that year, plus an additional $3,000 in losses per annum, with the remainder to be carried forward to future years.

Let me reference you once again to the current Schedule D tax form for the reporting of capital gains and losses (Exhibit 3D). If you look at line 18 of this form, you will note that it states: "If line 17 is a (loss), enter here as a (loss) and on Form 1040, line 13, the smaller of: (a) The (loss) on line 17; or (b)($3,000) or, if married filing a separate return,($1,500)." Part V, lines 28 to 43, is the area where you calculate the amount beyond this ($3,000) figure to be carried forward to future years.

This unlimited gain/limited loss business always seemed a bit unfair to me since it appeared as if the government was saying "if you win, we win, if you lose, we lose but only up to $3,000." It was somewhat more equitable prior to tax reform as long–term gains were only taxed at a 20% maximum tax rate. Now, however, all gains are taxed at ordinary rates, **and** the tax code has retained the policy of allowing only a $3,000 loss beyond income in any one year.

Unlimited Income/Limited Expenses: The PIG and His PAL

In the good old pre–tax reform days when men were men and tax shelters were tax shelters, you used to get a dollar per dollar write off for all business expenses. That is, of course, assuming that they met the IRS minimum standards for being ordinary, reasonable, legal, and necessary. In other words, the tax code looked at the **expense** and its necessity to the process of earning income. Back then all income, other than capital gains, was treated similarly, so were expenses.

Under pre–tax reform, if you bought a piece of rental property which had more expenses than income one year, you got to subtract the loss from your taxable income. Not so anymore. Now that we have passive activity income, we also must contend with passive activity loss.

Passive Activity Loss (PAL) can only be deducted against Passive Activity Income in any one year except for the year of disposition of the activity. That is, if you have expenses associated with a passive activity, you can only deduct them to the extent that you have income, and if you have more expenses than income in any one year, you must carry them forward to the next year with income, and if none, until disposition of the property. Thus, the PIG, or Passive Income Generator, or, any passive activity which can generate income in any one year for the main purpose of using up the otherwise wasted passive activity expenses, was born.

In the area of real estate, there is a minor exception to this passive activity rule. If you, as owner, actively manage the property and participate in such areas as the rental of units and other managerial duties, you may be allowed more of a deduction for expenses beyond income.

Chapter 6

Expenses Allowable As Deductions

"Dauntless Doug, The Duke of Deductions"

Introduction to the Audit

Throughout my years as a tax practitioner, I have dealt with a diverse and somewhat unusual client base. These clients have run the full gamut from several big time rock and roll stars to small business owners with a portfolio of varied investments and ordinary taxpayers. With this kind of exposure, I have seen many types of deductions by taxpayers, some legal, some not, and some questionable.

One of the very first jobs I had out of graduate school was with a sole proprietor CPA known to his colleagues as "Dauntless Doug, the Duke of Deductions." I can honestly say that this man taught me more about how to run and how **not** to run a CPA practice than anyone else I have met in the accounting field.

Doug's specialty was in two main types of clients. The first was medical accounts, doctors and dentists, and the second was entertainers, the rock and roll star type. But he would usually take on any legitimate account which either held his interest or could pay his bill.

He liked these two particular groups of clients for two reasons. Primarily, he **liked** entertainment clients because he was attracted to the fast lane in which they travelled. He **didn't** like them because they were erratic in paying their bills. One of these accounts would make it for a year or two, run up a big bill, and then fade before they had a chance to pay the entire amount. Medical and dental accounts were appealing to him for their dependability in making regular payments.

He worked with several assistants but he never became partners with any of them because, as Doug put it, "Between the city and the state, the IRS, and the tax courts, you have **enough** partners. Who needs any more?"

Doug had a unique way of building his practice. He always felt it was more important to add new clients to his base than to spend time servicing the ones he already had. He would tell me, "You can't please all the clients anyway, and the ones you do please aren't necessarily the ones you try to please. Besides, if you lose one client, but get two new ones every month, by the end of the year you will have increased your practice by 12 new accounts!" You couldn't argue with this kind of logic.

With this in mind, Doug spent most of his time outside the office developing the practice and leaving me and one other assistant to carry on the day–to–day management and deal with any problems that arose.

I had recently graduated from business school and received a Master's degree in accounting. I also had several years of "Big 8" audit experience, which is quite different than what you need to survive in a small CPA firm. The first day on the job with Doug I knew I was in for trouble.

I reported for work at 8:30 AM, as it was my habit to get in early, especially on my first day on the job. As I walked in, Doug was in the process of throwing his papers in his attache case and running out of the office. He handed me a note which read,

"I have to meet a client at 9:00, the IRS is coming in this morning to audit Dr. Esterman's tax return. (Not sure what years they want to see.) Files are in cabinet. Make them happy. I'll be back later. Good Luck!"

I panicked and, running after him to the elevator, yelled "Doug, I never prepared a tax return, let alone gone to an audit! I have no idea of what to do."

"I know that," he said, stepping in as the doors closed. "Relax. The auditor's a young girl, your age. She's been here before and she's as green as you are. Besides, she's getting married in two weeks and she's not going to concentrate too much on this audit. Just do whatever it takes to make her happy."

Bye, Doug.

His secretary arrived by 8:45. A sweet girl named Maria who tried awfully hard to do well but was somewhat impeded by a language barrier. English was her second language and she had a difficult time with it. This fact further complicated Doug's filing system which was a bit eccentric in and of itself.

It consisted of two sets of files for each year, the business clients in one set and the personal (non–business) clients in the other. This was OK, but Maria had problems classifying those personal clients who **also** had businesses. These files could end up in either of the two sets of cabinets or in a third set behind her desk for the clients she couldn't decide on.

When you factored in the language barrier you had total confusion. You see, in Spanish, the *e* is pronounced like *a*, the *i* like *e* and the *y* like *i*. It was a real treat to find a set of files for a client like Dr. Esterman, who had a personal return with a business, Schedule C, and had a name which started with an *e*, which Maria pronounced *a*. Then, you had to go through this process for each year the auditor might want. You could spend all day looking for a file, which usually wasn't in the file cabinet at all, but rather in Doug's office locked in one of his attache cases.

Miss Green, Field Agent for the local IRS Office, arrived at 9:00 sharp. I introduced myself and led her to a conference room down the hall which she was more familiar with than I was. She told me this was her fifth trip to our office. Doug had stood her up twice and could not find the files the third time. Actually this was only her second working visit.

She located the first year's tax return herself, being better acquainted with Doug's filing system than I. She also provided me with a list of two more years of returns and documentation she would need.

Since locating the files could be an all day task, I put Maria on it and went back to the conference room to let Miss Green know we were working on it. At this point I received my introductory lesson in "IRS Allowable Deductions."

Miss Green asked me if I was at all familiar with Dr. Esterman's situation. I said "no," and told her quite honestly that this was my first day on the job. What I didn't tell her was that this was one of the first tax returns I had ever seen.

She handed me the file and directed me to an area she was most interested in, that being the Schedule C – a secondary business of the taxpayer's wife.

This business, it seemed, was as an entertainer. I chuckled to myself, "This is great, here we have Doug's perfect client. A doctor who was married to an entertainer. She runs up the bills and he pays them."

Little did I know how close I was to the truth, or how close I was to the problem. But I was about to find out.

Miss Green asked me what I thought about a semi–retired entertainer who worked only twice a year in Puerto Rico making $200 an appearance for each weekend. I said I didn't think that was too bad, at least she would get a paid vacation twice a year in a nice spot for what doesn't seem to be too much work.

"Exactly," she replied, "it seems like a good deal to me too. But there's a major problem with this situation. You see, although there is income of only $400 – there are expenses of $19,500. This comes to a net business loss of $19,100 for the year. Then this $19,100 **business loss** is subtracted from the Doctor's earned income."

"I have a real problem with this," she continued. "Not only do I question whether or not this is a real business, which should be run to generate income, or just a hobby of a retired entertainer. But if we granted that it was a business, I would still have a problem with the expenses deducted here."

"Are they **necessary** in order for Mrs. Esterman to conduct business? Are they **ordinary** expenses which the average person would incur in conducting this business? And finally, are they **reasonable** for the type of business this is?"

Ah yes, I thought to myself, the old "Four Criteria Test" without number Four, **Legal**. I guess Miss Green assumed that everything a 65 year– old dancer could do, being semi–retired from 40 years of performing on the Borscht Belt circuit (Catskills, Monticello, N.Y.), would be legal.

The "Four Criteria Deduction Test"

Let's take a look at some of the expenses that were being examined that day and examine them within the context of this **"Four Criteria Deduction Test."**

Is the expense:
1) Necessary – to produce income;
2) Ordinary – in the normal course of doing business;
3) Reasonable – with regard to the income being produced; and
4) Legal – one allowed under federal or state statute?

The U.S. Master Tax Guide, Paragraph 902 states:

> Whether an expense is ordinary and necessary is based upon the facts surrounding each particular expense. An expense can be considered necessary if it was appropriate and helpful to the taxpayer's business or if it was clearly and reasonably related to the business. An expense can be considered ordinary if it was one that would normally be expected in the situation, even if the situation would seldom arise.[6]

As I had learned in school, and was reminded of on the fateful day of my first IRS audit, an expense must meet **all** of the **four** criteria to be allowed as a deduction on a tax return.

Mrs. Esterman had written off many expenses incurred in keeping herself looking good. This was done, she would later tell me, so that she could go on auditions. "The image is very important to an entertainer."

Well, in the course of earning the $400 income for that year, Mrs. Esterman had written off virtually every expense associated with the maintenance and upkeep of her body. There was the beauty parlor every week, the nail salon, the masseuse, the gym fees, the personal trainer, clothing, trips to the spa and the fat farm, and miscellaneous other services which even I had never seen.

There was also the new portable stereo and cassette tape library, in addition to the expenses for a vocal coach, dance and music lessons, and back–up band fees. She also paid her own way to and from Puerto Rico to audition. These deducted expenses included air fares and hotel expenses.

Were these expenses necessary, ordinary, reasonable, **and** legal?

Miss Green didn't seem to think so and, to be candid with you, at that time, neither did I. It sounded like a pretty good scam although I would never have admitted it to Miss Green. But somebody thought these expenses were appropriate, and, in fact, had bet some pretty heavy bucks that either the IRS would agree with them, or, perhaps, not notice. Well, they were wrong on at least one of the assumptions, the IRS **did** notice.

It was obvious to both of us, then, that I was not going to be of much help to Miss Green. Nor was I going to be able to answer any of the questions about the legitimacy of deductions at that time.

This was an effective ploy by Doug who knew she would have to return at a later date to finish up – perhaps much later because of her upcoming marriage and honeymoon. I later learned this was a carefully planned technique Doug often used in order to delay the IRS audit process as long as possible. In doing so, he hoped to wear down the auditor to try to get a compromised (and more favorable) settlement while at the same time giving himself more time to get the case together. (For further discussion of this see "Playing For Keeps With The IRS.")

By noon Maria had located one of two years which Miss Green had requested. Miss Green also had prepared a list of additional support she needed to arrive at her decision.

I brought in the one year of tax data which Maria had located. Handing it to Miss Green, I asked if she would be returning after lunch. She told me that she had phoned in to her office and that her supervisor wanted her to spend the afternoon at another one of her audit sites. Being that this would be her last week in the field before her annual vacation, he wanted her to tie together as many of her cases as possible.

She asked if it would be possible to photostat the prior year's return and supporting data. I told her that Maria would have it ready to pick up after lunch. I asked Miss Green if she wanted to join me for a bite to eat and pick up the material she requested afterwards.

My first mistake of the day. "Never invite an IRS auditor to lunch," as Doug would later instruct me. First of all, they are not allowed to accept your invitation for two reasons. If they allow you to take them to lunch it would be the equivalent of accepting a gift from a taxpayer. As it states in the Field Auditors Manual, this is not acceptable, as it would compromise their independence. The second reason is that you could be seen by someone who is familiar with the auditor and, even if the auditor paid for their own lunch, it might **look** as if their independence were being compromised.

Another and more practical reason, from the taxpayer's perspective is that you never want to spend more time with an IRS auditor than is absolutely necessary. You never want to put yourself in a position where you might say something which has not been asked and which might incriminate the taxpayer.

Luckily, Miss Green declined my invitation. She said I should have Maria photostat the return while she and I discussed the follow up points.

Some of the items she wanted to look at were the bills for most of the expenses over $50, including receipts, and other proofs of payment – such as canceled checks and credit card receipts. In addition she presented me with a questionnaire to complete that asked various questions about the nature of the business (see Exhibit 6A).

This questionnaire would be used to help her arrive at a decision as to the legitimacy of the business and the reasonableness and necessity of the expenses incurred. It asked questions such as:

1) When the business was started;
2) How was the business started or acquired;
3) Principal customers and suppliers;
4) Who runs the business;
5) If there are any other businesses in existence;
6) If this is a typical year in terms of income/loss;
7) What type of accounting system the business has;
8) Who keeps the books and records;
9) What comprises the books and records, i.e. general ledger, cash receipts, sales journals, etc.; and
10) Have there been any changes or major events during the past three years (the period most easily accessible to audit) to the business that the IRS should be aware of?

In other words, "Is this **really** a business here?"

Doug finally arrived back at the office at 4:00 p.m. I had taken several hours to go through the questions Miss Green had left, and had reviewed the return and supporting documentation. Doug asked me if I had made Miss Green happy to which I replied, "Well, you'd never know it if she was. She left a ton of questions and said she would have to come back at some future point to conclude the audit."

"Good," Doug replied. "That's just what I wanted."

Doug sat down with me and reviewed the auditor's requests. He said, "Why don't you call up Dr. Esterman this afternoon and get the particulars for the questionnaire Miss Green left. We will go through the rest of the return tomorrow morning when you get in and we are both fresh."

AGENT NAME

SCHEDULE C - FORM 1040

Business background (how started)

How do you obtain new business?

Principal customers or clients:

Principal suppliers:

Financial interests in other businesses

Is it the husband, or is it the wife that operates the business? _____

Is business still in operation? _____

Are this year's sales and net profit representative, or are the results larger
or smaller than normal?

Cash Basis _____   Accrual _____   Other _____

What books and records are kept? _____

_____ Cash Receipts Journal		_____ Deposit Tickets	
_____ Cash Disbursement Journal		_____ Sales Invoices	
_____ Purchases Journal		_____ Purchase Invoices	
_____ Sales Journal		_____ Receipts for Expenses	
_____ General Journal		_____ Accountant's Workpapers	
_____ Cancelled Checks		_____ Single Entry System	
_____ Checking Account Statements		_____ Double Entry System	

Has there been any unusual or extraordinary events during the last 3 years
(such as a fire, flood, loss of prime suppliers, customers)

Has there been any major expansion or remodeling of the business facilities
in recent years?   If so, what has been done?

Any future plans to expand or remodel?

Exhibit 6A

How To Examine a Doctor

"Before you make that call, there are two things I want to teach you about dealing with doctors. The first thing you have to know about anyone in the medical profession is to never call them 'Doctor.' It makes them feel like they're superior to you–something you don't want. You must make them feel that you are their equal. For that reason, always call them by their first name."

"Secondly, and even more important, never let them know that they are making more money than you. If they think that they are, they will treat you as a subordinate. Always let them know that you are doing as well as they are and, in fact, better."

Another gem by "Dauntless Doug." Again, you can't argue with this logic. And, as I would later discover, Doug not only "talked the talk, but also walked the walk." He had a beautiful office in the most fashionable section of the city, fully furnished with expensive items, even though he was hardly ever there. Whenever a client came to the office they could not escape without feeling that Doug was doing extremely well. This was also used to justify Doug's bills which were as high as any I've seen for comparable services in my entire career.

In addition, one of Doug's favorite ploys was to buy a new Cadillac every year. He would try to visit each of his doctor clients at least once a year, in his new car, just to let them know just how well he was doing.

So, it was no longer "Dr." Esterman. He and I had just become friends, according to Doug, and it was now Ben.

When I called Ben, however, he was not terribly friendly. He had been trying to get in touch with Doug for the last two weeks to get the status of his audit. Doug must have heard me repeat that Ben had been trying to get in touch with him and he mouthed the words to me "I'm not here." Another one of Doug's ploys. Always make the client think you are too busy to talk to him at their convenience, but rather that you will call them back. This lets the client know just how busy you are. Doug, however, would race in and out of the office several times each day and, as he did, Maria would hand him a batch of pink slips of paper with his messages on them. Unfortunately, Doug would never have time to completely go through each batch, and the pile would grow and grow. Once a week, on Friday afternoons, Doug would say, "Let's start over again next week," as he threw the remaining batch of messages in the garbage. Consequently, half of the time he never called a client back.

I spent the next 20 minutes on the phone with Dr. Esterman completing the questionnaire. By this time I was ready to leave for the day, and I took a copy of the Schedule C in question home with me so that I would be prepared for the following morning with Doug. I had a lot to think about that night, after my first full day of "accounting reality."

The next morning I arrived at 8:30 a.m. to find Doug in the office consulting with a prospective new doctor client. Doug had an arrangement with the people on the same floor in his office. They were an insurance company which specialized in insurance for the medical profession. The insurance agents would spend a good deal of their time in the hospitals meeting new residents in the hope of selling them insurance policies. They would convince the young residents that within the next few years they would indeed be making huge amounts of money and would need life insurance, disability insurance, practice continuation insurance, health insurance, liability insurance, and any other umbrella insurance policies they could think of.

Part of their sales pitch was to incorporate Doug in the decision–making process. They would bring new prospects in to Doug. Doug would proceed to do a five–year cash flow projection based on a "normal physician's" income expectancy. When the young docs were feeling pretty good about how much money they would be making, they were prime candidates for the insurance salesmen. At this point, they would usually purchase the various forms of insurance being sold and feel so good about Doug that they would immediately hire him as their accountant. This way they could be assured of getting the financial expertise and guidance necessary to attain their income projections.

Pretty good arrangement, huh? The insurance people got their catch and Doug got the account.

The Schedule C–Giving an Auditor the Business

While I was waiting for the group to break up in Doug's office, I proceeded to review the Schedule C of "Entertainer" Esterman and do a preliminary evaluation of the expenses in question (see Exhibit 6B). Although the tax return I am discussing was prepared for another year, I have transferred the figures onto a 1991 Schedule C. I've done this because it is much more useful for us to work with newer tax forms. In this manner we can become familiar with the appropriate forms for preparing our own tax returns and tax planning strategies.

64

Expenses Allowable as Deductions

SCHEDULE C (Form 1040)	Profit or Loss From Business	OMB No. 1545-0074
Department of the Treasury Internal Revenue Service (5)	(Sole Proprietorship) ► Partnerships, joint ventures, etc., must file Form 1065. ► Attach to Form 1040 or Form 1041. ► See Instructions for Schedule C (Form 1040).	19**91** Attachment Sequence No. 09

Name of proprietor: MRS. ESTHER ESTERMAN — Social security number (SSN) 123 45 6789

A Principal business or profession, including product or service (see instructions): ENTERTAINMENT
B Enter principal business code (from page 2) ► 9811

C Business name: SAME
D Employer ID number (Not SSN)

E Business address (including suite or room no.) ►
City, town or post office, state, and ZIP code

F Accounting method: (1) ☒ Cash (2) ☐ Accrual (3) ☐ Other (specify) ►

G Method(s) used to value closing inventory: (1) ☐ Cost (2) ☐ Lower of cost or market (3) ☐ Other (attach explanation) (4) ☒ Does not apply (if checked, skip line H) — Yes / No

H Was there any change in determining quantities, costs, or valuations between opening and closing inventory? (If "Yes," attach explanation.) — No ☒

I Did you "materially participate" in the operation of this business during 1991? (If "No," see instructions for limitations on losses.) — Yes ☒

J If this is the first Schedule C filed for this business, check here ► ☐

Part I — Income

1 Gross receipts or sales. **Caution:** If this income was reported to you on Form W-2 and the "Statutory employee" box on that form was checked, see the instructions and check here ► ☐	1	400
2 Returns and allowances	2	
3 Subtract line 2 from line 1	3	400
4 Cost of goods sold (from line 40 on page 2)	4	
5 Subtract line 4 from line 3 and enter the **gross profit** here	5	400
6 Other income, including Federal and state gasoline or fuel tax credit or refund (see instructions)	6	
7 Add lines 5 and 6. This is your **gross income** ►	7	400

Part II — Expenses (Caution: Enter expenses for business use of your home on line 30.)

8 Advertising	8		21 Repairs and maintenance	21	230
9 Bad debts from sales or services (see instructions)	9		22 Supplies (not included in Part III)	22	
10 Car and truck expenses (see instructions—also attach Form 4562)	10	2345	23 Taxes and licenses	23	
11 Commissions and fees	11		24 Travel, meals, and entertainment:		
12 Depletion	12		a Travel	24a	805
13 Depreciation and section 179 expense deduction (not included in Part III) (see instructions)	13	2450	b Meals and entertainment		2350
14 Employee benefit programs (other than on line 19)	14		c Enter 20% of line 24b subject to limitations (see instructions)		470
15 Insurance (other than health)	15	435	d Subtract line 24c from line 24b	24d	1880
16 Interest:			25 Utilities	25	
a Mortgage (paid to banks, etc.)	16a		26 Wages (less jobs credit)	26	
b Other	16b		27a Other expenses (list type and amount):		
17 Legal and professional services	17	1200	Backup Band 635		
18 Office expense	18	584	Rehearsal Studio 840		
19 Pension and profit-sharing plans	19		Salon + Nails 1265		
20 Rent or lease (see instructions):			Phys. Fitness 1450		
a Vehicles, machinery, and equipment	20a		Costumes 1850		
b Other business property	20b		Cleaning 435 + Misc 270		
			27b Total other expenses	27b	6745

28 Add amounts in columns for lines 8 through 27b. These are your **total expenses** before expenses for business use of your home ►	28	(16674)
29 Tentative profit (loss). Subtract line 28 from line 7	29	(16274)
30 Expenses for business use of your home (attach **Form 8829**)	30	(2826)
31 **Net profit or (loss).** Subtract line 30 from line 29. If a profit, enter here and on Form 1040, line 12. Also enter the net profit on Schedule SE, line 2 (statutory employees, see instructions). If a loss, you MUST go on to line 32 (fiduciaries, see instructions)	31	(19100)

32 If you have a loss, you MUST check the box that describes your investment in this activity (see instructions). If you checked 32a, enter the loss on Form 1040, line 12, and Schedule SE, line 2 (statutory employees, see instructions). If you checked 32b, you MUST attach **Form 6198**.
32a ☒ All investment is at risk. 32b ☐ Some investment is not at risk.

For Paperwork Reduction Act Notice, see Form 1040 instructions. — Cat. No. 11334P

Exhibit 6B

65

As we can see, on Line 1 and Line 7 is the $400 figure for gross income. We already know this was the income earned for two weekend appearances at the hotel in the Puerto Rico. On the expense side we see the following items.

LINE:

10) Car and truck expenses:	$2,345
13) Depreciation and Section 179 expense:	2,450
15) Insurance (other than health):	435
17) Legal and professional services:	1,200
18) Office expense:	584
20) Rental or lease:	2,826
21) Repairs and maintenance:	230
24) Travel, meals, and entertainment:	2,685
27) Other expenses:	
a. Backup band	635
b. Rehearsal studio	840
c. Beauty salon and nail sculpturing	1,265
d. Physical fitness and body work	1,450
e. Costumes	1,850
f. Cleaning	435
g. Miscellaneous	270
TOTAL EXPENSES	$19,500

In addition to substantiation of these expenses were these expenses **necessary, ordinary, reasonable, and legal**? She was going to evaluate each expense within this context, as well as within the overall representation made on the Business Information Questionnaire.

By this time I could hear the group breaking up in Doug's office, and I awaited Doug's input on these questions.

"Doug," I asked, "is it normal for someone with this low amount of income to incur such large expenses? Will the IRS accept these as ordinary business expenses?" Doug sat down and began to give me my first introduction to "IRS Allowable Deductions, According to Doug."

"Let's take a look," he said, and we proceeded to look at each deduction taken as a business expense.

1) Automobile Expense of $2,345. Legal? If the car was properly registered, of course. Necessary? She had to make trips

back and forth to her agent, the music store, the rehearsal studio, the beauty parlor, the gym, and any other place which might be an opening for potential work. "It appears," I said, "that she needed the car in order to carry out her business."

The U.S. Master Tax Guide, Paragraphs 945 and 946, defines Transportation and Automobile Expenses as follows:

> Transportation expenses are generally those incurred for the business use of a car; however, they also include the cost of travel by air, rail, bus, taxi, etc., but not the costs of meals and lodging or travel away from home. Business (including self–employed persons) may deduct ordinary and necessary transportation expenses from gross income (Reg. Section 1.162–1(a))...Commuting expenses between a taxpayer's residence and a business location within the area of his tax home generally are **not** deductible. However, a deduction is allowed for expenses incurred in excess of ordinary commuting expenses for transporting job–related tools and materials. An individual who works at two or more different places **may** deduct the costs of getting from one place to the other...The IRS has provided an exception to the general rule that commuting expenses are not deductible. If a taxpayer has at least one regular place of business, then daily transportation expenses for commuting between his residence and a temporary work location can be deducted...Expenses for gasoline, oil, tires, repairs, insurance, depreciation, parking fees and tolls, licenses, and garage rent incurred for automobiles used in a trade or business are deductible from gross income. The deduction is allowed only for that part of the

expenses that is attributable to business. An employee's unreimbursed expenses or those reimbursed under a non–accountable plan can be deducted only as an itemized deduction...All the principal items involved in deducting automobile expenses, or in allocating those expenses between business and non–business use, are reflected on Form 2106, Employee Business Expenses...A taxpayer can always substantiate automobile expenses by keeping an exact record of the amount paid for gasoline, tolls, and similar fees. However, methods are available that greatly simplify the amount of record keeping necessary and satisfy the substantiation requirements necessary to claim the deduction.[7]

Doug told me that he had allocated only a portion of total car expense for the year based on the exact number of miles driven in the course of business. Mrs. Esterman maintained an accurate log of each trip taken in this regard.

Were these expenses **ordinary**? In other words, would anybody conducting business in the entertainment field have similar expenses? This too appeared to be true. It was obvious to me that Doug had justification under the first three tests for taking the automobile expense deduction.

"But Doug, is this expense **reasonable**? Is it reasonable to expect someone to have so large an automobile expense with such a small amount of income?"

"Ah hah," Doug replied. "A good question."

And Doug had a real good answer. An answer which, in fact, would be the basis for deducting most of these expenses as well as a good deal of the expenses on future entertainers' tax returns.

"You see," Doug began, "an entertainer is a much different animal than the ordinary businessman. With a normal businessman there is the expectation that a profit will be generated within a reasonable period of time while conducting business. For an entertainer, however, this is not necessarily so. They can struggle for many years before they make any money at all. In fact, they can have a significant period of expenditures before any profit is generated if, in fact, it ever is. This does not mean that they are not **trying** to make money. It simply means that it may take them a much longer time to do it."

"This, I believe, is also quite fair," he continued, "because once they do make it, they make it **BIG** and the IRS has a veritable bonanza. Because they do not anticipate such a large amount of income all at once, the star–entertainer is usually not prepared for it in terms of tax planning. For this reason the IRS usually makes out as well as, if not better than, the entertainer himself."

"The normal test of whether or not an expense is reasonable, therefore, does not apply in the same sense to an entertainer as it would to another type of businessperson. What is reasonable expense for the entertainer is not necessarily reasonable for other types of businesses and vice versa."

"In fact, that Business Information Questionnaire which she gave you is also inappropriate. Miss Green doesn't know the first thing about the difference between a hobby and a business. She's going to try to present a case which argues that this is not really a business, but rather a hobby, because there has been no profit generated by Mrs. Esterman in the past three years. I'm not going to let her do that," he said, slamming his fist down on the pile of papers in front of us.

The U.S. Master Tax Guide defines a "Hobby Loss" as follows:

> Losses incurred by individuals, S corporations, and estates and trusts that are attributable to an activity not engaged in for profit (so–called hobby losses) are generally deductible only to the extent of income produced by the activity (Code Sec. 183, Reg. Sections 1.183–1 – 1.183–4).....An activity is presumed not to be a hobby if profits result in any three of five consecutive tax years ending with the tax year in question, unless the IRS proves otherwise (Code Sec. 183(d)).[8]

In other words, unless you have a profit in any business for three out of five years, that business is deemed to be a hobby? And, the IRS will not let you take deductions for any expenses incurred in the pursuit of that "hobby?"

"Wrong," Doug replied. "What this says is that if you **do** have a profit in three out of five years, the IRS will presume that you **do not** have a hobby. It is not a presumption that if you do not have a profit for three out of five years that it **is** a hobby. This is open to discussion and the IRS has the onus of proof that it **is** a hobby. It is not simply deemed to be one. As I already told you, an entertainer is a different type of businessperson and the IRS must recognize this. I've prepared hundreds of returns like this and I've never had a problem with any of them. Sometimes we will see many dry years without a single dollar of profit."

The Elvis Story

"I remember when Elvis Presley was first starting out in the 1950s. I had a reputation around Memphis as an aggressive but good tax practitioner. When Elvis had his first hit record, he said to his manager, Col. Tom Parker, 'Now I'm makin' some money. I can't use these local yokel accountants anymore. I want you to find me one of them Big Yankee Tax Accountants from New York who can do my return **right**.' And so I got involved with his tax returns for several years. The first thing I did was to file amended returns for the prior three years and to take **all** the losses he had been entitled to during those years. It seemed that the Nashville accountants were not aware how these things work. The IRS called me in to explain what was going on, and I simply let them know that good money had been spent in the years preceding the period in which he became a rock star. And, I was simply taking the expenses in those prior years which were valid. I just showed them the current year's return with all the income which was being reported and a projection of next year's tax return with even more income, and they agreed with me. There **was** a basis for taking several years of loss preceding several years of high taxable income. I have always used this as my guide for preparing entertainers' tax returns, regardless of whether or not they were successful."

"But Doug, has there ever been a court ruling in this area, specifically about entertainers?"

"Hell no! Nobody wants to waste the taxpayer's money by taking this thing to court; they know I'm right."

Here was the thing about Doug. I was never sure how much of what he told me about his experience was really fact or pure fiction.

To this day, I'll never know if the Elvis story was true. But as long as he was paying my salary and as long as he was willing to sign the tax returns as preparer, it didn't really matter. I would prepare them the way he wanted.

Now here is the most interesting part of this story. Several months ago, as reported in the *New York Times* "Tax Watch" column, there finally was a case involving this question of tax law interpretation for artists and entertainers. Some 12 years after the discussion I had with Doug, the Tax Court ruled in exactly the way Doug said they would. The Court agreed that in areas of artists, musicians, and other entertainers, a different standard must be used. "In determining whether or not a business exists for the purpose of generating income," it stated "you must first consider the nature of the business."

This particular case involved a woman artist who had painted for many years and had accumulated hundreds of her paintings as inventory. She had two years of high income eight years prior. Since then, she had incurred a great deal of expense with no profit, and had taken these expenses as deductions on her tax returns. In addition to supplies, studio rental, and other related expenses, she also paid monthly rent on a storage facility for housing her paintings. The IRS audited her return and concluded that this was no longer a viable business. She was now just painting as a hobby. It determined that she could no longer deduct expenses for a painting against her other income.

The Tax Court disagreed and ruled in favor of the taxpayer. They stated that in the case of an artist there are many peaks and valleys during the artist's career. Because of this, there often can be long, dry spells where no income is being generated. This is not to say that the artist is no longer in pursuit of income. In other words, they concluded that the artist could take those losses on her tax return.

Son of a gun! "The Duke" was right.

The Subjectivity Factor

Significance to the Investor

This taught me one very important lesson about expenses which has served me well throughout my career. The question of whether or not an expense is 1) **Normal**, 2) **Ordinary**, and 3) **Reasonable** is a very subjective one–a question which is open to interpretation and very much depends on the circumstances of each situation. The question of 4) **Legality** is somewhat more objective, and one which I will discuss further in the following sections.

With this in mind, let's look at the rest of the expenses deducted in Mrs. Esterman's business and evaluate them in the context of subjectivity. This exercise will give you the necessary methodology to use justifying your own expenses. This is very important in the tax planning process for you, **especially as an investor**, because there are so many expenses which are open to discussion and interpretation as to whether they are personal or business–related.

One of the best tax strategies I will give you in this book requires that you learn this method well because it involves turning your investment activities into a separate business. Pay close attention.

The Other Deductions

2) Depreciation and Section 179 Expense of $2,450 (to be defined below). Legal? If the item being depreciated is legal then certainly its depreciation will be.

The items which we are talking about for Mrs. Esterman were certain small pieces of business equipment purchased during the year in addition to the continual depreciation of items purchased previously. As you recall, I mentioned that she had purchased a new stereo and a cassette tape library of show tunes she performed in her act. As Doug and I reviewed the backup data in her file, Doug noted to me that he had deducted only a portion of the cost of these items.

This, he said, was even more conservative than was necessary. Although the equipment had been purchased exclusively for business use, Doug only deducted 55% of its cost. He explained to me that this was one of his favorite methods for cutting short audit adjustments. It was as he called it an "ace in the hole." In other words, if the IRS auditor tried to eliminate certain deductions, Doug would make them aware of the fact that he had been overly conservative in deducting this particular expense. And, if the auditor would not compromise, then Doug would insist on taking more of a deduction for these items.

The U.S. Master Tax Guide defines Property Subject to Depreciation as follows:

The law permits a deduction of a reasonable allowance for the exhaustion, wear and tear of property used in a trade or business, or of property held for the production of income (Reg. Section 1.167(a)–1). Depreciation is not allowable for property used for personal purposes, such as a residence or an automobile used solely for pleasure.

(For limits on depreciation for luxury automobiles and for certain property for which business use does not exceed 50%, see Paragraph 1211.)... Depreciation is allowable for tangible property, but not for inventories, stock in trade, land apart from its improvements, or a depletable natural resource (Reg. Section 1.167(a)–2)....An intangible asset such as a patent, copyright, license, franchise, contract, or similar asset having a limited useful life is also depreciable, but goodwill is not (Reg. Section 1.167(a)–3)... Depreciation based on a useful life is to be calculated over the estimated useful life of the asset while actually used by the taxpayer, and not over the longer period of the asset's physical life....Form 4562 is used to compute the recovery allowance (or an amortization deduction) and is attached to the taxpayer's tax return.[9]

To summarize, you can depreciate any equipment used in the course of your business over its useful life as determined by the IRS Code. In this way you can expense the cost of the machine on a year–to–year basis, rather than taking the write–off in one year. This is a fairer way to expense such equipment, the IRS feels, because its value lasts more than just one year. This principle is consistent with the matching concept of income and expense. The tax law purports that expenses should only be taken as they generate income. Because most machines produce value for a long period of time their cost should be matched against the value produced.

There is one exception to this rule, that being the case of "Section 179" expenses. The IRS Code currently allows a taxpayer to deduct the first $10,000 spent on business equipment in any one tax year as a one shot expense. There are certain limitations on this. If the taxpayer spends more than $200,000 in any tax year, the amount of Section 179 expense is phased out. Section 179 expenses are extremely useful and will be addressed again in my section on *Creating a Trading Business* (see Chapter 13). It is one of my favorite sections of the tax code. To further explain Section 179 expense, the U.S. Master Tax Guide states in Paragraph 1208:

> An expense deduction is provided for taxpayers (other than estates, trusts or certain non–corporate lessors) who elect to treat the cost of qualifying property, called Section 179 property, as an expense rather than a capital expenditure. The election, which is made on Form 4562, is to be attached to the taxpayer's original return (including a late–filed original return) for the year the property is placed in service and may not be revoked without IRS consent. Employees may make such election on Form 2106.
>
> The maximum Code Section 179 deduction is $10,000 ($5,000 for married persons filing separate returns). The $10,000 ceiling is reduced by the excess cost of qualified property placed in service during the tax year over $200,000.
>
> The total cost of property that may be expensed for any tax year cannot exceed the total amount of taxable income (determined after application of the investment limitation) derived from the active conduct of any

trade or business during the tax year. Costs disallowed under this rule may be carried forward an unlimited number of years subject to the ceiling amount for each year. To qualify as Code Section 179 property, the property must be Code Section 1245 property depreciable under Code Section 168 and property that is acquired by purchase for use in the active conduct of a trade or business.[10]

As a point of interest here, I should state that in the current tax law, as noted in the preceding paragraph, you can only use a Section 179 write–off to the extent that you have income. In other words, you cannot generate a business loss by writing off Section 179 assets. If you are in a business loss position, you must revert to depreciating the asset over its useful life.

You may wonder why Doug had taken Section 179 depreciation on Mrs. Esterman's Schedule C even though she had a $19,100 loss for the year. The answer to this question is simple. Back when this return was prepared, this stipulation was not in effect. You used to be able to take Section 179 expenses in full to the extent of its deductibility regardless of whether or not you were in a profitable business situation for the year. Now, Section 179 expenses can only be taken to the extent that the business shows a profit for the year.

So, Doug and I discussed the $2,450 expense item with regard to its being necessary, ordinary, and reasonable. Once again, it looked to me like Doug had his bases covered.

As an entertainer, Mrs. Esterman needed to expand her repertoire of musical numbers. She needed the stereo and tape library in order to do this. Other pieces of equipment which had been purchased in either this year or last, but which also were necessary to her business as an entertainer were as follows: the year before she had purchased a player piano for several thousand dollars; several years ago, she had additionally purchased a metronome in order to pace her act; and she had also acquired a xylophone; a pair of maracas; and three pairs of ebony castanets.

Necessary? She thought they were. Reasonable? As we have already determined, of course. Ordinary? Well, this depends. According to Doug, these items were quite ordinary for an entertainer as classy as Mrs. E.

3) Insurance (other than health) for $435. Mrs. Esterman had found some obscure insurance company which was willing to insure her legs against potential disability.

Reasonable? Ordinary? Necessary? And legal?
If she was a legitimate act and this was a legitimate business all these conditions were obviously met.

4) Legal and Professional Services for $1,200. These expenses were for services rendered by Doug as well as for an attorney who drew up the contracts between Mrs. Esterman and several business parties. Doug allocated a portion of his annual fee for accounting and tax services performed for Mrs. Esterman's business. The lawyer's fees were incurred as a normal course of business in dealing with the hotels, the backup musicians, and the music transcriber.

Again, we are looking at expenses which apparently met all four of the above criteria.

5) Office expense of $584. These expenses were incurred as a normal course of business for Mrs. Esterman. She purchased supplies for doing paperwork which directly related to potential job offers. In addition, these covered the expense of photostating letters and various other office related items. These, too, appeared to meet our four criteria test.

6) Rental or Lease Expense of $2,826. This amount was deducted as a "Home–Office expense." The law provides that a taxpayer may deduct expenses related to the upkeep of their home in proportion to the percentage of the home which is used in connection with a trade or business. There are two criteria which the IRS generally requires be met in order for the taxpayer to be entitled to the deduction. The portion of the home which is used for business (a) must be used **exclusively** for business; and, this portion of the home (b) must be the primary place in which business is conducted.

The U.S. Master Tax Guide, Paragraph 961, further expands upon the requirements necessary for a business use of home:

> A taxpayer is not entitled to deduct any expenses of using his home for business purposes unless they are attributable to a portion of the home (or separate structure) **used exclusively on a regular basis** as (1) the principle place of business carried on

by the taxpayer or (2) a place of business that is used by patients, clients, or customers in meeting or dealing with the taxpayer in the normal course of business (Code Section 280A(c)).

A specific portion of the taxpayer's home must be used solely for the purpose of carrying on a trade or business in order to satisfy the exclusive use test. Such requirement is not met if the portion is used for both business and personal purposes.

The Home Office Deduction is limited to the gross income from the activity, reduced by expenses that are deductible without regard to business use (such as home mortgage interest) and all other deductible expenses attributable to the activity but not allowable to the use of the unit itself. Thus a deduction is not allowed to the extent that it creates or increases the net loss from the business activity to which it relates. Any disallowed deduction may be carried over, subject to the same limit in carry over years (Code Section 280A(c)(5)).

Again, as in the Section 179 expense, we are currently limited in home office deduction to businesses with positive net income. We cannot use a home office deduction to generate or increase a loss. This is the current tax law. When Mrs. Esterman's return was prepared, this limitation was not in effect, therefore it did not matter that she had an overall loss of $19,100.

Doug led me through his calculation of this expense. Mrs. Esterman had used the basement of her house exclusively for business. She had her instruments set up permanently at this location and regularly rehearsed there with her band.

On the basis of square feet, the basement represented one-eighth of the total square feet of the house. On the basis of total rooms without regard to size, the basement represented one–tenth of the entire ten–room house. Being the conservative tax practitioner which he was, Doug once again used the conservative figure in calculating the Home Office Deduction.

He took one–tenth of all expenses incurred in the upkeep of the house, including utilities, real estate tax, and mortgage interest. He also depreciated the house in accordance with IRS guidelines and took one–tenth of the annual depreciation as an expense.

Again, Doug assured me, if there was a problem with the audit he would be able to use this as a bargaining chip. He could have actually used one–eighth of these expenses instead of one–tenth, as the IRS guidelines did not specifically spell out whether or not to use the allocation based on square feet or number of rooms.

Reasonable? He had me convinced. Normal and ordinary? Well, she needed someplace to practice. And, it certainly was legal to own property here in our good old capitalistic economy.

7) Repairs and maintenance expense of $230. This expense was incurred for tuning the piano which we expensed under the second category, Depreciation and Section 179 Expense. If the depreciation was appropriate, then so was the maintenance expense. Case closed.

8) Travel, meals and entertainment expense of $2,685.

The U.S. Master Tax Guide defines deductible travel, meals and entertainment expense in Paragraph 952, as follows:

> The following expenses paid or incurred while traveling away from home ordinarily are deductible: travel, meals, and lodging; transportation, plus a reasonable amount for baggage, necessary samples and display materials; hotel rooms, telephone and telegraph services, and public stenographers; and the costs of maintaining and operating an automobile for business purposes.
>
> The cost of taking a spouse along on a business trip is not deductible unless it can be shown that the presence of the spouse serves a bona fide busi-

ness purpose. Incidental services performed by the spouse such as the
occasional typing of notes, do not meet
bona fide business purpose requirements (Reg. Section 1.162–2(c)).

A taxpayer may deduct as part of
traveling expense reasonable expenditures for laundry, cleaning, and
pressing of clothing and for transportation between his place of lodging
and place of business at a temporary
or minor post of duty. When a taxpayer at such an assignment returns
to his family and distant residents on
intervening non–working days, expenses of the trip may not be deducted
to the extent that they exceed the cost
of meals and lodging that would have
been deductible had he remained at
his temporary location for those days.
The deduction for the cost of meals
and lodging while away from home on
business is limited to amounts that
are not lavish or extravagant under
the circumstances (Code Section
162(a)(2)).

As we already know, the amount of money deducted for this
category of expense was spent on several trips down to Puerto Rico
in search of work. Doug noted to me that she had scheduled at least
three auditions on each of the trips. In addition, he showed me a
schedule prepared by Dr. Esterman which backed out his travel and
meal expense. Doug was extremely proficient at documenting his
workpapers. He needed to be due to the somewhat aggressive
positions he took on many issues.

Legal? They did everything right. She only took expenses
relating to **her own** cost of the trip. Reasonable, ordinary, and
necessary? Again, things were starting to appear as if every expense
taken on this return was appropriate. If I was in a position to decide
the propriety of these expenses at this time, I would have issued a "no
change." The question was "would Miss Green?"

9) Other expenses:

    (a) Backup band for $635. She couldn't dance without music.

    (b) Rehearsal studio for $840. If I were Dr. Esterman I would testify to the necessity of a rehearsal studio after having my wife rehearsing all year in the basement.

    (c) Beauty salon and nail sculpturing for $1,265. Doug informed me that this was an area that he, in fact, had some hesitation about deducting. Mrs. Esterman assured him that if it weren't for her career she would not need such extensive beauty treatment. Doug was not sure he agreed.

    (d) Physical fitness and body work for $1,450. This expense included a personal trainer three times a week for two hours a day. Doug had seen the results of this regimen. In fact, he told me that Mrs. Esterman had lost 25 pounds that year and he was sure he could justify the expense in the money it saved on costumes. Because of the reduced size, Mrs. Esterman's costume designer was able to save approximately 25% on material used that year. Doug had all the documentation in the file.

    (e) Costume expense of $1,850. Mrs. Esterman, I'm told, performed a wicked "Queen of Sheba" routine turban and all. In addition, Doug told me her rendition of Ethel Merman's *Everything's Coming up Roses* couldn't be beat. She couldn't perform without a wardrobe.

    (f) Cleaning expense of $435. She had to clean the costumes. It is awfully hot in Puerto Rico. And besides, it cut down on perfume expense!

    (g) Miscellaneous expense of $270. This must have been the perfume. Doug wasn't sure, "but for $270," he said, "let them look for it."

"Well," Doug said, "it looks like we can justify almost everything. All we need now is her substantiation of having spent these amounts. We need to generate a letter to Mrs. Esterman requesting that she provide us with the invoices, canceled checks, receipts, credit card chits, and statements for as many of these expenses, over $50, as she can possibly locate."

Backup and Substantiation of Deductions

Over the next several weeks while Miss Green vacationed, got married, and honeymooned in the Caribbean, Doug and I commenced our own honeymoon, of sorts. Dr. and Mrs. Esterman were most cooperative in providing any documentation they could find in compliance with the auditor's request. In fact, "Ben" and I became close working friends as Doug had suggested.

The **automobile expense deduction** of $2,345 was fairly easy to substantiate. As I mentioned, Mrs. Esterman kept a log of dates, destinations, miles traveled, and purpose of business travel for the entire year. In arriving at the amount of expense, Doug had calculated that the standard mileage deduction for actual miles traveled was the most beneficial, and consequently deducted this amount on the tax return.

The way this works is that the taxpayer is given the choice each year of deducting the percentage of business use of actual expense incurred in the upkeep of the car, versus a standard amount per business mile which the government deems fair. This amount changes on a yearly basis since car upkeep varies from year to year.

As an example, I will illustrate how the "Duke" arrived at the amount he deducted on Mrs. Esterman's Schedule C. See Exhibit 6D, Form 4562 for this illustration, keeping in mind that I am using 1991 tax forms. On page 2, Part V, Section B, we are required to fill out information regarding the use of vehicles used for business. Line 27 asks for the total business miles driven during the year, not including miles used in commuting to your job. Line 28 requires the addition of commuting miles driven during the year. Line 29 includes other personal (non–commuting) miles driven. The IRS Code requires that you maintain a log which essentially substantiates the number of miles driven for business, Line 27. Lines 31, 32, and 33 ask for further information about the use of the vehicle so that the IRS can be assured it was used in accordance with the requirements for business use of automobile.

Although Form 4562 is used for depreciation and amortization of business property, Part V must be filled out whether or not you are depreciating the car or taking the standard mileage deduction.

In calculating the actual expense of the car used for business Doug arrived at this figure was by dividing Line 27 by Line 30, (total business miles/total miles driven). Mrs. Esterman had driven 14,210 miles for business, Line 27. Her total mileage for the year was 26,300, and the percentage of business miles over total miles was

81

The Serious Investor's Tax Survival Guide

Form 4562

Department of the Treasury
Internal Revenue Service (5)

Depreciation and Amortization
(Including Information on Listed Property)

▶ See separate instructions. ▶ Attach this form to your return.

OMB No. 1545-0172

1991

Attachment Sequence No. **67**

Name(s) shown on return: DR & MRS. BEN ESTERMAN

Identifying number: 123-45-6789

Business or activity to which this form relates

Part I — Election To Expense Certain Tangible Property (Section 179) (Note: If you have any "Listed Property," complete Part V.)

1	Maximum dollar limitation (see instructions)	**1** $10,000
2	Total cost of section 179 property placed in service during the tax year (see instructions)	**2** 1768
3	Threshold cost of section 179 property before reduction in limitation	**3** $200,000
4	Reduction in limitation—Subtract line 3 from line 2, but do not enter less than -0-	**4** —
5	Dollar limitation for tax year—Subtract line 4 from line 1, but do not enter less than -0-	**5** 200,000

(a) Description of property	(b) Cost	(c) Elected cost
6		

7	Listed property—Enter amount from line 26	**7** 1768
8	Total elected cost of section 179 property—Add amounts in column (c), lines 6 and 7	**8** 1768
9	Tentative deduction—Enter the lesser of line 5 or line 8	**9** 1768
10	Carryover of disallowed deduction from 1990 (see instructions)	**10**
11	Taxable income limitation—Enter the lesser of taxable income or line 5 (see instructions)	**11** 200,000
12	Section 179 expense deduction—Add lines 9 and 10, but do not enter more than line 11	**12** 1768
13	Carryover of disallowed deduction to 1992—Add lines 9 and 10, less line 12 ▶	**13**

Note: Do not use Part II or Part III below for automobiles, certain other vehicles, cellular telephones, computers, or property used for entertainment, recreation, or amusement (listed property). Instead, use Part V for listed property.

Part II — MACRS Depreciation For Assets Placed in Service ONLY During Your 1991 Tax Year (Do Not Include Listed Property)

(a) Classification of property	(b) Mo. and yr. placed in service	(c) Basis for depreciation (Business/investment use only—see instructions)	(d) Recovery period	(e) Convention	(f) Method	(g) Depreciation deduction
14 General Depreciation System (GDS) (see instructions):						
a 3-year property						
b 5-year property						
c 7-year property						
d 10-year property						
e 15-year property						
f 20-year property						
g Residential rental property			27.5 yrs.	MM	S/L	
			27.5 yrs.	MM	S/L	
h Nonresidential real property			31.5 yrs.	MM	S/L	
			31.5 yrs.	MM	S/L	
15 Alternative Depreciation System (ADS) (see instructions):						
a Class life					S/L	
b 12-year			12 yrs.		S/L	
c 40-year			40 yrs.	MM	S/L	

Part III — Other Depreciation (Do Not Include Listed Property)

16	GDS and ADS deductions for assets placed in service in tax years beginning before 1991 (see instructions)	**16** 682
17	Property subject to section 168(f)(1) election (see instructions)	**17**
18	ACRS and other depreciation (see instructions)	**18**

Part IV — Summary

19	Listed property—Enter amount from line 25	**19**
20	Total—Add deductions on line 12, lines 14 and 15 in column (g), and lines 16 through 19. Enter here and on the appropriate lines of your return. (Partnerships and S corporations—see instructions)	**20** 2450
21	For assets shown above and placed in service during the current year, enter the portion of the basis attributable to section 263A costs (see instructions) **21**	

For Paperwork Reduction Act Notice, see page 1 of the separate instructions. Cat. No. 12906N Form **4562**

Exhibit 6C

Expenses Allowable as Deductions

Page **2**

Part V Listed Property.—Automobiles, Certain Other Vehicles, Cellular Telephones, Computers, and Property Used for Entertainment, Recreation, or Amusement

If you are using the standard mileage rate or deducting vehicle lease expense, complete columns (a) through (c) of Section A, all of Section B, and Section C if applicable.

Section A.—Depreciation (Caution: *See instructions for limitations for automobiles.)*

22a Do you have evidence to support the business/investment use claimed? ☐ Yes ☐ No 22b If "Yes," is the evidence written? ☐ Yes ☐ No

(a) Type of property (list vehicles first)	(b) Date placed in service	(c) Business/ investment use percentage	(d) Cost or other basis	(e) Basis for depreciation (business/investment use only)	(f) Recovery period	(g) Method/ Convention	(h) Depreciation deduction	(i) Elected section 179 cost
23 *Property used more than 50% in a qualified business use (see instructions):*								
STEREO & TAPE Library		55 %	3215	1768				1768
		%						
24 *Property used 50% or less in a qualified business use (see instructions):*								
		%			S/L –			
		%			S/L –			
		%			S/L –			

25 Add amounts in column (h). Enter the total here and on line 19, page 1	25	
26 Add amounts in column (i). Enter the total here and on line 7, page 1.	26	1768

Section B.—Information Regarding Use of Vehicles—*If you deduct expenses for vehicles:*
- Always complete this section for vehicles used by a sole proprietor, partner, or other "more than 5% owner," or related person.
- If you provided vehicles to your employees, first answer the questions in Section C to see if you meet an exception to completing this section for those vehicles.

	(a) Vehicle 1	(b) Vehicle 2	(c) Vehicle 3	(d) Vehicle 4	(e) Vehicle 5	(f) Vehicle 6
27 Total business/investment miles driven during the year (DO NOT include commuting miles)	14210					
28 Total commuting miles driven during the year	1590					
29 Total other personal (noncommuting) miles driven	10500					
30 Total miles driven during the year— Add lines 27 through 29	26300					

	Yes	No	Yes	No	Yes	No	Yes	No	Yes	No	Yes	No
31 Was the vehicle available for personal use during off-duty hours?		X										
32 Was the vehicle used primarily by a more than 5% owner or related person? . .		X										
33 Is another vehicle available for personal use?		X										

Section C.—Questions for Employers Who Provide Vehicles for Use by Their Employees
(Answer these questions to determine if you meet an exception to completing Section B. **Note:** *Section B must always be completed for vehicles used by sole proprietors, partners, or other more than 5% owners or related persons.)*

	Yes	No
34 Do you maintain a written policy statement that prohibits all personal use of vehicles, including commuting, by your employees?		
35 Do you maintain a written policy statement that prohibits personal use of vehicles, except commuting, by your employees? (See instructions for vehicles used by corporate officers, directors, or 1% or more owners.) .		
36 Do you treat all use of vehicles by employees as personal use?.		
37 Do you provide more than five vehicles to your employees and retain the information received from your employees concerning the use of the vehicles?		
38 Do you meet the requirements concerning qualified automobile demonstration use (see instructions)? . .		
Note: *If your answer to 34, 35, 36, 37, or 38 is "Yes," you need not complete Section B for the covered vehicles.*		

Part VI Amortization

(a) Description of costs	(b) Date amortization begins	(c) Amortizable amount	(d) Code section	(e) Amortization period or percentage	(f) Amortization for this year
39 Amortization of costs that begins during your 1991 tax year:					

40 Amortization of costs that began before 1991	40	
41 Total. Enter here and on "Other Deductions" or "Other Expenses" line of your return. . . .	41	

Exhibit 6D

54.03 %. (14,210/26,300 = 54.03). This means Mrs. Esterman would have been entitled to 54.03% of the entire expense of maintaining the car for the year. This amount came out to $2,050 based on 54.04% of actual receipts and canceled checks, as well as 54.03% of depreciation.

However, it was more advantageous that year for Mrs. Esterman to take the standard mileage allowance of 16.5 cents per mile. This alternative calculation was done as follows: 14,210 miles X .165 = $2,345. This was the figure actually used on Line 10 of the Schedule C, Car and Truck Expenses.

The only question which could possibly be raised by an IRS auditor would be whether or not the information listed in the travel log was accurate. Since the total mileage traveled tied in to the calculation of automobile expense, it would be a question of fact to be determined by overall reasonableness of the deduction. Again, this question would revert to whether or not the IRS considered this to be a true business.

In calculating the **Depreciation and Section 179 Expense** of $2,450 we also turn to Form 4562 (Exhibit 6C). On Part 1 of this form we calculated the Section 179 Expense, Election to Expense Certain Tangible Property, rather than depreciating it. Line 1, the maximum dollar limitation is $10,000 (for 1991). The total limitation, as mentioned previously, goes on Line 3. This amount is $200,000. The total cost of property which is being expensed during the tax year goes on Line 2.

Mrs. Esterman provided us with the following bills for items purchased for business for the year. The stereo and cassette library for her act came to $3,215. We had the invoices for these amounts but no canceled checks as they were paid by Visa. She did not have the actual Visa slips for the individual purchases, but did retain the monthly statements. In addition, she had canceled checks for payments made to Visa which totaled slightly more than the amount deducted. This was because interest payments were included as well as other purchases not related to business.

As I mentioned, Doug was conservative in attributing only 55% of the use of these items to business. For that reason 55% of $3,215, or $1,768, would be listed on Line 2 as the total cost of Section 179 property placed in service during the tax year. On Lines 4 and 5 of Part 1 of Form 4562 we have zero, and $200,000, which represent products of addition of numbers. What this is telling us is that there was not an excessive amount of money spent on new equipment over $200,000 which would limit the allowable deduction.

On Line 6 there is space for the description of the property and the cost. If the property being expensed was not "listed property," the description and cost would be given here. Listed property is property which is subject to further scrutiny by the IRS since it has the potential of being abused by taxpayers in taking excessive deductions. These are items which may be considered to be used for amusement, entertainment, or recreation by the taxpayer. These items include automobiles (if we were taking actual depreciation rather than standard mileage deduction), cellular telephones, computers, and stereo and video equipment–items frequently used for personal activities.

Part V of Form 4562 (Exhibit 6D), Section A, Line 23 we have space for providing information about the listed property. As you can see, we have entered a 55% business use of the stereo system and cassette tape library of which we are expensing 100% of the business use amount in the current year. On Line 22A of Section A we are asked "Do you have evidence to support the business use claim?," and "If yes, is the evidence written?" to which we have answered yes on both counts. Mrs. Esterman has a detailed log of her practice sessions and the songs rehearsed as she maintained a very disciplined schedule. Doug felt certain that this would provide adequate written evidence of the business use of these items. The songs which were rehearsed and learned during the tax year were the same songs which were purchased as part of this cassette tape library.

On Line 7 $1,768 represents the total from Page 2, Part V, Line 26 (Exhibit 6D). Line 8 is the total carried down, as is Line 9. Line 10 is for any disallowed carry over deduction. Line 11 is the taxable income limitation which we previously discussed. At this time you are limited to taxable income in deducting Section 179 expense – i.e., you cannot generate or add to a business loss by taking the expense write–off in this section. As I mentioned before, this is now a limitation which was not in effect during the tax year in question. For purposes of this illustration I have entered $200,000 on this line, although if I were preparing a 1991 tax return I would have to enter "0."

Line 12 is the allowable Section 179 deduction which is the lesser of the amount spent or the limitation. In this case the amount was $1,768. Line 13 would have been the amount carried over to the next year if any amount of the expense could not be deducted in the current year due to limitations.

Next we will look at Part II, Page 1. In this section, we take depreciation expense for assets purchased for business use which could not be, or voluntarily were not, deducted as part of the Section 179 expense. We had no new assets for Mrs. Esterman which were not taken as a direct write–off, therefore this section was left blank.

Part III is for bringing forward any depreciation for items purchased in prior years but not fully depreciated in the past. Here, we have an amount of $682. This represents the portion attributable to the current year of depreciation for items purchased in prior years but not fully written off. The way this figure was arrived at was as follows: The piano which was purchased last year for $4,000 was estimated to have a useful life of ten years. It was therefore being written off at $400 per year. The castanets, maracas, metronome, and xylophone together had a annual depreciation of $282 per year. The only required amount to be reported on Form 4562 for all these amounts would be $682 ($400 + $282) on Line 16, Part 3.

The only substantiation necessary for this figure was a fully detailed depreciation schedule in the workpapers. If the expenditure were to be questioned we would have had to go back to the years in which the purchases were made and examine the support from those years. For this small amount of money, Doug did not feel, at this point, it would be worth our time. If Miss Green wanted us to do so at a future date, we would look into it.

The total figure for Depreciation and Section 179 Expense was consequently calculated as follows:

Section 179 Expense	$1,768
Depreciation of piano	400
Misc. musical instruments	282
Total expense, Line 20	$2,450

Documentation and substantiation for the actual **Insurance Expense** of $435 would be relatively straight forward. Mrs. Esterman provided us with two, six month invoices from the PennMutual Insurance Company for $217.50 each, plus canceled checks for those amounts.

Legal and Professional Service expenditures of $1,200 was also fairly easy to back up. There were schedules in the workpaper files to show the allocation of Doug's bill to Mrs. Esterman. Using the percentage of actual time spent on her business as compared to the time spent on the entire Esterman account, Doug came up with an equitable figure for accounting fees used for business purposes. She also submitted to us checks for the entire amount paid to him for the year.

The legal expenses incurred by Mrs. Esterman for the drafting of contracts and other legal documents were also supported by invoices and canceled checks.

The **Office Expense Deduction** of $584 for supplies and photostating was a bit harder to substantiate. Since most of the photostating was done at the library on the public copy machines there was no backup to support the figure she claimed.

Doug told me not to worry about this as Miss Green probably needed **something** to worry about. He said that she would probably waste her time focusing on this small expense and consequently not think very much about some of the larger expenditures.

The balance of this $584 figure consisted of small stationary purchases. Some of these purchases had support, some did not. So for this expense we would have to "wing it."

The **Home Office Expense Deduction** of $2,826 was easy to document. If Miss Green granted us the concept of having an existing business, then the actual documentation of this amount would be relatively simple. There were invoices and canceled checks for the payment of real estate taxes, fuel and electricity costs, and miscellaneous maintenance.

As we discussed previously, Doug used a conservative 10% allocation figure rather than a more aggressive allocation method based on square feet. The calculation of both these amounts was well documented in the workpaper files. Ten percent of all these expenses came to $1,176.

A significant portion of this expense was for depreciation of 10% of the actual cost of the house. There were depreciation schedules in the workpapers which provided support for the amount which we took on Form 4562, Part 3, Line 18, of $1,650.

In addition, there was reference in the current year's workpapers to the Esterman's permanent file which contained documentation of the original cost of the house, date acquired, and improvements made. This provided a basis for the depreciation, as well as the documentation we needed to support each years' write off.

Repairs and Maintenance Expense of $230 incurred for the tuning of her piano was supported by a bill from the piano tuner. There was no canceled check because she paid in cash.

Travel, Meals and Entertainment Deduction for $2,685 was also well documented. There were bills from hotels and restaurants in Puerto Rico. In addition, she had Visa chits from most of these establishments, as well as the Visa statements and canceled checks for payment of these Visa bills.

Another technique Doug advised all his clients to utilize was that of keeping a detailed diary with all of their appointments during business trips. He also advised clients to enter the results of those appointments in the diary to further substantiate the business purpose and outcome of the trips. Mrs. Esterman provided us with these detailed records.

The Other Expenses which were deducted were documented with varying degrees of detail. The expenses for a backup band of $635 and rehearsal studio of $840 had checks which totaled the amounts paid but no bills from the people the checks were written to.

The beauty salon had checks or credit card statements for approximately 50% of the amount deducted and no invoice. The trainer she employed for body work had little support other than appointment times written down in Mrs. Esterman's diary. The gym fees at the health club were evidenced by Visa statements.

The expense for the costumes of $1,850 had some substantiation but was not entirely backed up. Doug had filed a Form 1099 at the end of the year for $1,050 paid in fees to the dressmaker who worked as a costume designer for Mrs. Esterman. There was no bill from him, nor were there canceled checks as he was paid in cash on a production basis. There were no receipts for material purchased for the costumes he made.

The cleaning expense of $435 was documented with monthly statements from the dry cleaners. Unfortunately, all of her cleaning bills were on these statements and we could not identify the specific costumes which related to the various amounts. As I mentioned before, there was no documentation of a $270 expense labeled miscellaneous. Upon my inquiry, Mrs. Esterman informed that she believed this was for out–of–pocket tips and other gifts of cash or small items for people who had been helpful to her. Beyond this there were no records of these expenses.

Putting It All Together – The Audit Concludes

Well, that's our side of the story but, we still had to deal with Miss Green. By the time she got back from her vacation I felt fairly secure in my position as an "experienced tax accountant." She called our office and we set up an appointment for the following week. She asked if I had all the documentation she had requested and if I could forward it to her before the appointment date.

On Doug's instructions, I told her we had received the documentation, but were still in the process of putting together the information. We would have it available for her when she arrived at the office. Another one of Doug's audit techniques was to control as much of the paperwork as was possible. He never allowed an IRS auditor to get what they wanted without making them feel like he was putting a huge effort into the process. He felt this would serve as a further bargaining chip if it was necessary in arriving at a settlement.

By the time Miss Green arrived I had set up the conference room with the documentation organized by category. I was ready for her.

The first bit of data she requested was the Business Information Questionnaire I had completed on Mrs. Esterman. She looked through it briefly and asked if this was her copy to take back to the office. I indicated it was.

"Damn," I thought to myself, "she's not even going to look at this stuff."

She asked to see the documentation on all of the expenses she had earmarked for review. For the next three and a half hours we went through it dollar for dollar as I have analyzed it with you in the previous sections.

To summarize the results of that morning's audit, I will list the expenses one more time and give a brief synopsis of her reaction to them.

1. Automobile Expense of $2,345: She was impressed with the log and the attention to details which was evidenced by the records kept. She indicated she had no problem with the amount taken.

2. Depreciation and Section 179 Expense of $2,450: At first she questioned the necessity of a new stereo as a business expense. I indicated to her that Doug had only expensed 55% of the entire amount spent and that we felt this was a fairly conservative amount. I'm sure it was the detailed records of her practice sessions, including the dances rehearsed, that convinced her. After reviewing the documentation she indicated she would allow the full deduction. Miss Green had wanted to see some evidence of the actual payment

of $3,215 for the stereo and tape library. As I mentioned, we had invoices, but no canceled checks, since they were paid with a credit card. She had no problem with the payment method, however, we did not have the actual credit card chits to support payment. (The chits are the customers' copies of the actual purchase slips which are signed at the time of the purchase. They indicate a detailed record of what was actually purchased, as opposed to the monthly statements which only list the store to which the payment was made.) With the production of the monthly statements and the canceled checks we had evidence that payments had been made to the store, however, we could not ascertain from those two items alone what was being purchased. I did have detailed bills for the purchase of the stereo and tapes which tied into the statements on hand. Using this as alternate documentation the auditor was satisfied as to the propriety of the amount deducted.

Note the method of using **alternate documentation** as evidence when backup material requested by an auditor is not readily available. They will accept other forms of verification if you can be creative and satisfy them as to the propriety of deductions. They are not locked into a fixed mode and may use discretion on a case by case basis.

3. Insurance Expense of $435: Because we had the bills and canceled checks there was no question as to the propriety of the deduction.

4. Legal and Professional Service Expenditures of $1,200: We had the bills, we had the canceled checks, and we had the allocation schedules. She had no problem.

5. Office Expense Deduction of $584: This area could have been a potential problem as we had very little detail to substantiate the figure. Miss Green asked to look at Mrs. Esterman's diary in order to determine the volume of paperwork and related office supplies.

We produced more credit card statements which listed several payments made to an office supply company in the total amount of $350. Miss Green asked us if we could request duplicate invoices from the stationary store. I indicated that I would do this. She told me that if I could secure these invoices she would allow the entire deduction including photocopying fees. She felt that based on the amount of activity indicated in the diary the photocopying fees were reasonable.

90

6. Home Office Expense Deduction: The figures we had provided substantiated the entire amount. She was impressed with the detailed records we had in the permanent file relating the purchase of the house and the annual updating of this file for improvements made over the years. I did not think much of it when she said to me, upon concluding this area of the audit, "Well, I suppose if she **has** a business, she **would** need a place to conduct it." Later in the day when I mentioned this to Doug he smiled and said "So that's what she's got up her sleeve."

7. The Repairs and Maintenance Expense: this $230 was only supported by a bill from the piano tuner. I expected she would want something further, however, she surprised me by telling me not to worry about it in light of its immaterial amount.

8. Travel, Meals, and Entertainment Expense: this was another story. Having just returned from a vacation in the Caribbean, Miss Green felt she was the newly ordained expert on the "cost of vacationing in the Islands."

She felt that $2,685 might have been an excessive amount to have paid for three "business trips" to Puerto Rico. Air fare had been only $198 round trip each time, and the balance was spent on hotels and meals. Although she had no problem with the business nature of the trip, "if indeed this was a business," she felt there was a "substantial element of pleasure" associated with these trips.

The concept of "**substantial element of pleasure**" is one which the IRS uses in determining whether or not trips for business, charitable, and/or medical reasons are truly taken for the reasons stated. Or, if indeed, the trips are taken as vacations. Many people do try to write off vacations as having a business or charitable purpose in order to get "a free ride on the government." The IRS is aware of this and therefore has come up with this concept of "substantial element of pleasure," as a crucial test in this determination.

The IRS will allow you to deduct any expenses incurred while traveling away from home in the pursuit of business, charity, or valid medical reasons. These expenses are subject to certain limitations, such as allowing only 80% for meals and entertainment, rather than 100%; however, the IRS must be convinced that indeed the trip did not include a "substantial element of pleasure."

What this apparently means is that you can visit another city or country in the hopes of conducting business. You can take people out to dinner who are potential business contacts or clients. You can even have your picture taken with them in the restaurant by the house photographer. **But, if you do, you had better make sure you are not smiling**. This might lead the IRS to believe you are involved in an activity which is generating a "substantial element of pleasure."

There were no pictures of Mrs. Esterman smiling in Puerto Rico. I indicated to Miss Green that I felt she was wrong in thinking that this might have been a vacation. I also related to her that an entertainer must maintain the image of being successful and having "class." This might account for the fact that Mrs. Esterman spent a fair amount of money by staying at good hotels and dining in the finer restaurants.

We did provide pictures of Mrs. Esterman performing in costume at the hotel. However, Ms. Green did not seem convinced. In fact, she let me know that she would probably disallow a good part of the deduction as non–business related.

9. Other expenses:
   (a) Backup band for $635; and
   (b) Rehearsal studio for $840: We had the checks, but no bills. Miss Green indicated she would allow the entire amount if we could produce signed state– ments from the people to whom we paid the checks.
   (c) Beauty salon and nail sculpturing for $1,265; and
   (d) Physical fitness and body work for $1,450: We had checks made out to the beauty salon and credit card statements for half of the amounts deducted. We had no invoices. She once again requested Mrs. Esterman's diary and went through it with me week by week to verify appointments with the beauty parlor and physical fitness trainer. We also had the credit card statements for annual gym fees. I was very surprised when she turned to me and said, "This seems to be in order. Based on what I have seen as evidence, these appointments were kept, and, based on the normal fees for such appoint- ments, I am going to allow the entire amounts for both of these expenses."

"Son of a gun! This audit's going well," I thought to myself. "Must be some sort of beginner's luck."

(e) Costume expense of $1,850 and

(f) Cleaning expense of $435: Miss Green admitted she was impressed that we actually filed a Form 1099 at the end of the year for the costume designer.

Form 1099 is an informational return that must be filed with the IRS at the end of each year to let them know that you have paid somebody to work for you in some capacity during that year as an independent contractor. In addition, it informs them that you will be deducting the amount you have paid, that the IRS should be aware of this payment, and, in fact, they can look for it to be reported as income on the other person's tax return. It is required to be filed by anyone making a business payment to an individual which amounts to $600 or more in that tax year.

Because there is no payment due with this form and because there are relatively light penalties for non–filing of the form, many people do not take the time to file it. For this reason, I believe, it looks really good when you present a tax return which has deductions taken which are entirely substantiated by the filing of 1099s. Keep this point in mind as we will be discussing the technique of trading as a business, and, in doing so, the possibility of hiring family members to work for you as independent contractors. This will be discussed further in "This Business Of Trading."

In addition to the filing of 1099s, the IRS generally will appreciate a taxpayer's attention to small details.

One thing we did have going for us in this audit was certainly an abundance of small details. Because of this, and probably because it was getting close to lunch and her next appointment, Miss Green allowed these "expenses" to also pass without a problem.

She did want to see some invoices for the amounts spent on materials used to make the costumes. She wanted to be sure we did not have a stockpile of inventory which should be expensed over the course of the next few years. I agreed to look into obtaining them for her.

(g) Miscellaneous expense of $275: She said we would have to come up with something to call this as she could not allow an amount to be expensed, regardless of the amount, without knowing for sure what it was. If I could put together a schedule from Mrs. Esterman's diary indicating the amounts spent on various people and the items purchased for them, then she would reconsider this disallowance.

93

Where We Stood

After lunch I returned to the office and sat down to calculate exactly where I felt we stood in terms of the audit process. It looked rather solid to me, even the worst potential outcome. She appeared satisfied that the amounts in question were accurate. She passed on changing any of the figures, but was waiting for further documentation on several of the amounts. Even if she had decided to disallow all of the deductions which required further documentation, we still would come out looking pretty good.

The amounts in question which needed further substantiation were as follows.

1.	Travel, Meals, and Entertainment	$2,685
2.	Duplicate office supply invoices	350
3.	Backup band – signed statement	635
4.	Rehearsal studio – invoice	840
5.	Material used in costumes	800
6.	Miscellaneous gifts	275
	Total potential disallowance	$5,310

At a 45% tax rate, the bracket which the Estermans were in, the potential tax liability was only $2,389.50 + possible penalties for underpayment + interest calculated at 9% per year. In other words, the largest potential liability for the Estermans appeared to be less than $3,500. Out of a potential expense disallowance of $19,100, this did not seem too bad.

"Good work, Ted!" I thought to myself, as the theme from "Robin Hood" echoed through my mind. "What a way to begin your career as a defender of the people. A true crusader, on the side of the average citizen who must enter into battle with the all–powerful Internal Revenue Service."

By the time I finished patting myself on the back, "Dauntless Doug, the Duke of Deductions" had returned. He came over and asked me how it went with that "Green person from the IRS?"

I responded, "It couldn't have gone better. She still wants to see some documentation, but I think we have her beat. The most she can get out of us would be less than $3,500 and that would only be if we can't provide the statements she asked for. But I think we can. All we have to do is get Esterman to get some signed bills, and we are home free."

"You mean she has agreed with us that Mrs. Esterman is truly a legitimate business? You mean she's not going to try to disallow the entire loss as a hobby?," the Duke asked.

"She didn't say anything about that," I replied.

"Don't worry," Doug said, "she will. She's got nothing else to hang her hat on. She'll try to disallow the entire amount. I can just feel it. She's young, she's ambitious, she's green, and she's careless. She hasn't fully researched the case history on this. There is none. There has never been a case where the court has thrown out an artist's business for lack of producing income within three years."

"In fact," he continued, "this is just the way I've planned it. She's playing right into our hands. Because she is focusing on an area which she feels is most important she has obviously neglected areas which she feels are not. In other words, she has been quite generous to us with some of the points. She could have been a real stickler on some of these amounts, but she passed on them in hopes of getting the entire business thrown out on the grounds of a "hobby loss." I've seen this before and I've beaten it before. Watch, she will call you by the end of the week with more prodding questions on the nature of the business and will then disallow the entire loss on those grounds."

And, son of a gun, Doug was right! Again! That's exactly what happened. In the meantime, per Doug's instructions, I hadn't come up with any further documentation regarding the $5,310, and I mentioned this to her. She was not interested in this. She went right for the jugular as Doug predicted she would, and informed me that she did not believe we had a true business loss. Also, that she was considering a disallowance of the entire $19,100. She asked if it would be possible to arrange a conference with Doug present. I indicated to her it probably would be and that I would call her back later.

I congratulated Doug on his accurate assessment of the situation and told him it was "showdown time at O.K. Corral." He said to arrange the conference as soon as possible – he was ready. The conference was set up for first thing in the morning. With a sense of anticipation, I looked forward to finally seeing "the Duke" in action.

Before I left that evening Doug gave me one more lesson in "The IRS Audit, According To Doug." Doug told me to remember that the audit process was nothing more than a discussion between two people. Each person is entitled to his or her own opinion, and these opinions are likely to differ from time to time.

95

He told me that he felt Miss Green had something to prove, being that she was somewhat new to the Service. He also believed that she was not prepared to stand her ground on the issue of a "hobby loss," and that if she could come away from the audit looking good with something to show for it, she would be happy.

Although, in principle, auditors are not supposed to trade issues, often they do. In other words, she should not negotiate the allowance of one amount for the disallowance of another. But, if we presented a strong case for the existence of a business and we yielded on some of the items she was questioning, she would probably not be prepared to take this issue to a higher level.

And you know something, Doug was three for three!

That next morning at the audit Doug told her that he had filed hundreds of returns just like he did this one, and although he had been through numerous audits on them, he had never once been disallowed a business status due to lack of income.

He complemented her on coming up with the points she raised and on the possible adjustment to income of $5,310. He also mentioned that her supervisor would probably be happy with getting this as a settlement. And, in fact, Doug mentioned him by name just to make sure that she knew that he knew who her supervisor was. Doug also mentioned that he was prepared to take the issue of hobby loss versus business loss all the way to the top and would request an appointment with the supervisor if they could not reach an agreement that day.

But, he was willing to agree with the changes of $5,310 without contention, although he felt confident that they were all appropriate. If Miss Green was willing to agree to these changes, we would go no further in trying to document them.

She agreed and prepared a Form 870, Waiver of Restrictions on Assessment, to close the case. It was then that I knew why they called him "Dauntless Doug, the Duke of Deductions."

The Lessons Learned

"...here I sit so patiently, waiting to find out what price, you have
to pay to get out of, going through all these things twice."

Bob Dylan
"Stuck Inside of Mobile
With the Memphis Blues Again"

Relevance to the Investor

From the story of Dauntless Doug, and my first tax audit,
there are several important lessons which we can glean:

    a)   First of all, we have had our basic introduction into
          what constitutes an expense;

    b)   Secondly, we see what the IRS looks for in terms of
          backup and substantiation; and

    c)   Finally, by going through the audit process we have
          gained insight into the ultimate resolution of the
          propriety of an expense.

As investors it is extremely important for us to know precisely
what we **can** and what we **cannot** legitimately take as write offs
against income. We must understand this process, not so much to
memorize a list of the specific deductions, but rather so that it
becomes almost second nature to us. We must think in terms of
structuring our lives so that as much of what we spend sustains a
valid business purpose as is possible. Hopefully, in doing so, we can
write off many ordinary and necessary **living** expenses as a cost of
doing business. For example, since we all have to eat, doing business
while dining with a client, potential business contact, or investment/
tax advisor transforms the meal into a deductible business meal. We
must also be aware of the type of documentation and record keeping
required to substantiate such deductions.

Furthermore, it is important for us as taxpayers and as investors,
to understand exactly how the audit process works. In this way, we
will be in the best position to **avoid** an audit, while at the same time
being prepared for any inquiry from the IRS, or even a full scale audit
should one ever occur. We want to deal from a position of strength
which justifies and substantiates whatever is being examined.

The Great Houdini Tax Act

Saving money on taxes does not come from finding tax loopholes, using smoke and mirrors, or resorting to cheating on your tax returns. It is the product of acquiring specific tax knowledge and of using whatever is available under the current law to our fullest advantage. Good tax planning can be translated directly into significant tax savings. Instead of waiting for Congress to act to slash the capital gains tax once again or to pass some other new and more favorable tax act for the investor, we must constantly keep ourselves aware of the possibilities which already exist.

In this next section we will summarize what we have just learned in these last few chapters, namely:

1) The different classes of income, and
2) The various types of expenses which can be used to reduce taxable income.

Not all of these expenses will apply to all investors, but at the very least we will be aware of them and on the lookout for their existence. In addition, we will take a look at the specific tax forms which are used to deduct these expenses, when each form is appropriate, and how to keep track of your income and deductions throughout the year so that you can be more in tune with the actual tax savings achieved through each deduction.

I will then discuss the subject of **legality** and how it applies to our task in "How Far Can We Go?" I will examine how the Government looks at this concept and how it has dealt with several familiar cases and some not so familiar.

The section after this will recap the points touched on previously on handling an IRS tax audit. There was a great deal of wisdom in the way Doug handled the IRS. We will summarize these techniques and add to them in the section entitled, "Playing For Keeps With The IRS."

After this section, we will then examine several general tax strategies and the various concepts associated with each in the sections addressing how to shelter your wealth and legally reduce your tax liability. Here we will discuss retirement planning, transferring wealth to future generations, and this business of trading.

With these techniques under our belt, we will reexamine the portfolio I previously discussed. As a tune up for our own tax restructuring, we will investigate the changes which were made and the results achieved.

We will then shift the focus to our own tax objectives. That is, we will investigate tax strategies we can use in our own lives. I will give you 50 specific methods for reducing your tax burden which you can start using today in handling your investments and in conducting your everyday life.

Chapter 7

Recap of Income and Expenses

Summary Listing

Let's recap some of the areas I've covered about **income** and **expenses**. I will summarize them for you in a check list and reference them to their proper form on the tax return. My objective here is to provide a quick reference for you.

Description	Form
1. **Salary**: Wages from Employment. Expenses not reimbursed by employer, such as: union dues, tools, books, seminars, etc., are deductible from wages.	1040, Page 1, Line 7 Exhibit 3F 2106, Page 1 Exhibits 7A&B
2. **Fees, Commissions, Business Income**: Received as non–employee. Expenses associated with production of income must be reasonable, ordinary, necessary, and legal. Examples include: automobile, travel and entertainment, office rent, insurance, professional fees, equipment, etc.	1040, Page 1, Line 22 Exhibit 3F If expenses, must report both income and expenses on Schedule C, Page 1, Income, Line 1, Expenses, Lines 8–27 Exhibit 6B. If Schedule C, then Line 12, Page 1, 1040. Also, Schedule SE Exhibit 7C
3. **Interest**: All taxable interest and all non–taxable interest. Expenses incurred in production of	1040, Page 1, Line 8A 1040, Page 1, Line 8B Exhibit 3F

income, such as investment advisory fees, are deductible.

Schedule A, Line 20
Exhibit 3H
If interest is over $400 must use Schedule B, Pt 1, Exhibit 7D

4. **Dividends**: All taxable dividends and all non–taxable dividend expenses same as above.

1040, Page 1, Line 9
1040, Page 1, Line 9
Over $400, Schedule B

5. **Capital Gains**: Expenses same as above.

1040, Page 1, Line 13
Must use Schedule D to report detail of transactions. Exhibit 5A

6. **Rental Income, Royalties, Trusts, Partnerships, Sub S Corporations**: Deductible expenses reported on Schedule E.

Sch. E, Pages 1&2,
to 1040, Page 1,
Line 18
Exhibits 7E&F

7. **Income from Retirement Plans and Pensions**: Premature distributions subject to penalty. Expenses such as IRA fees reported as itemized.

1040, Page 1, Lines 16A, 16B, 17A & 17B
Exhibit 3F
Form 5329, Exhibit 7G
Schedule A, Exhibit 3H

8. **Non–Taxable Income**:
a) Tax–free interest
b) Tax–free insurance proceeds
c) Gifts
d) Inheritances
e) Non–taxable portion of Social Security

1040, Line 8B, Exhibit 3F
Non–reportable
Non–reportable
Non–reportable
1040, Line 21a,
Exhibit 3F

9. **Deductions Reducing Income**:
a) IRA Contribution
b) Retirement Plan Contribution
c) Self–Employee Deduction such as health insurance and half the Self–Employment Tax
d) Alimony paid
e) Penalty for early withdrawal of savings account

1040, Line 24a&b
1040, Line 27
1040, Line 26
1040, Line 25

1040, Line 29
1040, Line 28–All in Exhibit 3F

Form **2106**

Department of the Treasury
Internal Revenue Service (X)

Employee Business Expenses

▶ **See separate instructions.**

▶ **Attach to Form 1040.**

OMB No. 1545-0139

19 91

Attachment
Sequence No. **54**

Your name	Social security number	Occupation in which expenses were incurred

Part I Employee Business Expenses and Reimbursements

STEP 1 Enter Your Expenses

		Column A Other Than Meals and Entertainment		Column B Meals and Entertainment	
1	Vehicle expense from line 22 or line 29	1			
2	Parking fees, tolls, and local transportation, including train, bus, etc.	2			
3	Travel expense while away from home overnight, including lodging, airplane, car rental, etc. **Do not** include meals and entertainment	3			
4	Business expenses not included on lines 1 through 3. **Do not** include meals and entertainment	4			
5	Meals and entertainment expenses. (See instructions.)	5			
6	**Total expenses.** In Column A, add lines 1 through 4 and enter the result. In Column B, enter the amount from line 5.	6			

Note: If you were not reimbursed for any expenses in Step 1, skip line 7 and enter the amount from line 6 on line 8.

STEP 2 Enter Amounts Your Employer Gave You for Expenses Listed in STEP 1

7	Enter amounts your employer gave you that were **not** reported to you in Box 10 of Form W-2. Include any amount reported under code "L" in Box 17 of your Form W-2. (See instructions.) . . .	7			

STEP 3 Figure Expenses To Deduct on Schedule A (Form 1040)

8	Subtract line 7 from line 6	8			
	*Note: If **both columns** of line 8 are zero, **stop here.** If Column A is less than zero, report the amount as income and enter -0- on line 10, Column A. See the instructions for how to report.*				
9	Enter 20% (.20) of line 8, Column B	9			
10	Subtract line 9 from line 8	10			
11	Add the amounts on line 10 of both columns and enter the total here. **Also enter the total on Schedule A (Form 1040), line 19.** (Qualified performing artists and individuals with disabilities, see the instructions for special rules on where to enter the total.) . . . . ▶	11			

For Paperwork Reduction Act Notice, see instructions.

Cat. No. 11700N

Form **2106** (1991)

Exhibit 7A

Form 2106 (1991)   Page **2**

Part II   Vehicle Expenses (See instructions to find out which sections to complete.)

Section A.—General Information		(a) Vehicle 1	(b) Vehicle 2
12	Enter the date vehicle was placed in service	/ /	/ /
13	Total mileage vehicle was used during 1991	miles	miles
14	Miles included on line 13 that vehicle was used for business	miles	miles
15	Percent of business use (divide line 14 by line 13)	%	%
16	Average daily round trip commuting distance	miles	miles
17	Miles included on line 13 that vehicle was used for commuting	miles	miles
18	Other personal mileage (add lines 14 and 17 and subtract the total from line 13)	miles	miles

19   Do you (or your spouse) have another vehicle available for personal purposes? ☐ Yes ☐ No

20   If your employer provided you with a vehicle, is personal use during off duty hours permitted? ☐ Yes ☐ No ☐ Not applicable

21a   Do you have evidence to support your deduction? ☐ Yes ☐ No   21b   If "Yes," is the evidence written? ☐ Yes ☐ No

Section B.—Standard Mileage Rate (Use this section only if you own the vehicle.)

22   Multiply line 14 by 27.5¢ (.275). Enter the result here and on line 1. (Rural mail carriers, see instructions.)   **22**

Section C.—Actual Expenses		(a) Vehicle 1	(b) Vehicle 2
23	Gasoline, oil, repairs, vehicle insurance, etc.		
24a	Vehicle rentals		
b	Inclusion amount		
c	Subtract line 24b from line 24a		
25	Value of employer-provided vehicle (applies only if 100% of annual lease value was included on Form W-2. See instructions.)		
26	Add lines 23, 24c, and 25		
27	Multiply line 26 by the percentage on line 15		
28	Enter amount from line 38 below		
29	Add lines 27 and 28. Enter total here and on line 1		

Section D.—Depreciation of Vehicles (Use this section only if you own the vehicle.)		(a) Vehicle 1	(b) Vehicle 2
30	Enter cost or other basis. (See instructions.)		
31	Enter amount of section 179 deduction. (See instructions.)		
32	Multiply line 30 by line 15. (See instructions if you elected the section 179 deduction.)		
33	Enter depreciation method and percentage. (See instructions.)		
34	Multiply line 32 by the percentage on line 33. (See instructions.)		
35	Add lines 31 and 34		
36	Enter the limitation amount from the table in the line 36 instructions		
37	Multiply line 36 by the percentage on line 15		
38	Enter the **smaller** of line 35 or line 37. Also enter the amount on line 28 above		

Exhibit 7B

SCHEDULE SE	**Self-Employment Tax**	OMB No. 1545-0074
(Form 1040)	▶ See Instructions for Schedule SE (Form 1040).	19**91**
Department of the Treasury Internal Revenue Service (X)	▶ Attach to Form 1040.	Attachment Sequence No. 17

Name of person with **self-employment** income (as shown on Form 1040)	Social security number of person with **self-employment** income ▶

Who Must File Schedule SE

You must file Schedule SE if:

- Your *net earnings from self-employment from other than church employee income* (line 4 of Short Schedule SE or line 4c of Long Schedule SE) were $400 or more; **OR**
- You had church employee income (as defined in the instructions) of $108.28 or more;

    AND

- Your wages (and tips) subject to social security AND Medicare tax (or railroad retirement tax) were less than $125,000.

Exception: If your only self-employment income was from earnings as a minister, member of a religious order, or Christian Science practitioner, AND you filed **Form 4361** and received IRS approval not to be taxed on those earnings, DO NOT file Schedule SE. Instead, write "Exempt–Form 4361" on Form 1040, line 47.

Note: *Most people can use Short Schedule SE on this page. But you may have to use Long Schedule SE on the back.*

Who MUST Use Long Schedule SE (Section B)

You must use Long Schedule SE if ANY of the following apply:

- You received wages or tips **and** the total of all of your wages (and tips) subject to social security, Medicare, or railroad retirement tax plus your net earnings from self-employment is more than $53,400;
- You use either "optional method" to figure your net earnings from self-employment (see Section B, Part II, and the instructions);
- You are a minister, member of a religious order, or Christian Science practitioner and you received IRS approval (by filing Form 4361) not to be taxed on your earnings from these sources, but you owe self-employment tax on other earnings;
- You had church employee income of $108.28 or more that was reported to you on Form W-2; **OR**
- You received tips subject to social security, Medicare, or railroad retirement tax, but you did not report those tips to your employer.

Section A—Short Schedule SE (Read above to see if you must use Long Schedule SE on the back (Section B).)

1	Net farm profit or (loss) from Schedule F (Form 1040), line 37, and farm partnerships, Schedule K-1 (Form 1065), line 15a	**1**
2	Net profit or (loss) from Schedule C (Form 1040), line 31, and Schedule K-1 (Form 1065), line 15a (other than farming). See instructions for other income to report	**2**
3	Combine lines 1 and 2	**3**
4	**Net earnings from self-employment.** Multiply line 3 by .9235. If less than $400, **do not** file this schedule; you **do not** owe self-employment tax. **Caution:** *If you received wages or tips, and the total of your wages (and tips) subject to social security, Medicare, or railroad retirement tax plus the amount on line 4 is more than $53,400, you cannot use Short Schedule SE. Instead, use Long Schedule SE on the back* . . . . ▶	**4**
5	**Self-employment tax.** If the amount on line 4 is: • $53,400 or less, multiply line 4 by 15.3% (.153) and enter the result. • More than $53,400, but less than $125,000, multiply the amount in excess of $53,400 by 2.9% (.029). Add $8,170.20 to the result and enter the total. • $125,000 or more, enter $10,246.60. Also enter this amount on Form 1040, line 47	**5**

Note: *Also enter one-half of the amount from line 5 on **Form 1040, line 25**.*

For Paperwork Reduction Act Notice, see Form 1040 instructions.	Cat. No. 11358Z	Schedule SE (Form 1040) 1991

Exhibit 7C

105

The Serious Investor's Tax Survival Guide

OMB No. 1545-0074   Page **2**

Name(s) shown on Form 1040. (Do not enter name and social security number if shown on other side.) | Your social security number

Schedule B—Interest and Dividend Income

Attachment Sequence No. **08**

Part I
Interest
Income

(See pages 15 and 43.)

If you received more than $400 in taxable interest income, or you are claiming the exclusion of interest from series EE U.S. savings bonds issued after 1989 (see page 43), you must complete Part I. List ALL interest received in Part I. If you received more than $400 in taxable interest income, you must also complete Part III. If you received, as a nominee, interest that actually belongs to another person, or you received or paid accrued interest on securities transferred between interest payment dates, see page 43.

Interest Income	Amount
1 Interest income. (List name of payer—if any interest income is from seller-financed mortgages, see instructions and list this interest first.) ▶	

Note: If you received a Form 1099-INT, Form 1099-OID, or substitute statement, from a brokerage firm, list the firm's name as the payer and enter the total interest shown on that form.

	1	
2 Add the amounts on line 1	2	
3 Enter the excludable savings bond interest, if any, from Form 8815, line 14. Attach Form 8815 to Form 1040	3	
4 Subtract line 3 from line 2. Enter the result here and on Form 1040, line 8a . ▶	4	

Part II
Dividend
Income

(See pages 16 and 43.)

If you received more than $400 in gross dividends and/or other distributions on stock, you must complete Parts II and III. If you received, as a nominee, dividends that actually belong to another person, see page 43.

Dividend Income	Amount
5 Dividend income. (List name of payer—include on this line capital gain distributions, nontaxable distributions, etc.) ▶	

Note: If you received a Form 1099-DIV, or substitute statement, from a brokerage firm, list the firm's name as the payer and enter the total dividends shown on that form.

	5	
6 Add the amounts on line 5	6	
7 Capital gain distributions. Enter here and on Schedule D* .	7	
8 Nontaxable distributions. (See the inst. for Form 1040, line 9).	8	
9 Add lines 7 and 8	9	
10 Subtract line 9 from line 6. Enter the result here and on Form 1040, line 9 . ▶	10	

*If you received capital gain distributions but do not need Schedule D to report any other gains or losses, see the instructions for Form 1040, lines 13 and 14.

Part III
Foreign
Accounts
and
Foreign
Trusts

(See page 43.)

If you received more than $400 of interest or dividends, OR if you had a foreign account or were a grantor of, or a transferor to, a foreign trust, you must answer both questions in Part III. | Yes | No

11a At any time during 1991, did you have an interest in or a signature or other authority over a financial account in a foreign country (such as a bank account, securities account, or other financial account)? (See page 43 for exceptions and filing requirements for Form TD F 90-22.1.) . . .

b If "Yes," enter the name of the foreign country ▶ ....

12 Were you the grantor of, or transferor to, a foreign trust that existed during 1991, whether or not you have any beneficial interest in it? If "Yes," you may have to file Form 3520, 3520-A, or 926 .

For Paperwork Reduction Act Notice, see Form 1040 instructions.

Schedule B (Form 1040) 1991

Exhibit 7D

SCHEDULE E	**Supplemental Income and Loss**	OMB No. 1545-0074

SCHEDULE E
(Form 1040)

Department of the Treasury
Internal Revenue Service (X)

Supplemental Income and Loss
(From rents, royalties, partnerships, estates, trusts, REMICs, etc.)
▶ Attach to Form 1040 or Form 1041.
▶ See Instructions for Schedule E (Form 1040).

OMB No. 1545-0074

Attachment
Sequence No. **13**

Name(s) shown on return   Your social security number

Part I **Income or Loss From Rentals and Royalties** Note: *Report farm rental income or loss from* **Form 4835** *on page 2, line 39.*

1	Show the kind and location of each **rental property**:		2	For each rental property listed on line 1, did you or your family use it for personal purposes for more than the greater of 14 days or 10% of the total days rented at fair rental value during the tax year? (See instructions.)		Yes	No
A					A		
B					B		
C					C		

Rental and Royalty Income:

			Properties			Totals (Add columns A, B, and C.)
			A	B	C	
3	Rents received	3				3
4	Royalties received	4				4

Rental and Royalty Expenses:

5	Advertising	5				
6	Auto and travel	6				
7	Cleaning and maintenance	7				
8	Commissions	8				
9	Insurance	9				
10	Legal and other professional fees	10				
11	Mortgage interest paid to banks, etc. (see instructions)	11				11
12	Other interest	12				
13	Repairs	13				
14	Supplies	14				
15	Taxes	15				
16	Utilities	16				
17	Wages and salaries	17				
18	Other (list) ▶	18				
19	Add lines 5 through 18	19				19
20	Depreciation expense or depletion (see instructions)	20				20
21	Total expenses. Add lines 19 and 20	21				
22	Income or (loss) from rental or royalty properties. Subtract line 21 from line 3 (rents) or line 4 (royalties). If the result is a (loss), see instructions to find out if you must file **Form 6198**	22				
23	Deductible rental loss. **Caution:** *Your rental loss on line 22 may be limited. See instructions to find out if you must file* **Form 8582**	23	(	)(	)(	)
24	**Income.** Add rental and royalty income from line 22. Enter the total income here					24
25	**Losses.** Add royalty losses from line 22 and rental losses from line 23. Enter the total losses here					25 ( )
26	Total rental and royalty income or (loss). Combine lines 24 and 25. Enter the result here. If Parts II, III, IV, and line 39 on page 2 do not apply to you, enter the amount from line 26 on Form 1040, line 18. Otherwise, include the amount from line 26 in the total on line 40 on page 2					26

For Paperwork Reduction Act Notice, see Form 1040 instructions.   Cat. No. 11344L   Schedule E (Form 1040) 1991

Exhibit 7E

Schedule E (Form 1040) 1991   Attachment Sequence No. **13**   Page **2**

Name(s) shown on return. (Do not enter name and social security number if shown on other side.)   **Your social security number**

Note: *If you report amounts from farming or fishing on Schedule E, you must enter your gross income from those activities on line 41 below.*

Part II   **Income or Loss From Partnerships and S Corporations**

If you report a loss from an at-risk activity, you MUST check either column **(e)** or **(f)** of line 27 to describe your investment in the activity. See instructions. If you check column **(f)**, you must attach **Form 6198**.

27 (a) Name	(b) Enter P for partnership; S for S corporation	(c) Check if foreign partnership	(d) Employer identification number	Investment At Risk? (e) All is at risk	(f) Some is not at risk
A					
B					
C					
D					
E					

	Passive Income and Loss		Nonpassive Income and Loss		
	(g) Passive loss allowed (attach Form 8582 if required)	(h) Passive income from Schedule K–1	(i) Nonpassive loss from Schedule K–1	(j) Section 179 expense deduction from Form 4562	(k) Nonpassive income from Schedule K–1
A					
B					
C					
D					
E					
28a Totals					
b Totals					

29   Add columns (h) and (k) of line 28a. Enter the total income here **29**

30   Add columns (g), (i), and (j) of line 28b. Enter the total here . . . . **30** (   )

31   Total partnership and S corporation income or (loss). Combine lines 29 and 30. Enter the result here and include in the total on line 40 below **31**

Part III   **Income or Loss From Estates and Trusts**

32 (a) Name	(b) Employer identification number
A	
B	
C	

	Passive Income and Loss		Nonpassive Income and Loss	
	(c) Passive deduction or loss allowed (attach Form 8582 if required)	(d) Passive income from Schedule K–1	(e) Deduction or loss from Schedule K–1	(f) Other income from Schedule K–1
A				
B				
C				
33a Totals				
b Totals				

34   Add columns (d) and (f) of line 33a. Enter the total income here **34**

35   Add columns (c) and (e) of line 33b. Enter the total here . . . . **35** (   )

36   Total estate and trust income or (loss). Combine lines 34 and 35. Enter the result here and include in the total on line 40 below **36**

Part IV   **Income or Loss From Real Estate Mortgage Investment Conduits (REMICs)—Residual Holder**

37 (a) Name	(b) Employer identification number	(c) Excess inclusion from Schedules Q, line 2c (see instructions)	(d) Taxable income (net loss) from Schedules Q, line 1b	(e) Income from Schedules Q, line 3b

38   Combine columns (d) and (e) only. Enter the result here and include in the total on line 40 below   **38**

Part V   **Summary**

39   Net farm rental income or (loss) from **Form 4835**. (Also complete line 41 below.). **39**

40   TOTAL income or (loss). Combine lines 26, 31, 36, 38, and 39. Enter the result here and on Form 1040, line 18 . . . . ▶ **40**

41   **Reconciliation of Farming and Fishing Income:** Enter your **gross** farming and fishing income reported in Parts II and III and on line 39 (see instructions) **41**

Exhibit 7F

Form **5329**	**Return for Additional Taxes Attributable to Qualified Retirement Plans (Including IRAs), Annuities, and Modified Endowment Contracts** (Under Sections 72, 4973, 4974 and 4980A of the Internal Revenue Code) ▶ **Attach to Form 1040. See separate instructions.**	OMB No. 1545-0203 **19**91
Department of the Treasury Internal Revenue Service		Attachment Sequence No. **29**

Name of individual subject to additional tax. (Enter the name of **one** individual only. See the instructions for "Joint Returns.") | Your social security number

Address (number and street). (Enter P.O. box no. if mail is not delivered to street address.) | Apt. No.

City, town, or post office, state, and ZIP code | If this is an Amended Return, check here ▶ ☐

Part I **Excess Contributions Tax for Individual Retirement Arrangements (Section 4973)**

Complete this part if, either in this year or in earlier years, you contributed more to your IRA than is or was allowable and you have an excess contribution subject to tax.

1	Excess contributions for 1991 (see instructions). Do not include this amount on Form 1040, line 24a or 24b	**1**	
2	Earlier year excess contributions not previously eliminated (see instructions)	**2**	
3	Contribution credit. (If your actual contribution for 1991 is less than your maximum allowable contribution, see instructions for line 3; otherwise, enter -0-.).	**3**	
4a	1991 distributions from your IRA account that are includible in taxable income	**4a**	
b	1990 tax year excess contributions (if any) withdrawn after the due date (including extensions) of your 1990 income tax return, and 1989 and earlier tax year excess contributions withdrawn in 1991.	**4b**	
c	Add lines 3, 4a, and 4b	**4c**	
5	Adjusted earlier year excess contributions. (Subtract line 4c from line 2. Enter the result, but not less than zero.)	**5**	
6	Total excess contributions (add lines 1 and 5).	**6**	
7	Tax due. (Enter the **smaller** of 6% of line 6 or 6% of the value of your IRA on the last day of 1991.) Also enter this amount on Form 1040, line 51.	**7**	

Part II **Tax on Early Distributions (Section 72)**

Complete this part if a taxable distribution was made from your qualified retirement plan (including an IRA), modified endowment contract, or annuity contract before you reached age 59½. **Note:** *You must enter the amount of the distribution on the appropriate line (or lines) of Form 1040 or Form 4972.*

8	Early distributions included in gross income attributable to:		
a	Qualified retirement plans (including IRAs)	**8a**	
b	Annuity contracts	**8b**	
c	Modified endowment contracts	**8c**	
d	Prohibited transactions	**8d**	
e	Pledging of accounts as security	**8e**	
f	Cost of collectibles	**8f**	
g	Total distributions (add lines 8a through 8f)	**8g**	
	Note: *Include this amount on line 16b or 17b of Form 1040 or on the appropriate line of Form 4972.*		
9	Exceptions to distributions subject to additional taxes (see instructions):		
a	Due to death (does not apply to modified endowment contracts) . . .	**9a**	
b	Due to total and permanent disability	**9b**	
c	As part of a series of substantially equal lifetime periodic payments . .	**9c**	
	Lines 9d through 9f DO NOT apply to distributions from IRAs, annuities, or modified endowment contracts.		
d	Due to separation from service in or after the year of reaching age 55 .	**9d**	
e	Distributions to the extent of deductible medical expenses	**9e**	
f	Made to an alternate payee under a qualified domestic relations order . .	**9f**	
g	Other (specify) _____	**9g**	
h	Total amount excluded from additional tax (add lines 9a through 9g)	**9h**	
10	Amount subject to additional tax (subtract line 9h from 8g)	**10**	
11	Total section 72 tax (multiply line 10 by 10% (.10)). Enter here and on Form 1040, line 51. . . .	**11**	

For Paperwork Reduction Act Notice, see page 1 of separate instructions.   Cat. No. 13329Q   Form **5329** (1991)

Exhibit 7G

The Serious Investor's Tax Survival Guide

Part III Tax on Excess Accumulation in Qualified Retirement Plans (Including IRAs) (Section 4974)

12	Minimum required distribution (see instructions)	12
13	Amount actually distributed to you	13
14	Subtract line 13 from line 12. If line 13 is more than line 12, enter -0-	14
15	Tax due (multiply line 14 by 50% (.50)). Enter here and on Form 1040, line 51	15

Part IV Tax on Excess Distributions From Qualified Retirement Plans (Including IRAs) (Section 4980A)

Complete lines 16 through 19c for regular distributions ONLY.

16	Enter the total amount of regular retirement distributions		16
17a	Enter the applicable threshold amount ($136,204 or $150,000) (see instructions)	17a	
b	1991 recovery of grandfather amount (from Worksheet 1 or 2)	17b	
c	Enter the **greater** of line 17a or 17b		17c
18	Excess distributions (subtract line 17c from line 16. (If less than zero, enter -0-.)		18
19a	Tentative tax (multiply line 18 by 15% (.15))		19a
b	Section 72(t) tax offset (see instructions)		19b
c	Tax due (subtract line 19b from line 19a). Enter here and on Form 1040, line 51		19c

Complete lines 20 through 23c for lump-sum distributions ONLY.

20	Enter the total amount of your lump-sum distributions		20
21a	Enter the applicable threshold amount ($681,020 or $750,000) (see instructions)	21a	
b	1991 recovery of grandfather amount (from Worksheet 1 or 2)	21b	
c	Enter the **greater** of line 21a or 21b		21c
22	Excess distributions (subtract line 21c from line 20. (If less than zero, enter -0-.)		22
23a	Tentative tax (multiply line 22 by 15% (.15))		23a
b	Section 72(t) tax offset (see instructions)		23b
c	Tax due (subtract line 23b from line 23a). Enter here and on Form 1040, line 51		23c

Acceleration Elections (see the instructions for Part IV, Worksheet 1)

1 If you elected the discretionary method in 1987 or 1988 and wish to make an acceleration election beginning in 1991 under Temp. Regs. section 54.4981A-1T b-12, check here ▶ ☐ .

2 If you previously made an acceleration election and wish to revoke that election, check here ▶ ☐
Note: *If you checked 2 above, see the instructions for filing amended returns on page 2.*

Please Sign Here Under penalties of perjury, I declare that I have examined this return, including accompanying schedules and statements, and to the best of my knowledge and belief, it is true, correct, and complete. Declaration of preparer (other than taxpayer) is based on all information of which preparer has any knowledge.

Your signature (Sign and date only if not attached to your income tax return.)	Date

Paid Preparer's Use Only

Preparer's signature ▶	Date	Check if self-employed ▶ ☐	Preparer's social security no. (see instructions)
Firm's name (or yours, if self-employed) and address ▶		E.I. No. ▶	
		ZIP code ▶	

Exhibit 7H

The first part of this chapter will serve as a summary and quick reference for you in determining the major sources of income and deductions as well as a guide to the forms used for reporting these items. Using a similar summary, I will now provide you with a form and a method for estimating your **marginal tax bracket**.

Your marginal tax bracket will provide you with ongoing information as to how much your additional income will be taxed and how much will be saved from deductions which you generate. I use this form to categorize and keep track of my income and deductions throughout the year. Hopefully, it will assist you in making wiser investment decisions and stimulate you to think in terms of generating valid tax deductions.

Marginal Tax Bracket Calculation

Table C
1. **Federal Marginal Tax Rate** (From Table D) .... _____
2. **State Marginal Tax Rate**(6% or 11% if high tax rate)_____
3. **Add 1 + 2 = Combined Marginal Tax Rate** .... _____

Federal Tax Rate Schedules For 1991/1992

Table D

	Taxable Income	Marginal Rate
1. **Single**:	$0 - $20,349	15%
	$20,350 – $49,299	28%
	Above	31%
2. **Married**:		
Filing Jointly:	$0 – $33,999	15%
	$34,000 – $82,149	28%
	Above	31%
Separately:	$0 – $16,999	15%
	$17,000 – $41,074	28%
	Above	31%
3. **Head of Household**:		
	$0 – $27,299	15%
	$27,300 – 70,449	28%
	Above	31%

111

The Taxable Income Summary Worksheet

1. **Salary and Wages**... _____
Employee Business Expenses:
    a) Job Related Travel .... _____
    b) Commuting Expense to Second Job.. _____
    c) Professional Dues........................... _____
    d) Professional Journals .... _____
    e) Continuing Professional Education... _____
    f) Other Job Related .... _____
Total 2106 Expenses (Lines 1(a)–1(f) Less 2% of AGI) .. (_____)
2. **Business, and Other Fees or Commissions** .... _____
Expenses Related to Self Employment:
    a) Automobile Expense to Promote
       Business.. _____
    b) Books, Subscriptions, Journals .... _____
    c) Commissions and Professional Fees . _____
    d) Insurance and Business Interest ...... _____
    e) Rent, Office Expense,& Maintenance _____
    f) Equipment Expense (or Depreciation)_____
    g) 80% of Business Meals...................... _____
    h) Other Business Related .... _____
Total Schedule C Expenses (Lines 2(a)–2(h)) ....(_____)
3. **Interest, Dividends, & Capital Gains**...................... _____
Expenses Related to Investment Income:
    a) Investment Advisor Fees .... _____
    b) Dues, Subscriptions, Books .... _____
    c) Computer Expense, Data, Analysis ... _____
    d) Other Investment Related .... _____
Total Schedule A Misc. (Lines 3(a)–3(d)Less 2% AGI) ... (_____)
4. **Income From Rentals, Partnerships, Trusts, Sub S**
   Corps, Royalties, Net of Expenses on Schedule E _____
5. **Other Taxable Income**.. _____
6. **Less Adjustment for Alimony Paid,**
   Retirement Plans, Etc. .... (_____)
7. **Less Other Itemized Deductions:**
    a) Medical less 7 1/2 % Adjusted Gross _____
    b) Taxes–State, Real Estate, Other ...._____
    c) Mortgage Interest, Investment Interest
       (less limitation to interest) ...._____
    d) Contributions .... _____
    e) Other ...._____
Total Other Schedule A Exps.(Lines 7(a)–7(e)).............. (_____)
8. **Less Personal Exemptions** ($2,300 each) .... (_____)
                     TAXABLE INCOME .... _____

State Taxation

Of the 50 states and the District of Columbia, all but nine have income tax. The rates go from as low as a 1 1/2% to as high as 15% (including the local city tax). The average state tax rate is approximately 6%. You can use this number in the calculation above, or if you know your state rate, you can use the exact amount. In any event, unless you are a resident of one of the high tax states, such as New York, California, or the District of Columbia 6% is a reasonably accurate estimate.

In his book *More Wealth Without Risk*[11], Charles Givens tells the story of his first experience filing a tax return. He relates,

> At 19, I dropped out of Millikin University after one semester, far short of the $300 tuition necessary to remain enrolled. Needing money to help support my mother and brother, I went to work in a foundry dumping slag–molten metal waste–from the furnaces. If you ever want a job that will motivate you to do something with your life, work in a foundry for a while. That same year I started a rock–and–roll band – Chuck Givens and the Quintones – and I was soon making more money playing music on weekends than I made working in the foundry all week. Then came my first shocking experience with the tax system. My record–keeping skills were almost nonexistent, but I put together what I had and headed for the tax preparer's office. After only five minutes, I left with an assurance I could pick up my completed tax return in a week. When I returned, I got the shock of my life.
>
> "I've got some good news and some bad news," muttered the CPA. "The good news is your tax return is completed. The bad news is you owe the IRS an extra $2000."
>
> At the tender age of 19, I had never seen $2000 in one place at one time and knew that I had absolutely no chance of putting that much money together anytime in the foreseeable future. My mind played visions of police cars and prisons.
>
> In self–defense, I drove to the Federal Building in Decatur, not to turn myself in, but to pick up every publication the IRS would give away free. I was determined to learn something about a tax system that was about to put me

under. I didn't realize what I had asked for and carted two full armloads of IRS material to the car. During the next three months, I scoured the pages looking for tax relief. Constantly, it seemed, I came upon possible deductions the CPA had never mentioned. At the end of the three months, right before April 15, I completed another return myself. Based on my calculations, I did not owe the IRS the extra $2000, and was entitled to a refund of some of the taxes that had been withheld from my paychecks at my full-time job. I was sure I'd made a mistake.

Returning to the CPA's office, I asked, "Where did I go wrong?"

"You're not wrong, "he said, "you're absolutely right."

The shock must have registered on my face. "What do you mean?" I said. "You had me scared to death, owing the IRS $2000 I don't have, and yet when I do my own return, I get money back."

With a look of disgust, he came halfway out of his chair. "Let me tell you something, son! I am a tax preparer, not your financial adviser. You are paying me to take your numbers and put them on the tax forms. If you don't know how to tell me about what you are doing, I have no reason or responsibility to take the deductions."

The light went on; I got it! If I ever wanted to protect myself from overpaying income taxes, I must learn everything possible about the tax system. No one, not even a tax preparer or a CPA, was going to do it for me the way it needed to be done. That experience has probably saved me more in income taxes than most people make in a lifetime.

As you keep track of your income and deductions, you will be surprised how quickly tax planning becomes an integral part of your life. And it needs to be, because if you don't keep track of what is yours, no one else will. In fact, if you try to deal with the tax system in this country without a strategy and some degree of tax knowledge, you will be, as a former client of mine used to say, "running around like a head without a chicken!"

Now that we have a general foundation in basic taxation, I will give you one other methodology which will come in handy. I call the technology "Total Return Investment Planning," or "TRIP," and the concept is extremely important.

This technique will help you evaluate investment alternatives in a more accurate way. Now that you have the ability to calculate your marginal tax rate, you have all the tools you need to proceed with the calculation of your "TRIP." I will first present the theory and then provide you with another handy worksheet for its practical application.

Chapter **8**

Total Return Investment Planning or "TRIP"

Calculation of True Yield

Since illustrations always make concepts much clearer, let's start right off by comparing two investments, a fully taxable versus a 100% non–taxable bond. These bonds are both 10–year bonds and pay interest of 10% and 8% per annum, taxable and non–taxable, respectively. For the purpose of this illustration, let us further assume that they are purchased by two investors in the same federal tax bracket, 31%, and who live in the same state with a 15% tax rate.

Investor #1 purchases the taxable bond for par value, $10,000, paying 10% per year. Using conventional terms, the yield on this investment would be $1,000. Using Total Return Investment Planning, however, we also consider the taxability of this income to determine the after tax, **true yield,** on this investment. The added steps deduct the net taxes on the interest earned each year:

Interest Per Year	$1,000
Federal Tax Rate	X .31
Federal Tax on Interest	$ 310
Interest Per Year	$1,000
State Tax Rate	X .15
State Tax on Interest	$ 150

State Tax on Interest	$ 150
Federal Tax Rate	X .31
Credit to Federal Tax	$ 47*
Interest Per Year	$1,000
Less: Federal Tax	(310)
Less: State Tax	(150)
Credit for Deduction	47
Net Total Return	$ 587

The result of our calculation demonstrates that the true after–tax yield on our investment is really 5.87%, not 10% as we believed it was:

TRUE YIELD:	**Total Return After Taxation**	$587
divided by	**Amount of Investment**	$10,000
equals	**Yield**	5.87%

Compare this to the tax–free investment purchased by Investor #2. This is an 8% **tax–free** $10,000 municipal which, because of its 100% tax–free status, actually has a **true yield** of 8%. We calculate the yield as follows:

TRUE YIELD:	**Total Return After Taxation**	$800
divided by	**Amount of Investment**	$10,000
equals	**Yield**	8%

The numerator, "Total Return After Taxation," is the huge variable. It's calculation not only depends on the type of investment and its taxability, but also on the federal tax bracket the investor is in and the state income tax rate in the state where he or she lives. In other words, it will differ from investor to investor as will the tax status.

---

*The one step which may be unclear to some of you is the add–back of $47 for credit for taxes paid to the state. The federal government allows, as an itemized deduction, the amount of tax paid to the state. In this case, assuming the 15% tax rate on $1,000, $150 would be paid to the state. If we deducted this $150 from federal taxable income, which was taxed at a 31% rate, the net effect on federal tax would be a credit of $47 ($150 X .31), assuming that the taxpayer itemizes deductions.

Of course, there are all sorts of permutations and variations on this theme, such as the partially tax–free bond, the state tax–free bond (U.S. Treasuries), and the Private Activity (AMT addback) bond. But the method is the same. You basically need only six pieces of information to calculate **true yield**:

1. Amount of Investment;
2. Annual Return;
3. Federal Taxability of Return;
4. State Taxability of Return;
5. Marginal Federal Tax Bracket (From Section 7C, Line 1); and
6. Estimated State Tax Bracket (From Section 7C, Line 2) (use 6%, if unknown).

I will now give you a format and a sample worksheet on which all of the above calculations can be done.

Worksheet For Calculating Your "TRIP"

1. Amount Invested .... _____
2. Annual Projected Income From Investment .... _____
3. Federal Taxable Percent of Income[12] .... _____
4. Amount of Income Taxed on Federal Tax Return
    (Line 2 X Line 3) .... _____
5. State Taxable Percent of Income[13] .... _____
6. Amount of Income Taxed on State Tax Return
    (Line 2 X Line 5) .... _____
7. Federal Tax Rate (From Section C, Line 1) .... _____
8. Projected Federal Tax on Return of Investment
    (Line 4 X Line 7) .... _____
9. Estimated State Tax on Return of Investment
    (Line 6 X State Rate or .06 If Unknown) .... _____
10. Federal Credit for State Tax Paid
    (Line 9 X Line 7) .... _____
11. Annual Return Net of Tax
    (Line 2 – Line 8 – Line 9 + Line 10) .... _____
12. True Yield (Line 11/Line 1) .... _____

Let's now look at the same two examples, Investor #1 and Investor #2, and calculate the **true yield** of their investments using the format just described:

	Investor #1	Investor #2
1. Amount Invested	$10,000	$10,000
2. Annual Projected Income From Investment	$1,000	$800
3. Federal Taxable Percent of Income	100%	0%
4. Amount of Income Taxed on Federal Tax Return (Line 2 X Line 3)	$1,000	$ 0
5. State Taxable Percent of Income	100%	0%
6. Amount of Income Taxed on State Tax Return (Line 2 X Line 5)	$1,000	$ 0
7. Federal Tax Rate (From Section C, Line 1)	31%	31%
8. Projected Federal Tax on Return of Investment (Line 4 X Line 7)	$ 310	$ 0
9. Estimated State Tax on Return of Investment (Line 6 X .15)	$ 150	$ 0
10. Federal Credit for State Tax Paid (Line 9 X Line 7)	$ 47	$ 0
11. Annual Return Net of Tax (Line 2 – Line 8 – Line 9 + Line 10)	$ 587	$ 800
12. True Yield (Line11/Line 1)	5.87%	8%

Before we did this calculation it looked like Investor #1 had made the better investment choice. Who do you think is better off now? Clearly, it is Investor #2 with a greater **true yield** on his investment of 8% compared to Investor #1 at 5.87%.

Let's look at one more example. In this case, Investor #3 is considering a 10–year, $10,000, partially tax–exempt bond, (75% taxable by the federal government, 50% taxable by the state), paying 9% per year which he can purchase at par value or $10,000. This investor is in a 15% federal tax bracket and lives in a lower tax state (3%). What would the **true yield** of this investment be for him?

Lets look at the facts as we have them. First, the six items needed for the "TRIP" calculation are as follows:

1. Amount of Investment	$10,000
2. Annual Return	$900[14]
3. Federal Taxability	75%
4. State Taxability	50%
5. Marginal Federal Tax Bracket	15%
6. State Tax Bracket	3%

That's all we need! Plugging in our formula, we easily arrive at the investment's **true yield**.

1. Amount Invested	$10,000
2. Annual Projected Income From Investment	$900
3. Federal Taxable Percent of Income	75%
4. Amount of Income Taxed on Federal Tax Return (Line 2 X Line 3)	$675
5. State Taxable Percent of Income	50%
6. Amount of Income Taxed on State Tax Return (Line 2 X Line 5)	$450
7. Federal Tax Rate	15%
8. Projected Federal Tax on Return of Investment (Line 4 X Line 7)	$101
9. Estimated State Tax on Return of Investment (Line 6 X .03)	$14
10. Federal Credit for State Tax Paid (Line 9 X Line 7)	$2
11. Annual Return Net of Tax (Line 2 – Line 8 – Line 9 + Line 10)	$787
12. True Yield (Line 11/Line 1)	7.87%

This variation demonstrates the simplicity of the calculation even with a seemingly involved tax situation. An investment which apparently had a 9% return only had a **true yield** of 7.87%.

121

The Risk/Reward Ratio Revisited

We have now explored a standard and more accurate method of evaluating investment return. At the very least, this should help us tremendously in making more accurate investment choices. It should also assist us in making **wiser** choices, because when we evaluate the risk/reward potential of any investment, we now can use a more precise figure for "total return."

Space here does not allow me to go into great detail on the concept of risk/reward. This is a book strictly on the taxation of investments and not on their comparative analysis. I do feel it is necessary, however, that we understand the basic concepts involved in this area and how they relate to investment selection as filtered through tax considerations.

When we examine the yield of any investment, we see the need to consider its **true yield**, as opposed to "pre–tax yield." In doing so for all our potential investments we reduce them to their lowest common denominator. Therefore, when we speak of the financial speed of an investment or the rate at which it grows, we have a more realistic figure to work with.

The question of "if a 7% yield is good, is a 10% yield better?" can be restated in terms of post–tax yield. We no longer have to compare apples and oranges, such as in the case of a 10% **taxable**, versus a 7% **non–taxable** investment. This has always been confusing, and in fact, misleading. We can translate these percentages into meaningful comparisons, and, hence, consider the associated risk in a more consistent manner.

Just to give you some idea of the significance of this calculation of "return on investment" over a period of time, I'd like to continue with the example of the two investors. Investor #1 purchases a 10% fully taxable bond, where as Investor #2 purchases the 8% tax–free bond. The tax considerations are the same as the first illustration so that the **true yield** comes out to be only 5.87% for the investor with the 10% investment.

Let us further assume, for the purpose of this illustration, that the investments are in a **bond fund** as opposed to in a single bond so that the interest will be hypothetically reinvested annually at the same rate of return. We will now look at an entire ten–year period instead of just one year. You may be surprised at the significance that the method of calculation makes in the potential return on investment over the ten–year period.

Calculation Comparison of Return on Two Investments

Using Old Terminology for "Yield on Investment"

Year	Investor #1 (10% taxable)	Investor #2 (8% non–taxable)
1. Principal:	$10,000	$10,000
Interest:	$1,000	$800
2. Principal:	$11,000	$10,000
Interest:	$1,100	$864
3. Principal:	$12,100	$11,664
Interest:	$1,210	$993
4. Principal:	$13,310	$12,597
Interest:	$1,331	$1,008
5. Principal:	$14,641	$13,605
Interest:	$1,464	$1,088
6. Principal:	$16,105	$14,683
Interest:	$1,611	$1,175
7. Principal:	$17,716	$15,869
Interest:	$1,772	$1,269
8. Principal:	$19,487	$17,138
Interest:	$1,949	$1,371
9. Principal:	$21,436	$18,509
Interest:	$2,144	$1,481
10. Principal:	$23,579	$19,990
Interest:	$2,358	$1,599
End Principal:	$25,937	$21,589

The figures we would use in estimating the comparative ten–year return on these two investments, without tax consideration, are $15,937 on the 10% versus $11,589 on the 8% investment[15]. These amounts would also be used in evaluating the risk/reward ratio for each. A total return of $15,937 on an investment of $10,000 is a 159% return on capital. This looks much better than the $11,589, or 116% return on capital received by Investor #2. One would probably take a greater risk to achieve this return than he would if he knew the real story.

In the next illustration, we will see how radically the picture changes with the introduction of **true yield**.

Using True Yield to Determine Risk/Reward

Year	Investor #1 (5.87% taxable)	Investor #2 (8% non–taxable)
1. Principal:	$10,000	$10,000
Interest:	$587	$800
2. Principal	$10,587	$10,800
Interest:	$621	$864
3. Principal:	$11,208	$11,664
Interest:	$658	$993
4. Principal:	$11,866	$12,597
Interest:	$697	$1,008
5. Principal:	$12,563	$13,605
Interest:	$737	$1,088
6. Principal:	$13,300	$14,693
Interest:	$781	$1,175
7. Principal:	$14,081	$15,869
Interest:	$827	$1,269
8. Principal:	$14,908	$17,138
Interest:	$875	$1,371
9. Principal:	$15,783	$18,509
Interest:	$926	$1,481
10. Principal:	$16,709	$19,900
Interest:	$981	$1,599
End Principal:	$17,690	$21,589

In other words, the ten–year total return on the investment for Investor #1 has just gone down by $8,247[16] when you include the effect of taxes.

Risk/Reward Ratio Meets the "Tax Factor"

Investor #1 experienced a 46% reduction in income, or to put it another way, total return was overstated by 107%.[17] How good does the 76.9%[18] ten–year return on investment for Investor #1 look now as compared to the 116% return for Investor #2? Would you be willing to risk as much for an investment which returned 159%? I know I wouldn't!

In evaluating a risk/reward ratio, it is apparent that we'd better use accurate figures to evaluate whether or not an investment is worth the associated risk. Generally, we would require the yield to increase in direct proportion to risk.

Modern portfolio theory states that there are historical rates of return for all investments which can be quantified. To accomplish this, models have been developed which evaluate the risk/reward ratios of most investments. It is generally believed that the investor can customize his or her own portfolio to reflect specific needs and tolerance to risk. Up until now, there has been no inclusion of the tax factor in this calculation.

Under the old definitions of yield and total rate of return a financial planner would look at a portfolio and determine that, for example, an investment has a 10% rate of return with a standard deviation of 4%. What this means, in layman's terminology, is that there is a 68 1/4% chance that the rate of return will be between 6% and 14%, depending on future market fluctuations. What this also means, however, is that there is a 31 3/4% chance that the investment will return less than 6% and there is still a further chance, however remote, that it may not return anything at all.

The point I'm trying to make here is that when we evaluate investments, we want to know whether the return is really 8% or 5.87%. Will we earn $15,937 during ten years, or really just $7,690, net of taxes. We need to know this in order to properly determine whether or not it is worth the investment risk!

Chapter 9

How Far Can We Go?
A Question of Legality

Story of the Legitimate Prostitute and the Illegitimate Hearse Driver

Two of the more memorable clients I have encountered during my career as a tax practitioner have been the two I refer to as **the legitimate prostitute** and **the illegitimate hearse driver**.

The first of these was a woman who ran what I shall refer to as "an escort service." In fact, she did quite well at it, grossing several hundred thousand dollars a year. I was a bit surprised, however, when a colleague of mine contacted me to relate that she had engaged his services. Most women of this profession keep their income "off the books." Since this is a cash industry, it is easy enough to do so. Madam Y, as we shall refer to her, was quite interested however in running a "legitimate service business."

Because of the rather unusual nature of this business and because my colleague had never encountered a situation quite like this, he questioned the proper way of handling an account such as this. Was this a **valid** business? It was certainly not an entirely legal one. Was this really taxable income? And how about the expenses? If this was in fact a real business, and the income was taxable income, wouldn't all the expenses be deductible?

These were questions we had to deal with in setting up this "new business."

I related to him my recollections of one very infamous tax evader, Al Capone. As you may recall, he was a Chicago–based prohibition era "organized businessman" who made his fortune in bootlegging and racketeering. The government tried for many years to put him behind bars for these illegal activities, but they were unsuccessful in doing so. They could not prove the illegal source of his income. The only way they were able to bust Al Capone was by proving that he had, in fact, **received** the income, and that it had gone **unreported** on his tax returns. In fact, it was a Treasury agent who ultimately nabbed Al Capone for tax evasion thus making him a very visible example of the government's attitude towards people who earn income illegally **and** do not report it on their tax return.

In convicting Al Capone, the government's case was based on the fact that he had a great deal of unreported income. They did not, however, go into detail as to what he should have done to keep himself out of jail. One can only speculate that had he reported the income, they would have kept on trying to convict him on bootlegging and racketeering charges. However, this was not the issue we had to deal with. We were not lawyers trying to keep a woman out of jail who might be performing illegal services. Rather, we were engaged to assist her in properly reporting this income. With that in mind, our responsibility, therefore, became how to keep this woman out of jail for **tax evasion**.

I suggested that since we were treating the income as legitimate "earned" income, we should be consistent in our approach. Since the income was legitimate for tax purposes, all her expenses would also have to be considered valid. What we did at that point was to set up an accounting system whereby we deducted any normal, ordinary, and reasonable expenses associated with the production of income. The issue of legality pertained to the expenses, not the income.

Expenses such as telephone; utilities; a portion of apartment rent and; the purchase of linens, sheets and pillow cases, and their cleaning were all valid expenses in the production of taxable income. In addition, she had some rather unusual writeoffs, specific to her profession. We faced the question of how to label items such as condoms and sex toys on the tax return, not whether they were fully deductible. We resolved this dilemma by calling them "Escort Service Expenses," and assigned a rather conservative life period for items being depreciated.

Using this as a guide, we prepared her business tax returns in a consistent manner. If any expense met three of the four criteria for deductions and was appropriate in the production of income, then it was a legitimate expense. We filed tax returns for Madam Y for many years until she ultimately retired from the business. Never once were we questioned by the IRS as to the nature of any of these expenses and, as far as we know, neither was she.

The second client I would like to discuss, **the illegitimate hearse driver,** was a different story. Here the income was perfectly acceptable by the IRS, however, there was a problem with one of the expenses related to the production of income. In this case, the particular expense met three of the criteria for deductions. It was **necessary** in the production of income, it was **reasonable** in the amount of the expense in comparison to the income generated, and it was **ordinary** in this line of work. The issue, however, was the legality of the expense.

The question of whether or not this particular expense was allowable came up during an audit of the client's tax return. In preparing his return we never questioned the deductibility of the expense in question. The client gave us a figure every month which he categorized as "parking expenses." We accepted this at face value and deducted a total amount for the year as being an expense related to the use of a business vehicle. In this case, the hearse.

The return in question was that of a funeral parlor which had four hearses as business assets. When somebody contacted the funeral director to inform him of a death and the need for the funeral parlor's services, he would send one of the hearses out to pick up his client, in this case the corpse.

One of the major problems incurred in running this type of business in New York City was what to do with the hearse while running upstairs to pick up the body? If any of you have ever tried to find a parking space in Manhattan you'll know what I'm talking about. It is very difficult to park a car anywhere in Manhattan, let alone in a specific location. It would be very peculiar, I imagine, to see the hearse drivers walking down the street carrying a corpse to where they parked the hearse. Therefore, it was necessary to leave the hearse directly in front of the "client's" apartment. What they ended up doing was either parking in a bus stop, in a fire hydrant zone, in a space reserved for diplomats, in a space that no one can park in, or simply double–parked in the middle of the street. It was an accepted convention in this line of work to incur regular parking violations as part of the cost of doing business. They considered it to be a "parking expense." This cost was factored into their fees and was a necessary part of producing income.

The problem, however, was that while these parking violations were **necessary**, **ordinary**, and **reasonable**, they were **not**

129

legal. The law specifically states that any payment made directly or indirectly as a result of breaking a government regulation is **not** a deductible business expense.

When the IRS auditor asked for a breakdown of the $12,500 "parking fee" expense we were made aware of the fact that the funeral director had been classifying traffic violations as parking fees.

The Master Tax Guide states, relating to Fines and Penalties that:

> A fine or a penalty paid to a government for the violation of any law is not a deductible business expense (Code Sec. 162(f); Reg. Section 1.162–21). No deduction is allowed for any payment made directly or indirectly to any person if the payment is a bribe, kickback, or other illegal payment under any U.S. law or under any generally enforced state law that subjects the payor to a criminal penalty or to the loss of license or privilege to engage in a trade or business (Code Section 162(c)(2); Reg. Section 1.162–18). For all the above purposes, a kickback includes a payment in consideration of the referral of a client, patient or customer (Code Section 162(c)(3); Reg. Section 1.162–18). No deduction is allowed for a federal tax penalty. Penalties paid in connection with the violation of a federal civil statute are deductible if they are compensatory, rather than punitive, in nature.[19]

"Fear of Frying" – The Fear Factor

The end result of the auditor's discovery of these "parking fees" was a disallowance. The funeral director was forced to reclassify all of these parking violation fines as miscellaneous non–tax–deductible costs of doing business. There was no mention by the auditor of a word which people fear the most, the word **fraud**. It was a simple misunderstanding by the taxpayer of what constitutes and what does not constitute a legitimate business tax deduction.

Most people in this country are tax–ignorant. They do not really know what they are entitled to in terms of allowable deductions. Those that do know what they are entitled to are often held back from doing what they can do in terms of maximizing their tax strategies.

Government officials have talked about what motivates taxpayers. Ask most IRS employees, off the record, and they will agree that the most effective method through which they can achieve tax compliance is by instilling fear. This four–letter word, FEAR, is what keeps most people from utilizing the tax law to their fullest advantage.

Many of my friends have either worked for the IRS or are acquainted with someone who has. They tell me that unless you are an outright tax cheater, you have very little to worry about. Many people have an irrational fear about going to jail or losing everything they have because of the IRS.

The IRS likes it this way. Believe me, it is a far better position for them. But when you look at the nature of the penalties for all types of offenses, from a simple mistake to undeniable fraud, you will see that this fear is not based entirely in reality.

Don't get me wrong, you want to avoid penalties for several reasons. They can be costly, they make your return more susceptible to audit, and, if serious enough, the penalties can involve prison terms. But on balance, the two most serious penalties, fraud and negligence, are well-defined and fairly easy to avoid.

As you will see in the following summary, penalties are not given arbitrarily or used to punish taxpayers without reason, but rather as a threat to taxpayers who intentionally try to cheat or to hide unreported income. Interest and penalties are assessed only on the taxes which are currently due, not on the total tax which was been paid, nor on your total taxable income.

Another type of honest taxpayer mistake is that imposed for filing of your tax return. Your tax return is due, except for certain extenuating circumstances, by April 15 of each year. You may file an extension for this return by the due date. If you do not, the late filing penalty is 5% per month up to 25% maximum of the tax due. Generally there is no penalty unless you owe money.

PENALTIES AND INTEREST ON TAX RETURNS
Interest   Currently charged for underpayment of tax is the 3-month T–bill Rate + 3%.
Penalties Currently charged by the IRS (note that some of these penalties are overlapping, i.e., one type will often reduce the   other):

1. Unpaid taxes–5% per month up to 25% + interest.
2. Negligence–5% of underpayment + interest.
3. Failure to file return–$100 or taxes due (60–day grace period).
4. Bad check charge–1% of check.
5. Frivolous or incomplete return–$500.
6. Frivolous lawsuit against the IRS–$5,000.
7. Overvaluation of property–10% to 30% of underpayment.
8. Intent to evade taxes–75% of underpayment + additional 50% of interest due.
9. False withholding information–$500.
10. Failure to file partnership return–$50 each partner per month, maximum 5 months.

Criminal Violations:
1. Willful failure to pay or file–Up to $25,000 + 1 yr. prison.
2. Willfully falsifying return–Up to $100,000 + 3 yrs. prison.
3. Intent to evade taxes–Up to $100,000 + 5 yrs. prison.
4. False withholding information–Up to $100,000 + 1 yr. prison.

"Only the Little People Pay Taxes"

The question most often asked the week Leona Helmsley was sentenced to five years in jail was: "Why has Harry Helmsley dimmed the lights at the top of the Empire State Building all week?" Some people answered, "he did it in deference to Leona and to show his disgust with the penalty given to his wife." But the true answer I hear,

132

from those who really know about such things, is that Harry turned down the lights at the top of the Empire State Building so that Leona couldn't find her way back to New York.

Why was Leona Helmsley convicted of tax evasion? Was it because she was so flagrant a tax evader that the government had to teach her a lesson? Or was it because she was such a well known figure that the government could not let anyone believe that she could get away with it, and therefore had to make an example out of her? It is true that she allegedly broke the law. Leona remodelled her estate, purchasing many hundreds of thousands of dollars of new items. This is no crime. The crime was that she apparently wrote these items off as business expenses.

In other words, she purchased them through the business, for personal use, but nonetheless took them as valid **business** expenses. This reduced the taxable income of the business which she and her husband own, and consequently the tax payable on this income.

I believe the answer to the question of why she was convicted and given what many people consider an extremely harsh jail sentence for a woman her age, was a combination of factors. Yes, she was a tax evader, yes she overstated deductions and understated income, and yes she was a well known figure. But, I feel that the clincher was the six little words which comprise the title of this section "Only the Little People Pay Taxes." In other words, Leona was saying that people of her class status did not have to pay taxes, only those people who were **not** of her class. A class which, incidentally, she married into.

I think it was mainly these six words that locked in a jail sentence for Leona Helmsley. The testimony of an ex–employee that Leona made that statement whenever questioned about taxes was so damaging that it mandated prison time. The government could not afford to let someone walk away from tax evasion after rubbing the "little peoples'" collective faces in the mud. It would have been far too damaging a blow to the legal system in general and to the IRS specifically.

I have been told that the IRS is generally obsessed with keeping taxpayers and tax preparers nervous and honest. Often, the IRS is often quite willing to spend $50,000 to prove a $2,000 intentional omission. In the publication *The IRS Confidential Report*, Randy B. Blaustein relates:

> They (IRS) are interested in punishment, not rehabilitation. They usually will not plea bargain. They will ask for jail time rather than probation. And they are not impressed by a taxpayer's exemplary record.... But they will be conciliatory if they do not have enough evidence to build a solid case. In 1980, for example, there were only 80 acquittals out of 1,874 cases disposed of at trial. The IRS is anxious to protect that winning image.

NEGLIGENCE OR TAX FRAUD? Failure to report income deposited in a bank could be considered careless. Carelessness is punishable by a 5% negligence penalty. But, when the omitted income represented deposits made in a bank in a different state, one court regarded the omission as a fraudulent, willful attempt to conceal income.

TAX FRAUD: WHO GETS CAUGHT? Executives, lawyers, doctors, and other high–income professionals are accused of tax fraud more often that the general population. Charges stem from IRS challenges that there was willful or intentional failure to file, understatement of income, or claiming of fraudulent deductions. About one out of every five charges brought by the IRS in one recent year involved a professional or business executive. The average claim for back taxes is nearly $70,000.

	Investigations	Convictions
Total	8,901	1,476
Of which:		
Business owners	2,059	328
Other executives	485	94
Company officers	438	94
Attorneys	299	46
Dentists & doctors	199	33
Non–CPA accountants	164	40
CPAs	89	13

Less than 20% of IRS fraud investigations end in convictions. Other cases are dropped, the Justice Department refuses to prosecute, or they end with acquittal or dismissal."[20]

Well, unfortunately for Leona, she was one of the "chosen few."

How the IRS Builds a Criminal Case

In an article in the publication *IRS Confidential* entitled "How the IRS Builds a Criminal Case," R.B. Blaustein states that criminal tax investigations are the ultimate weapon in the IRS enforcement system. They are conducted by IRS Special Agents who can show up at a taxpayer's home or business without any notice. They usually work in pairs so that they can corroborate each other's testimony about facts or statements that the taxpayer makes.

They will usually give you a Miranda warning to let you know that anything you say can be used against you in court and that you do not have to answer questions without an attorney present. The fact is, however, that many taxpayers are afraid that if they do not answer a question they will appear guilty. In addition, the agents are very persistent and will usually press for answers. As a resuly, the taxpayer will often make statements he later regrets.

They will ask questions such as "have you reported all of your income," "where do you keep your savings and checking accounts," "what is the procedure for reporting sales in your business," "what kind of car do you own," "do you gamble" and other seemingly low-key questions. They will try to make you believe that if you help them they will close your case and you will be done with them. Guess again!

Be extremely wary as any false or misleading statements you make in answering these questions may be a crime.

What the agents are trying to establish in this particular kind of investigation is whether or not a taxpayer failed to report income or misreported income, and that the error or omission was done willfully. They will ask for copies of your checking account statements, canceled checks, saving account booklets, and/or deposit and withdrawal tickets.

They may speak to neighbors and business associates and will look at public records to find out whether or not a taxpayer owns real estate, cars, boats, or any other large, expensive item. They will also examine insurance records which indicate possession of furs and jewels. The IRS will also use mail surveillance to try to determine who a businessperson's customers and suppliers are. Although they will not open your mail they can obtain a great deal of information by just looking at the outside of the envelope.

Mr. Blaustein also discusses a procedure which is used in order to analyze a taxpayer's net worth. The agent will take the value of all the taxpayer's property at the beginning of the year and subtract from it his end–of–year assets. The difference between these two figures, with adjustments for non–taxable items and other factors, represents the increase in net worth for the year. It is generally correct to assume that the taxpayer had income which was at least enough to generate that increase in net worth.

In this article, he goes on to reveal a technique which oftentimes incriminates the taxpayer. Sometimes during the initial interview with the IRS agent a taxpayer is asked how much cash and property he had at the beginning of the year. A taxpayer who does not want to appear very prosperous may state that he only had a few hundred dollars and no other property to speak of. This allows the IRS to then claim that everything which was owned at the end of the year was acquired during that year and, hence, should have been reported as income.

Sneaky! Very sneaky, but effective.

The way to deal with this type of investigation is to give the Special Agent as little information as possible when you are asked questions about your opening net worth. The IRS does not have as much information on most individuals as we believe. It must get information from the taxpayer or other knowledgeable third parties. The most effective legal strategies for dealing with the IRS focus on keeping information out of their hands.

The Taxpayer's Bill of Rights

Over the years the IRS has had a public relations problem and has recently taken steps to spruce up its image. As a result, the IRS has formally given us certain rights ensuring that we are treated fairly.

The first indication that something has changed is evident whenever you receive correspondence from the IRS requesting payment of delinquent taxes. Along with the bill there is a four–sided document enclosed entitled "Your Rights as a Taxpayer." This is put out by the Department of the Treasury, Internal Revenue Service, and is called "Publication No. 1."

Here it states: "As a taxpayer you have the right to be treated fairly, professionally, promptly, and courteously by Internal Revenue Service employees. Our goal at the IRS is to protect your rights so that you will have the highest confidence in the integrity, efficiency, and fairness of our tax system. To ensure that you always receive such treatment, you should know about the many rights you have at each step of the tax process."

This pamphlet contains a great deal of information and you should, if ever given the chance, read these four pages carefully. It goes into subjects such as the type of assistance available to you through the IRS in preparing your tax returns including many valuable publications and how to obtain information on the Volunteer Income Tax Assistance (VITA) program in your area.

The VITA service is offered above and beyond the direct assistance of IRS employees who are available to answer questions by phone (but in whom I have very little confidence). In fact, studies have shown in recent years that IRS employees will disseminate inaccurate information over 50% of the time. The VITA program, on the other hand, is comprised of tax professionals in private practice as well as other knowledgeable tax preparers who are generally better informed than Internal Revenue Service employees. In fact, I used to be among the ranks of VITA tax preparers.

Other information contained in "Publication No. 1" are facts about your rights to privacy and confidentiality, representation by someone else to the IRS, the line of authority you can access to appeal a decision you believe is unfair, the rights you have as a taxpayer to set up payment arrangements with the IRS, and your responsibility to them if such arrangements are established. This publication also informs you of your right to the cancellation of penalties such as the ones referenced previously for certain mitigating circumstances. It states:

> You have the right to ask that certain penalties (but not interest) be canceled (abated) if you can show reasonable cause for the failure that led to the penalty (or can show that you exercised due diligence, if that is the applicable standard for that penalty).
>
> If you relied on wrong advice you received from the IRS employees on the toll–free telephone system, we will cancel certain penalties that may result. But you have to show that your reliance on the advice was reasonable. If you relied on incorrect written advice from the IRS in response to a written request you made after Janu-

ary 1, 1989, we will cancel any penalties that may result. You must show that you gave sufficient and correct information and filed your return after you received the advice.[21]

The best way to have the IRS accept responsibility for the conveyance of inaccurate information is to have them state it to you in a written document. From my own experience it is very difficult to establish a case that you were given misleading information verbally from an IRS official even if you record the name of the employee and the date on which you spoke with him.

An alternative to this is to request a written response to the question by telephone or a written inquiry by you in lieu of a telephone call. The safest method of all is to never ask the IRS anything. Get your information from a qualified tax professional in the field.

Another publication on taxpayer rights and penalties is Notice No. 746 also put out by the Internal Revenue Service. It states:

> **Elimination of Penalty – Reasonable cause**. Except for certain cases of the Underpayment of Estimated Tax Penalty and for Fraud and Negligence penalties, the law provides that the penalties explained below can be removed if you have an acceptable reason. If you believe you have a good reason but have not yet sent us an explanation, please send it to us. The explanation should be signed by the taxpayer or person having a power of attorney. We will review your explanation and let you know what our decision is. If a penalty or any portion of a penalty is the result of written advice of the Internal Revenue Service, that penalty or portion of the penalty will be "removed." To have the penalty "removed," you should complete Form 843, requesting that the

penalty be removed. Submit the Form 843 to the service center where your tax return was filed for the tax year in which you relied upon erroneous advice from the IRS. Attach the following documents to the Form 843: a copy of your original request for written advice from the IRS; a copy of the erroneous written advice you received from the IRS; and a notice (if any) showing assessment of the penalty that you wish to have removed.[22]

Specific Mitigating Circumstances

In the March 1992 issue of *Tax Avoidance Digest*, there is an article entitled "File two years late and not pay a penalty?" This article tells us that you don't always have to get hit with penalties when a tax return is filed late. As spelled out in Notice 746, a late filing penalty can be waived for reasonable cause. In fact, IRS regulations tell us that late filing will be excused if you "exercised ordinary business care and prudence and were still unable to file on time".[23] Specific instances considered reasonable causes, are discussed.

One generally accepted reasonable cause is that of **illness**. If you are very ill or an immediate family member is gravely ill, the IRS usually excuses late filing of a tax return until that person either recovers or dies. As you can see, death is not a reasonable cause!

In addition, the IRS considers only a spouse, child, parent, or sibling a close relative. If you are unusually close to a friend or a cousin, you may have a problem with reasonable cause.

I have done a good deal of work with taxpayers who are recovering alcoholics and consequently have not filed tax returns for several years. The approach I take when filing past due tax returns is to be totally honest with the IRS and to reveal to them the extenuating circumstances surrounding each particular case. I go in with the goal of helping the taxpayer "wipe the slate clean." Generally, the IRS cooperates. They usually agree that alcoholism is an illness and demonstrates reasonable cause. The results do vary, however, based on circumstances, and also on the agent handling the case.

139

Another reasonable cause cited in this article is **not having documents available**. If your tax records were destroyed in a fire, storm, hurricane, or war, your penalties will probably be waived until you have had a reasonable opportunity to reconstruct them. Also, if you are dependent on someone else to generate items such as a W–2 or a 1099, and that information is late, you usually are given a waiver of penalty.

If you did not get around to organizing and putting together your tax records, however, that is **not** reasonable cause!

Travel may be a reasonable cause when it results in an **unavoidable absence**. Business and vacation travel are not reasonable causes no matter how important. You are expected to plan around these absences. But, if you have to go out of town to care for a sick or dying relative, the IRS will sympathize.

The article does state that "if you are out of the country on business and get stuck in a civil war, you can probably get the penalties waived."[24] This has never happened to me so I can't say for sure that it is true, yet it seems to make sense.

Other reasonable causes listed in this article include: mailing the return on time, but with insufficient postage; filing a return with the wrong IRS district address; getting erroneous information from an IRS official; not receiving the requested forms from the IRS; and unsuccessfully trying to get assistance from the IRS after personally visiting an IRS office.

Another reasonable cause which usually works. Blaming a tax professional. This is one reasonable cause I would generally not recommend you use, especially if you are my client! However, many businesses get penalties waived for poorly prepared tax returns as well as for filing other required documents late by saying that the filing was left up to their accountant, or that failure to file was based on professional advice.

The article sums it all up by stating that "there is no foolproof way to get penalties waived. Some IRS employees seems to waive penalties if you offer almost any excuse. Others don't ever want to waive penalties. The point is that you should not meekly accept a penalty no matter how late your return is. State your reason to the IRS employee and you might get the penalty waived."[25]

I will conclude this section on penalties by relating a true story about a situation I was involved with several years ago. I had just starting working with a very competent tax manager in a relatively new position in the tax department of an accounting firm.

This man was an amazing worker and, in fact, did the work of about three men. This was both a blessing and a curse for the department because it meant was that several other people in the firm got by without necessarily pulling their own weight.

As a result of his diligence he was over-worked, over-stressed, and over-burdened. This naturally affected his health, and when he became suddenly ill on April 13th one year in the middle of filing extensions for some 100 clients, no one in the department knew what to do. And, since I had very recently joined the firm neither did I.

But there I was, on April 13th, with over 100 federal extensions and corresponding state extensions to file by midnight April 15th. I was familiar with some of these clients, but not on top of all their tax situations. I rounded up whatever people I could to help me with this task and within two days we filed all of the federal and state extensions.

The one problem, however, was that some of the estimated tax liabilities we claimed were incorrect. They were the best we could do under the circumstances; however, in some cases, the amounts were grossly insufficient to cover the amounts actually due.

You should be aware that an extension to file your tax return does not constitute an extension to pay your tax liability late as well. When you extend a tax return, both for federal and state purposes, you are expected to pay your full tax liability. If you do not do this and underpay your liability by more than a certain amount (usually 5%), you will invalidate the extension which was granted and create penalties for underpayment of taxes as well as for late filing.

We had 100 or so taxpayers being granted automatic extensions. However, a good part of these extensions would be become useless because of underpayment of estimated tax liabilities due. As a result, these taxpayers could owe a great deal of money in penalties and interest.

After the returns had been filed and the IRS and the states sent us notices of deficiency for the penalty amounts, we responded. We advised them of the extenuating circumstances surrounding the filing of these extension requests. We also told them that we felt these circumstances constituted reasonable cause for the waiving of any related penalties. We sent explanatory letters to IRS centers and the various state offices in all parts of the country. These taxpayers were scattered throughout the U.S. and had been required to file in many different locations.

141

The results of requesting almost 50 of these penalty waivers was as follows: We were **not denied** the waiver of one single penalty by **any** federal agent who reviewed the case at **any** IRS center. They were all waived. However, we were **not granted** the waiver of one single penalty by **any** state we applied to.

That's right, the IRS granted every one of our requests and every state we applied to denied them! And, if my memory serves me well, this included approximately 15 states.

So, if you always thought that the IRS was tougher to deal with than state tax departments, you are wrong. The IRS is generally more understanding of such matters whereas state and local governments are not so flexible.

This was an important lesson for me to learn. It taught me that if you are honest and treat the IRS fairly, they will usually do the same for you. It is the state and local governments which are the real problems whenever you have a situation which requires a judgement call!

Your New Rights As A Taxpayer

Another excellent publication put out by Agora, Inc., the publishers of the *Tax Avoidance Digest* newsletter is called *Tax Liberty* by Robert Carlson, J.D., CPA. In this publication, they list "199 loopholes that accountants overlook, ignore, or refuse to use." This publication talks about the new bill of rights you as taxpayers now have. It states:

> **One of the most significant actions Congress took in 1988 was passing the Taxpayer Bill of Rights**. Though this is a watered–down version of what was originally proposed and what is needed, the law makes a number of significant changes.
> Taxpayers now have some important protections that were not available a year ago, and some of the worst IRS abuses now are curbed. More importantly, Congress has sent a message to the IRS. The message is that deficit reduction is not so important that the IRS can do whatever it wants to taxpayers.

142

Most of the Taxpayer Bill of Rights provisions became effective over the last few months, and the IRS has issued some rules in this area, so this is a good time to review what your new rights are. There are so many provisions of the Taxpayer Bill of Rights that we cannot cover them all in one article. Here are the major benefits.

Knowing your rights. The first big change is that the IRS actually has to describe your rights in writing at the beginning of an audit or other interview. In the past, many people thought they had to talk to the IRS and didn't know that they could refuse to say anything or turn over evidence. The IRS plans to give everyone a copy of Publication 1, "Your Rights as A Taxpayer," to meet the requirement. The publication explains both the audit and collection processes and what your rights are during each process.

Audits and interviews. The new legislation also makes clear that you can be represented at an IRS proceeding by anyone who is qualified to represent taxpayers before the IRS. This means attorneys, CPAs, and enrolled agents. In fact, you are allowed to seek representation at any time, and the IRS is required to suspend an interview if you so request to allow you to consult with your representative.

Most importantly, in most cases you do not have to appear at an audit. That had been the IRS' longstanding policy. But a few years ago the IRS tried to change the policy, particularly when business taxpayers were involved. The IRS manual told agents

143

that taxpayers were likely to make misstatements and other mistakes at an initial interview, so taxpayers should be told to attend the initial meeting themselves even if a representative would be handling most of the audit...

The IRS Ombudsman is an important change for many taxpayers who have problems with the IRS. A common complaint among taxpayers who have been burned by the IRS is that their problems could have been resolved quickly, but the IRS employees involved did not pay attention to important facts until many months had passed. The result was a lot of headaches for the taxpayers and perhaps a loss of the taxpayer's business.

The Problem Resolution Office was set up a few years ago to deal with such problems, but that office had no real powers. Now each PRO has an ombudsman. This employee can intervene in any IRS enforcement action when the taxpayer is "suffering or about to suffer a significant hardship as a result of the manner in which the Internal Revenue laws are being administered." The Ombudsman can issue a Taxpayer Assistance Order, which is legally binding on the IRS.

If you have a problem that you think requires the Ombudsman's help, you should look up the PRO of your IRS district office in the telephone book under "United States Government, Internal Revenue Service." Call or write the PRO and ask for Form 911. When you receive the form, complete and return it according to the instructions. The Ombudsman will then look into you situation and decide what, if any, action should be taken.

But be warned that the PRO will act only in extreme situations. The IRS recently reported that over 50,000 requests for action by the Ombudsman had been received so far, and the Ombudsman had taken action in less than 100 cases...

Suing the IRS. You can sue the IRS when certain specified conditions are met. The general rule is that a government cannot be sued except when it specifically gives consent to be sued. The government has agreed that it can be sued when the IRS knowingly or negligently fails to release a lien when there was an error in the filing of the lien. The IRS also can be sued when an IRS employee acts recklessly or negligently in disregard of any provision of the tax code or regulations. But you can only recover actual economic damages and court costs under this provision, and your reward is limited to $100,000.

These are the major provisions of the TBR. Taxpayers are no longer faced with a completely one–sided system that is stacked against them, though the IRS still is in a better position than the taxpayer. It is possible that IRS abuses will continue and another TBR will be needed in the future.[26]

Significance to the Investor

What does this all mean to you and me? My interpretation of all this new tax legislation is that the IRS wants to be perceived as a more flexible institution. Although it will still maintain an intimidating

145

appearance in pursuing all tax fraud perpetrators, it will, I believe, listen to reason.

Therefore, it is necessary, as I've mentioned many times in this publication, to acquire as much tax law knowledge applicable to your situation as is possible. Armed with this knowledge you will be in a strong position to support any position you take within reasonable limits.

Charles Givens discusses this subject further in his book *More Wealth Without Risk.* He says that in pursuing the objective of lowering ones taxes, it is never necessary to resort to tax cheating or loopholes. He further states that there is a tremendous difference between cheating, loopholes, and tax strategies. I am firmly concur with Mr. Givens.

He defines tax cheating as understating your income or claiming deductions for assets you don't own for expenditures you never make. Leona Helmsley, of course, is a glaring example of such abuse.

Loopholes, as defined by Mr. Givens, are gray, untested areas of the tax law that allow you to claim deductions that Congress and the IRS might have ruled against had they had the foresight to see the potential for abuse. Since a specific "no" does not exist, you create a loophole by saying "yes" to a shaky deduction. Loopholes are often sought after by desperate, high income taxpayers who have never taken the time to plan their tax situations. Some loopholes are used entirely out of greed and others are taken because of the taxpayers' gambling instinct. Chuck Givens states unequivocally, and I once again concur, that there is only one "do" about loopholes, and that is "don't."

Tax strategies on the other hand, as defined in this book, are positive and legal uses of the tax laws to reduce your income taxes. Tax strategies arise from knowledge of the tax law. They are actions which are taken to automatically and legally qualify a taxpayer for additional deductions. These strategies can include opening up a retirement account, starting a small business, buying a rental property, among many other options. Many of these possibilities are straight forward and obvious. Other methods, such as travelling on tax deductible dollars, or creating a tax deductible college education for your children, are just as legal, just as easy to use, but less understood. Mr. Givens states:

146

One question I am asked over and over again: "Is paying less taxes really legal, patriotic, and moral?" For some reason many people seem to confuse our tax system with the United Way Fund, whose slogan is "Pay your fair share." By following the tax laws and regulations when you use tax strategies, you automatically pay your fair share, even if your share amounts to zero. Two neighboring families, each with a $30,000 annual income and two children, could both be paying their fair share of income taxes, even if one family paid $5,000 and the other paid nothing at all. It's the way the American tax system was designed.

We have a system that imposes taxes, not on your total income, but on a far smaller amount known as your taxable income; your residual income after you subtract your exemptions, adjustments, and deductions. Within the difference between total income and taxable income lies your opportunities for applying legal, powerful tax–reducing strategies.

Not long ago on the "Donahue" show, during one of the best national discussions on tax strategies in which I have ever participated, a lady caller said she thought reducing your taxes was cheating. She made $15,000 working, didn't have an IRA, and her husband was even a tax attorney! Her feeling was that she wanted to pay taxes to help the homeless. This may come as a surprise to you, as it did to her, but very few of your federal tax dollars go to the homeless or many other places you might prefer the money to go. By learning legal strategies for reducing her taxes, she could have given her tax savings directly to the homeless herself.

Another woman in the studio audience felt that paying more taxes was patriotic. The courts say that paying taxes has nothing to do with patriotism whether you pay a lot or none at all. The money goes into the economy whether paid to the government or used by you for a deductible purpose. The question of legality and morality of tax deductions was settled once and for all over 40 years ago by the United States Circuit Court of Appeals in an opinion written by Judge Learned Hand.

> Anyone may so arrange his affairs
> that his taxes shall be as low as pos-

> sible. He is not bound to choose a
> pattern that will best pay the Trea-
> sury. No one owes any public duty to
> pay more than the law demands.[27]

The decision as to how to handle your tax affairs should directly influence your tax plan and attitude. Rearranging your affairs to create deductions where you had none before is the secret to paying less taxes. I will discuss several general and quite a few specific tax strategies in this book. Which you use is your choice and depends on which one best suits you. Mr. Givens further states his own opinion about deducting expenses. As he puts it,

> Most taxpayers think they are doing themselves a
> favor by being ultraconservative in taking deductions. Noth-
> ing could be further from the truth. If you are tax deduction
> shy not only do you end up spending thousands of dollars in
> unnecessary taxes, you don't even reduce your chances for
> audit. Most audits are done at random and have little to do
> with whether you take all of your allowable deductions or
> only a few.
>
> If you want to reach your financial goals you must
> adopt the winning tax strategy: WHEN IN DOUBT, DEDUCT
> IT. Take everything the law allows. Follow the rules, but
> deduct all gray areas in your favor. Gray areas are not
> loopholes or an attempt to get around the tax laws, but are
> areas of ambiguity and uncertainty about what Congress or
> the IRS really meant. You have just as much chance of
> winning your point as the IRS does. You'll be surprised, as
> you learn about taxes, at how much of the code is ambiguous.
> Simple recordkeeping and tax strategies will always have you
> prepared to win your point.[28]

Michael Milken

A discussion of legality would not be complete without a brief glance at of one of my favorite criminals, Michael Milken. As investors, you should recall that Mr. Milken was convicted on several counts of fraud relating to the sale of junk bonds. Without going into too many of the details of his case, Mr. Milken became a hero to some and a nemesis to others, depending on where you got in on the purchase of these bonds. Some of his closest friends apparently made millions and some who were not lost an equal amount.

But there are two minor issues here I feel are somewhat relevant–one of which is directly relevant to the discussion of legality of deductions.

As you may recall, Mr. Milken, as part of the settlement with the courts agreed to pay approximately $500 million to settle a securities fraud suit. If this amount of money is considered a **fine or penalty** then it would not be deductible on Milken's tax returns.

However, since Michael Milken declared all of this ill begot income on his tax return and consequently paid taxes on it, he was not indicted for tax evasion. And, since he paid taxes on income which he must now return, should he not be entitled to either a credit on future tax returns or a return of the tax he paid on this income?

The law states that a taxpayer cannot deduct a fine or a penalty, but does say that he can deduct the return of misappropriated funds which were previously included in income. According to the tax code, since this payment is not considered a fine or penalty, the $500 million should apparently be deductible.

What this ultimately means is that if the deduction is allowed, Mr. Milken will not pay taxes again for a very long time. It is expected that he will request a ruling from the IRS before finalizing the settlement.

Chapter 10

Playing For Keeps With The IRS

What Criteria Are Most Important in the Selection of Tax Returns for Audit?

This next section deals with an unpleasant but necessary situation–what to do in case you are audited. The first part of this chapter will discuss **who** gets audited, the second part will further discuss methods to **lessen your chances** of an audit, and the third part will address **what to do** in case you are audited. This section will summarize some of the concepts and ideas already discussed throughout this book and will add many new ones. Even the most conservative taxpayers are selected for IRS audits due to no fault of their own. I will put together a workable plan of attack on what to do if, or rather when, your return is eventually examined.

No one I know can say for sure what factors are directly responsible for your tax return being selected for audit. People often try to avoid an audit by being overly conservative on their tax returns and sometimes not even taking those deductions to which they are entitled. This is a mistake, and may, in fact, not even help lessen the chances.

Audited returns are analyzed afterwards from all angles so that we might figure out the factors which contributed to their having been selected. Several of the ways they have been classified are as follows:

Audit Chances Based on Income

What are your real chances for being audited in one year? Out of approximately 100 million individual tax returns, less than three million returns are audited. Even so, it is important to know the rules of the game. Based on past performance of the IRS, here are your percentage chances for being audited by income and profession.

Your Income/Profession	Chance for Audit[29]
Under $50,000	2%
Over $50,000	8%
Professionals	25%
Known criminals	50%

Other Targeted Occupations

An interesting table comes from another of my favorite publications "The IRS Confidential" report. This table gives some idea of how specific professions are rated as far as probability for audit. This table is called "The IRS Hit List" and was prepared by Ralph J. Pribble, former IRS agent and president of The Tax Corporation of America.[30]

In addition to doctors, dentists, lawyers, and CPAs, who are all good targets for the IRS due to a generally high income level, the following list represents professions who are also subject to investigation and the areas most likely to be examined.

a. Salespeople: Outside and auto salespeople are particular favorites. Agents look for, and often find, poorly documented travel expenses and padded promotional figures.

b. Airline pilots: High incomes, a propensity to invest in questionable tax shelters, and commuting expenses claimed as business travel make them inviting prospects.

c. Flight attendants: Travel expenses are usually a high percentage of their total income and often aren't well documented. Some persist in trying to deduct pantyhose, permanents, cosmetics, and similar items that the courts have repeatedly ruled are personal rather than business expenses.

d. Executives: As a group they are not usually singled out. But if the return includes a Form 2106 showing a sizable sum for unreimbursed employee business expenses an audit is more likely. Of course, anyone whose income is over $50,000 a year is a higher priority target just because of the sums involved.

e. Teachers and college professors: Agents pounce on returns claiming office–at–home deductions. They are also wary of educational expense deductions because they may turn out to be vacations in disguise.

f. Clergymen: Bona fide priests, ministers, and rabbis aren't considered a problem group. But if W–2s show income from nonchurch employers the IRS will be on the alert for mail–order ministry scams.

g. Waitresses, cabdrivers, etc.: Anyone in an occupation where tips are a significant factor is likely to get a closer look from the IRS nowadays.

Audit Selection by Geographic Location

Depending on where you live, your risk of audit will vary. In the Manhattan district, for example, several years ago, 1.98% of all individual tax returns filed were audited, whereas in Dallas the rate was only 1.2%. The following table, taken from "The IRS Commissioner's Annual Report" for 1989,[31] shows the percentage of returns audited in various IRS districts. It will give you an idea of which areas are the most audit prone in the country.

IRS District	Percent of Returns Audited
Albany	.88
Anchorage	2.48
Atlanta	1.21
Baltimore	.99
Boston	.69
Chicago	.98
Cincinnati	.75
Dallas	1.20
Denver	1.37
Detroit	.90
Jacksonville	1.36
Los Angeles	1.88
Manhattan	1.98
Nashville	1.14
Newark	1.34
New Orleans	1.30
Philadelphia	.82
Phoenix	1.44
Salt Lake City	1.97
San Francisco	2.17

153

Types of Audit Selection Processes

The selection process is done in several ways, both by computer and manually. And, as I said before, no one knows for sure exactly how returns are selected. However, these four procedures are generally believed to constitute most of the selection process:

a. **Random Selection**. This is what is commonly known as the TCMP audit or taxpayer compliance measurement program. In this case it does not matter what income level you are or what deductions you take. Everyone has an equal chance of being selected for a TCMP audit. Reports state that approximately 40,000–50,000 out of 100 million returns are selected for the TCMP audit.

The IRS uses this type of audit to discover where taxpayers make mistakes or tend to cheat on their tax returns. The IRS will sometimes make you prove everything on the tax return–even the children you claim. This audit has been described as the most grueling type imaginable because of the thoroughness of it.

It is also true, however, that a good percentage of people selected for the TCMP audit actually receive a refund as a result of this audit.

b. **Target Group Selection**. This is the second group of taxpayers which is regularly selected for audit. The IRS has found that certain professions tend to provide the greatest amount of income for them per man hours spent on an audit. In other words, the IRS feels that it can collect the most tax dollars from these groups with the least amount of audit work. As I previously mentioned, these groups include doctors, dentists, lawyers, accountants, and other high income groups.

c. **Discriminant Function System**. This is a point system the IRS has developed as a third criteria for audit selection. Deductions on your return are compared to what the IRS considers to be normal for a person of your profession in your area of the country and with your income. The greater the difference between your tax return and what is considered normal, the higher the number of points you are assigned. If your DFS score gets too high, you may be chosen for an audit.

Reportedly, if you are selected by the discriminant function system by computer, two IRS employees must agree that there is a good chance of collecting additional taxes before you are actually sent an audit notice.

d. **Document Compliance Selection**. The last area which has resulted in tax returns being selected is one I call the document compliance selection process, or DCS. What this means is that another entity, such as a business or a bank, reports income to the IRS through the processing of such forms as W–2s (for salary) or 1099s (for commissions or interest).

A computer matching process is performed at the IRS and if these amounts are not reported on your tax return it may result in some form of an audit. Many times this will only lead to a desk audit. A desk audit is generally done through the mail and can be as simple as a request by the IRS for more information on the breakdown of a figure, such as interest, on your tax return.

It goes without saying that the more unreported items the IRS finds, the greater the chances of triggering a full scale audit of your tax return. If several items are missed, it would indicate carelessness or sloppy preparation of your tax return to the IRS.

Ten Ways To Reduce Your Chances of Being Audited

Although, in general, the greater your income, the greater your chances of an audit, there are specific methods which have been proven over the years to help the taxpayer avoid being audited. This is not to say that it will guarantee nonselection in the audit process. But, if two returns are identical in certain areas, there are steps that can be taken to ensure that the other one is the more likely to be selected.

1. **Be specific** in categories which are apt to be questioned. Suppose you have freelance income of some kind, and it is merely reported as "other income." It would be to your advantage to put down the specific source of this income, such as non–1099 Income–"Income from Investment Seminars."

There is one school of thought which believes it is best to avoid the Schedule C (form for reporting business income from self–employment). These people believe that if the expenses associated with this income are minimal, it is best to not report it as a business, but rather as simply "other income" with detail as explained above on line 22 of your tax return (see Exhibit 3F, line 22).

Nonetheless, I know of many instances when a Schedule C can provide much greater benefit than exposure. I will discuss this further "The Schedule C – Born To Be Filed."

2. One way to avoid the problem of a Schedule C is by **incorporating** or **finding a partner** if you are self–employed. There are several advantages to doing this, the most significant being that as a corporation or a partnership you will be a small fish in a big pond, whereas non–incorporation may put you in a more conspicuous situation as your income grows. The IRS generally concentrates its corporate auditing on the very largest corporations. There are pros and cons to the incorporation process and it is best to have an attorney handle the formality.

If you do not incorporate, **attach any explanation** to the return when your total income does not equal the sum of your W–2s and/or 1099s. For example, many businesses mail their checks on December 31 to get the deductions in the current year, and they will include these payments on the 1099s filed for that year. However, if a check is received by you in the next year, and you report income on a cash basis, you are not required to report the income until the year you receive it.

The way to deal with this is to reconcile the figure reported on your tax return with the 1099(s) filed on your behalf. This will demonstrate to the IRS that you are not understating your income, but rather are reporting it consistently from year to year. Be absolutely certain that your federal income tax returns are consistent with state income and sales tax returns. The IRS is able to examine these reports in many states without even notifying you.

3. **File your tax return as late as possible**. The later a return is filed, the less chance it has of being selected for audit. This is not what most non–tax professionals believe. I have heard many clients whose return I have extended say, "But won't filing after April 15th make my return look suspicious, and thereby increase my chance of an audit?"

This could not be further from the truth. A tax return filed on or before April 15th generally has a greater chance of being audited than one being filed on October 15th (the last extension date). This is because the IRS schedules audits about a year and a half in advance. As returns are filed and scored according to the methods I have discussed, local IRS offices submit their forecasts for returns with audit potential.

Before the age of the computer, it was probably best to file your return between April 1st and April 15th, just about when half the returns are filed. At that time the IRS was generally inundated with returns and your tax return had the best chance of being overlooked in the audit selection process.

But because the computer does the bulk of the selection process during this period, filing between April 1st and April 15th will not reduce your risk of audit, but rather will increase it. As I mentioned, each year the IRS establishes an estimate of what percentage of returns should be audited. The ones that are filed first are the ones first chosen. In fact, the later your return is filed, the greater the chances are that the quotas for returns in your particular category will have already been met.

You would think that the IRS would be wise to this ploy. But even if they were and tried to make the selection process as fair as possible, they could not fully accomplish it. Therefore, it makes sense to try to be part of the group which has the smallest chance of being audited.

In the February issue of *Tax Avoidance Digest*, it is reported that the IRS recently did a study which confirmed that it was not worth the cost to try to change its audit procedures.

> They stated: "It's better to get an automatic extension to August 15 using Form 4868 (Exhibit 10A), and even better to get an additional two–month extension to October 15 for "reasonable cause " on Form 2688 (Exhibit 10B). By the time your return gets into the computer and gets an audit score, chances are the IRS employees will already have more returns assigned to them than they can handle in that audit cycle. A few years ago when the IRS saw that the number of returns seeking extensions was rising, it did a study to see if audit selection procedures should be adjusted to include these returns. Then

The Serious Investor's Tax Survival Guide

Form **4868**		**Application for Automatic Extension of Time**		OMB No. 1545-0188
Department of the Treasury Internal Revenue Service		**To File U.S. Individual Income Tax Return**		**1991**

	Your first name and initial	Last name	Your social security number
Please Type or Print	If a joint return, spouse's first name and initial	Last name	Spouse's social security number
	Present home address (number, street, and apt. no. or rural route). (If you have a P.O. box, see the instructions.)		
	City, town or post office, state, and ZIP code		

Note: *File this form with the Internal Revenue Service Center where you are required to file your income tax return, and pay any amount(s) you owe.* **This is not an extension of time to pay your tax.**

I request an automatic 4-month extension of time to August 17, 1992, to file Form 1040A or Form 1040 for the calendar year 1991 (or if a fiscal year Form 1040 to ...., 19 ...., for the tax year ending............................, 19 ....).

1 Total tax liability for 1991. This is the amount you expect to enter on line 27 of Form 1040A, or line 53 of Form 1040. If you do not expect to owe tax, enter -0- **1**

    Caution: *You* **MUST** *enter an amount on line 1 or your extension will be denied. You can estimate this amount, but be as exact as you can with the information you have. If we later find that your estimate was not reasonable, the extension will be null and void.*

2 Federal income tax withheld **2**

3 1991 estimated tax payments (include 1990 overpayment allowed as a credit) . . **3**

4 Other payments and credits you expect to show on Form 1040A or Form 1040 . . **4**

5 Add lines 2, 3, and 4 . . . . **5**

6 **BALANCE DUE** (subtract line 5 from line 1). *To get this extension, you* **MUST** *pay in full the* **balance due with this form.** (If line 5 is more than line 1, enter -0-.) . . . . . ▶ **6**

If you expect to owe gift or generation-skipping transfer (GST) tax, complete line 7 (and 8a or 8b if applicable). Do not include income tax on these lines. (See the instructions.)

7 If you or your spouse plan to file a gift tax return (Form 709 or 709-A) for 1991, } **Yourself** ▶ ☐
generally due by April 15, 1992, see the instructions and check here . . } **Spouse** ▶ ☐

8a Enter the amount of gift or GST tax that **you** are paying with this form **8a**

  b Enter the amount of gift or GST tax that **your spouse** is paying with this form **8b**

Signature and Verification

Under penalties of perjury, I declare that I have examined this form, including accompanying schedules and statements, and to the best of my knowledge and belief, it is true, correct, and complete; and, if prepared by someone other than the taxpayer, that I am authorized to prepare this form.

Signature of taxpayer ▶ _____ Date ▶ _____

Signature of spouse ▶ _____ Date ▶ _____
         (If filing jointly, BOTH must sign even if only one had income)

Signature of preparer
  other than taxpayer ▶ _____ Date ▶ _____

If correspondence regarding this extension is to be sent to you at an address other than that shown above, or to an agent acting for you, please enter the name of the agent and/or the address where it should be sent.

	Name
Please Type or Print	Number and street (or P.O. box number if mail is not delivered to street address)
	City, town or post office, state, and ZIP code

General Instructions

Paperwork Reduction Act Notice.—We ask for the information on this form to carry out the Internal Revenue laws of the United States. You are required to give us the information. We need it to ensure that you are complying with these laws and to allow us to figure and collect the right amount of tax.

The time needed to complete and file this form will vary depending on individual circumstances. The estimated average time is: **Recordkeeping,** 26 min.; **Learning about the law or the form,** 11 min.; **Preparing the form,** 20 min.; and **Copying, assembling, and sending the form to the IRS,** 20 min.

If you have comments concerning the accuracy of these time estimates or

suggestions for making this form more simple, we would be happy to hear from you. You can write to both the **Internal Revenue Service,** Washington, DC 20224, Attention: IRS Reports Clearance Officer, T:FP; and the **Office of Management and Budget,** Paperwork Reduction Project (1545-0188), Washington, DC 20503. Do not send this form to either of these offices. Instead, see **Where To File.**

Cat. No. 13141W   Form **4868** (1991)

Exhibit 10A

Form **2688**	**Application for Additional Extension of Time To File**	OMB No. 1545-0066
	U.S. Individual Income Tax Return	**1991**
Department of the Treasury Internal Revenue Service	▶ See instructions on back. ▶ Be sure to complete all items.	Attachment Sequence No. **59**

Please type or print. File the original and one copy by the due date for filing your return.	Your first name and initial	Last name	Your social security number
	If a joint return, spouse's first name and initial	Last name	Spouse's social security number
	Present home address (number, street, and apt. no. or rural route). (If you have a P.O. box, see the instructions.)		
	City, town or post office, state, and ZIP code		

1 I request an extension of time until .... , 19........ , to file Form 1040A or Form 1040 for the calendar year 1991, or other tax year ending .... , 19......... .

2 Have you previously requested an extension of time to file for this tax year? . . . . ☐ Yes ☐ No

3 Explain why you need an extension ▶..
....
....
....
....

If you expect to owe gift or generation-skipping transfer (GST) tax, complete line 4.

4 If you or your spouse plan to file a gift tax return (Form 709 or 709-A) for 1991, generally due by } **Yourself** . . ▶ ☐
April 15, 1992, see the instructions and check here . . . . **Spouse** . . ▶ ☐

Signature and Verification

Under penalties of perjury, I declare that I have examined this form, including accompanying schedules and statements, and to the best of my knowledge and belief, it is true, correct, and complete; and, if prepared by someone other than the taxpayer, that I am authorized to prepare this form.

Signature of taxpayer ▶ _____ Date ▶ _____

Signature of spouse ▶ _____ Date ▶ _____
(If filing jointly, BOTH must sign even if only one had income)

Signature of preparer
other than taxpayer ▶ _____ Date ▶

File original and one copy. The IRS will show below whether or not your application is approved and will return the copy.

Notice to Applicant—To Be Completed by the IRS

☐ We **HAVE** approved your application. (Please attach this form to your return.)

☐ We **HAVE NOT** approved your application. (Please attach this form to your return.)
However, because of your reasons stated above, we have granted a 10-day grace period from the date shown below or due date of your return, whichever is later. This grace period is considered to be a valid extension of time for elections otherwise required to be made on returns filed on time.

☐ We **HAVE NOT** approved your application. After considering your reasons stated above, we cannot grant your request for an extension of time to file. (We are not granting the 10-day grace period.)

☐ We cannot consider your application because it was filed after the due date of your return.

☐ We **HAVE NOT** approved your application. The maximum extension of time allowed by law is 6 months.

☐ Other ....

Director

_____ By _____
Date

If the copy of this form is to be returned to you at an address other than that shown above or to an agent acting for you, enter the name of the agent and/or the address where the copy should be sent.

Please type or print.	Name	
	Number and street (include suite, room, or apt. no.) or P.O. box number (if mail is not delivered to street address)	
	City, town or post office, state, and ZIP code	

For Paperwork Reduction Act Notice, see back of form.   Cat. No. 11958F   Form **2688** (1991)

Exhibit 10B

the number of extension requests started dropping, and the IRS con- cluded that it did not need to change its audit procedures".[32]

4. Another technique to reduce your chances of being audited is to **avoid certain items** which are universally thought to trigger special IRS scrutiny. One of these such deductions is Home Office Expense. There are instances, however, where these deductions are absolutely justified, and when they are, they should be taken.

Whenever I have an item which is apt to raise a red flag, such as Home Office Expense, I will generally **put an explanation right on the tax return** to justify my reasons for taking the deduction. I also do this when an item appears to be out of line in the sense of being too large or too small.

For example, a client who had a retarded son spent many thousands of dollars to send him to a special school for the disabled. This deduction qualified under the tax code as a valid medical expense. For a taxpayer in her tax bracket the expense appeared to be inordinately large, especially in light of the fact that she had deducted significant sums of money for medical insurance.

The medical insurance did not, of course, cover the tuition and I attached the explanation, and even included documentation in the form of a copy of the paid bill to a special school for the handicapped. This technique reduced the possibility of an audit for the taxpayer and avoided further questions from the IRS .

Another example of the way I handle certain large dollar amounts for expenditures which might raise red flags is to attach explanatory notes. If the amount appears to be large and might generate questions, I will always attach an explanation with a reference to "See Statement 1." I then attach this statement to the return to further explain and break down these expenses.

If, for example, I am an investor who spends substantial amounts on investment software, data retrieval, and on–line data fees, I will provide further explanations on "Statement 1" as to the nature of these expenses and their relevance in the production of income.

I have been using this technique for years. It makes sense to let the IRS know that you pay attention to details and are familiar with the tax law. Any explanation or breakdown of figures on your tax return which shows how they were calculated will help convince the IRS that you knew what you were doing. Therefore, they will, hopefully, be convinced that there is no reason to spend anymore time on your return than they already have!

Other areas which might raise questions include taking large expense deductions as Unreimbursed Employee Business Expenses and Casualty Loss Deductions. Historically, these deductions have triggered audits. If you have a reason for taking them, include an explanation as I have just discussed.

In addition, you should try to have your employer reimburse you for as many of these expenses as possible, rather than taking them as deductions. You can attempt to work out an arrangement with your employer which would reduce your salary by a corresponding amount.

If you have casualty losses, make sure that they are properly documented and be aware that the IRS may be able to make a case that you actually received a gain from the insurance proceeds, even though you believe you had a loss.

5. **Choose your tax return preparer very carefully.** When the IRS suspects a tax preparer of incompetence or other wrong–doing, it can force them to produce a list of their clients. You would not want to be on this list regardless of how honest you are in preparing your tax return.

6. **Answer all questions** on your tax return completely. The IRS computer generally flags down returns with unanswered questions or inconsistent answers. For example, on Schedule B (see Exhibit 5B, part 3), there are questions asking you about foreign bank accounts. It is important, even if you do not have foreign bank accounts to answer these questions. You do not want to make anyone at the IRS **have** to look at your tax return more than once.

7. **Fill in your return neatly** and carefully. A sloppy return may indicate a careless taxpayer to the IRS. Furthermore, if they cannot clearly read any figure on your return it will make your return subject to further scrutiny. The IRS may continue to examine the return to make sure that the carelessness did not lead to any other mistakes. As I said above, you do not want to make anyone at the IRS look at your tax return more than once.

8. **Avoid putting large amounts of money in very general categories** such as "Miscellaneous Income" or "Miscellaneous Expense" without a more detailed explanation. Avoid such terms as "miscellaneous," "general," "sundry," or "various" on your tax re-

turn. If you cannot be specific about a deduction, the IRS may decide that you cannot substantiate it.

9. **Avoid round numbers** on your tax returns. A deduction rounded off to the nearest hundred or thousand may raise IRS suspicions. It will appear as if you are guessing at the deduction instead of determining it from accurate records.

10. **Take all your entitled deductions**. Not taking all your deductions actually increases your risk of an audit. According to *Tax Avoidance Digest*, many people believe that it is better to leave off legitimate deductions. In truth, it is not. The IRS is trained to look at tax returns which are out of the ordinary. Missing deductions are out of the ordinary.

For example, they describe an automobile dealership. The owner knew that entertainment deductions increased the chance of an audit, so he didn't take any. The return was referred to an auditor who decided to examine the auto dealer's book in detail. This probably would not have happened had a reasonable amount been deducted for entertainment expenses. The auditor went through the books and eventually found that there were other deductions which were not appropriate, and he disallowed them.[33]

The IRS knows that a sales business should have entertainment expenses and expects to see them deducted. Another example of this, which supposedly comes straight from the IRS manual, shows that someone reporting capital gains from the sale of stock most likely has dividend income to report; someone reporting property tax deductions most likely has a mortgage interest deduction; and someone who deducts medical insurance premiums should probably not have very large medical expense deductions. If you do not have corresponding deductions when you should, or you have them when you should not, an explanation is appropriate.

I want to mention one more thing in this section before I move on to discuss specific strategies for handling the audit. Many people have asked me when they can be sure that they have not been selected for an audit. Generally, the IRS will not audit you more than three years after April 15th, or the date your return was filed, whichever is later.

The normal audit policy is to send out the majority of notices approximately 18 months after April 15th of each year. Audit notices for tax returns filed by April 15th, 1992, should be sent out in the fall of 1994. You can begin to feel good about not being audited about 20 months after the return has been filed.

Playing In The Major Leagues

I have heard that if you take the entire tax code and place it on a shelf along with the tax regulations, it would stretch out to approximately 50 feet, or about 60,000 pages. This is the reason informed people consider the system to be such a mess. The IRS itself is even confused by the tax laws.

As I previously stated, IRS representatives have a reputation for providing incorrect information over the telephone. It was reported in a recent survey taken by *USA Today* that this is indeed the case. The publication hired CPAs to call the IRS with a list of ten questions. The IRS gave the wrong answer to these questions 40% of the time. Although these facts are not particularly comforting, they do demonstrate that IRS professionals are human beings and make mistakes just as you or I do. With this in mind, we can deal with the potential audit a bit more comfortably.

Dauntless Doug's Dos and Don'ts

Remember my first audit experience with "Dauntless Doug, the Duke of Deductions?" A significant part of this book has covered the audit process and the valuable lessons which Doug impressed upon me back them.

1. **Delay the audit as long as possible**. Federal law allows that the time and place for an audit must be convenient to both parties. Your best strategy is to delay the audit for as long as possible.

You recall that Ms. Green had been to our office five times without having done very much work. This was the way Doug delayed the audit. I would not necessarily use the same approach, yet I would send a registered letter to the IRS letting them know that I could not meet with them at the time they had set.

This response will automatically postpone the audit and after several postponements you will receive a noncomputer generated letter or a call from an IRS employee. At the very least this will give you much more time to prepare your records.

Once the audit has begun, the postponements will put pressure on the auditor to finish. Auditors usually have their time blocked out for them by their supervisors, and due to inadequate staffing, have fairly tight schedules. In order words, they must meet deadlines, just like you and me.

163

Doug believed, and I have found this to be true from my own experience, that "when they are behind the eight ball they're willing to talk to you." In addition to the time constraints, continual postponements tend to wear an auditor down. Consequently, he or she may be in the mood to compromise more readily in certain areas.

Tex Colson, one of ex–President Nixon's henchmen, was no favorite of mine. However, I'll always remember him for one thing and one thing only. He had a sign on the wall behind his desk quite visible to anyone entering his office. It said,

> "When you have them by the balls,
> Their hearts will follow."

Doug believed this was particularly true of the audit process.

2. **The IRS is a business, and should be treated as such**. Granted it is a big collection business, run by the government, but nonetheless its existence depends on its ability to generate income for itself. The IRS auditor is an employee who would like to please his or her supervisor. The way this can be assured is by creating revenue for the business.

With this in mind it is much easier to approach the audit, as you are now aware of a major motivating factor involved in the audit process. The auditor must, at some time, evaluate their chances of winning on each point. Contrary to popular opinion, they are willing to trade allowances and disallowances of certain items if it will help achieve their overall success.

3. Keep talking, try to get the auditor to see things your way. Don't expect, however, to walk out of an audit without owing anything. **You must set your sights on the large, important items and be willing to compromise on some of the smaller ones.** If you are convinced that an item the auditor would like to disallow is an appropriate deduction, be firm.

Don't give up until he reduces the adjustment. Even the most stubborn agent will give in somewhat if you stand your ground. Keep in mind that the agent's ultimate goal is to close the case, obtain some additional taxes from you, and move on to the next audit.

As you recall in the Esterman audit, the most important question was whether or not the business was in fact legitimate or whether it was simply a hobby for Mrs. Esterman. This was the focus of our approach. Any of the other disallowances in and of themselves would not have been that important to us. Because of this, we allowed Ms. Green to have the adjustments she wanted without much resistance.

4. **If you're at an impasse with the auditor let them know that you will be willing to go above their head if necessary**. It is best never to outwardly threaten or antagonize an IRS agent. This would be more aggravation than it's worth, however, this technique can be accomplished in a much subtler manner.

In the final showdown between Ms. Green and Doug, he let her know outright that he knew who her supervisor was and, in fact, had worked with him before. This indicated that if she did not reach an agreement with us, there would have been no hesitation by Doug to contact her supervisor in reaching this agreement.

At the end of this section I will discuss the various ways you can handle an audit where you feel that you have not been treated fairly and the different levels to which you can take it (see point #10, in the next section, "Ten Other Winning Audit Techniques").

5. **Never give an auditor original documents to take with them either to photocopy or to take back to their office**. The IRS is not responsible if the original documents are lost, regardless of how it happens. If by some chance an auditor misplaces the documents, that will not excuse you from having to produce substantiation.

In addition, you do not want the auditor to have possession of anything more than he is entitled to. Only give him what he asks for and never give him free reign of your documents or backup material.

Only let the auditor look at each of your documents once. Under a recent court ruling, if the auditor wants to look at your papers a second time, written permission must be obtained from the United States Secretary of the Treasury. This can be done, but the auditor usually will not go to the trouble if you mention the rule.

In the Esterman audit we only provided documents which were requested, and when providing them to Ms. Green we made certain that Maria, Doug's secretary, did the photocopying. We never allowed an original document to go out of the office.

6. **Use alternate documentation if the substantiation requested by the auditor is not available**. For example, if an auditor requests an original invoice for the purchase of one of the items you have deducted and you cannot locate that invoice and cannot get the store to reproduce it, an auditor will usually accept

165

a credit card statement and receipt (chit) which specifically itemizes the expenditure.

We used this technique in the audit when Ms. Green had requested a bill for the stereo and tape cassette library. In addition, we provided the cancelled check used to pay the credit card bill for these items. This is not necessary, as you do not have to actually pay the credit card company in the year of the purchase to be entitled to a deduction. However, the more documentation you can provide to substantiate an expenditure, the more believable it will be to the auditor. As a result, the more probable the chances will be of having the auditor accept the alternate documentation.

7. When preparing a return, never consciously omit deductions to which you are entitled. However, upon reviewing a return which is in audit, **if you discover that deductions were inadvertently overlooked or calculations were made on a very conservative basis, make note of it**. This can provide a bargaining chip for you if needed in reaching a settlement with the auditor.

In the Esterman audit, Doug pointed out several areas which he felt could be raised if we needed them. One of these was the allocation of home office on a lesser basis than could have been done. Another area was the allocation of certain other depreciable items with a lower percentage put to business use than was actually the case. Doug was ready to bring these points to the auditor's attention if we needed them to effect a more favorable settlement.

8. **If a trip for business, charity, or medical purposes is challenged, be prepared to provide proof of the nature of this trip**. For example, if, as a trader, you had to travel to Chicago for a trading seminar, you would want to provide backup on the seminar and why it was necessary for your business. Syllabus, notes, and manual should be kept on hand for substantiation.

If you are travelling for business or charitable reasons, provide documentation that the work was actually performed. An example of this was a client I had who organized renovating projects for various underprivileged area facilities throughout the country.

When the expenses for travel were deducted as charitable contributions on the client's tax return the deduction was questioned. We provided photos of his group renovating a drug rehabilitation center located several hundred miles from the taxpayer's residence. You will recall the concept of "substantial element of pleasure," so make certain that if there are photos you do not appear to be having too good a time! I know of at least one case where a charitable travel deduction was disallowed for just that reason.

In the Esterman audit we provided pictures of Mrs. Esterman performing in costume at one of the hotels where she was hired. Be prepared to provide similar types of documentation for any large or questionable expenses you may incur.

9. **Save the toughest items to substantiate for last**. As the audit progresses and the agent gets closer to a settlement, they may be willing to compromise or overlook these items. Provide documentation for the easiest items first. In addition to delaying the process of investigating the questionable items, this will provide the auditor with a feeling that you have done a tight job in keeping your backup.

First impressions are generally strongest, so provide your tightest and neatest backup first. You want to start off with the auditor thinking that you are a good record keeper.

As we got towards the end of the Esterman audit, there were certain items requested by Ms. Green I never needed to provide her. I was encouraged by Doug not to spend any time obtaining these items as he seemed to sense that first of all, we would not be able to, and second of all, we would not have to produce them.

10. **Never invite an auditor to lunch**. You do not want to spend more time with them than you must as you might say something which could work against you—assuming they would accept your offer.

Auditors are not supposed to accept gifts or favors from taxpayers. Besides, it would look bad if somebody familiar with the audit spotted the two of you having lunch or socializing. Also, it might make you look like you have something to hide if you try to be too nice to the agent.

This was the first mistake I made during my initial audit while working for Doug. It was also the last time I ever asked an auditor to lunch.

Ten More Winning Audit Techniques

The following points represent a compilation of ten other strategies I have learned in dealing with the IRS. Some of these are original and some I have borrowed from other sources (as noted).

167

1. **Try to schedule an audit before a three–day weekend if at all possible**. The auditor may be less interested in the audit than he is in the holiday. Another good time to schedule an appointment is at the end of the month.

If an auditor has not closed enough cases that month, he or she may be inclined to go easy on you to gain a quick settlement and close another case. For the same reasons an auditor may be willing to compromise on certain points.

In her book, *How To Beat The IRS*, Ms. X, Esq., a former IRS agent, states that "although the timing of an audit may seem ridiculous in fact it may provide you with a real advantage.

As for the best time of day, most experienced tax professionals like to start an audit at about ten o'clock in the morning. By the time it comes to discussing adjustments with the auditor it will be close to lunch time. If you are persistent, the auditor may be willing to make concessions just to get rid of you so as not to interfere with lunch."[34]

2. **Good records are the key to success and should be as complete as possible**. However, do not concede an issue if the paperwork is not perfect. Philip Storrer, in *The Tax Fighters Guide* states:

"Under the 'Cohan Rule', you are allowed to use approximations in determining deductible expenses. You must however, establish that you did legitimately incur the expense, and that your records are incomplete or unavailable. Many agents will not be open about the Cohan Rule and will try to disallow some of these expenses. Do not accept a disallowance which you think should be allowed."[35]

The Cohan Rule does not apply to expenses for overnight travel, business entertainment, or gifts. These must be fully documented to sustain a deduction. The documentation does not necessarily have to be in the form of receipts. Many times it is acceptable to provide a diary with the expenditure written in with details in the appropriate slot, especially if it is for an amount of $25 or less.

3. **Try to get the audit transferred to another district if it is at all feasible**. In other words, you would not want to ask for a New York case to be arbitrarily transferred to Fresno, CA without some believable reason. However, if you have a client being audited in a local branch of the IRS , say an hour or so away, you would be best off not making the drive to have the case done there. If they will agree to it, you should try to bring it to your local office.

168

The IRS Confidential by Boardroom Books states:

"Don't expect the IRS to admit it, but transferred cases often fall between the cracks and never get worked on, even though the taxpayer has been notified of the examination. Delays caused in processing the case file between districts, combined with the fact that the case is likely to go to the bottom of the pile when it is assigned to a new agent, may bring help from the statute of limitations. Rather than asking the taxpayer to extend the statute of limitations, as is the usual practice, many agents are inclined to take the easy way out and close transferred cases without auditing them."[36]

4. **Do your homework and be adequately prepared for the audit**. Make sure that each paper which supplies detailed figures of amounts on your tax return adds up correctly and ties in to the exact amounts on your tax return.

Take the time to provide added details on this backup, as appropriate, such as how and when you made the expenditure, or how and when you earned the income. By meticulously preparing whatever records you have available, you will establish your credibility with the auditor. In an audit, credibility is everything. It will thereby become a bit easier for him to accept non–documented items.

5. **Try to limit the items the agent examines by persuading him to do a test check of your expenses**. Let the auditor choose a three–month period for detailed examination. Or talk him into limiting the audit to items over, say, $100. Make sure you can document all items in the test check period or in the amount being examined.

Travel and entertainment is a very common expense chosen for audit. This technique works extremely well in this and provides a double benefit. A test check cuts your work in assembling backup data and it prevents the agent from rummaging through all your travel and entertainment expenses, which can be quite time consuming.[37]

6. **If an IRS field agent comes to your door, unannounced, do not invite him in**. The IRS has issued new guidelines as to what field auditors can do when visiting a taxpayer's home or place of business.

Agents may only enter premises when they are invited in by the rightful occupant. This rule has arisen from the IRS' concern about taxpayer lawsuits for violation of privacy rights.[38]

7. **Never go to an audit until you are advised of the reasons for the audit in writing**. The IRS is obliged to provide you with written answers to questions concerning a proposed audit of your tax return.

       a. They must tell you **why** they are auditing it.

       b. They must tell you **which** parts are being audited.

       c. They must tell you **what** they want to see.

8. **Try to look relaxed, even if you're not**. Body language and nonverbal communication is extremely important in any business interaction. This is particularly true in the case of an audit where an agent will try to ascertain your credibility as part of the audit process. Say little, smile a lot, and never volunteer information.

9. If you have been audited numerous times in the last few years, let the auditor know that this has occurred. **The IRS is not allowed to engage in a "hassle audit."**

If you are audited on any part of your return and the audit produces no change, or only a small change, you should not be audited on the same part of your return for at least three years. The IRS should be made aware of this situation if it exists, as oftentimes they are not.

10. **If you are unfairly treated, or if you feel you can justify items which were disallowed by the agent, go over his head**. The first level above the IRS agent is that of his **immediate supervisor**.

Auditors will generally make decisions in favor of the IRS in unclear areas. Supervisors generally will be more open to ruling in favor of the taxpayer. In addition, supervisors are generally more knowledgeable and familiar with the subtler nuances of the tax code.

Whenever an auditor shows some uncertainty as to an area of the tax code I feel should be in my favor, I immediately request that it be discussed with the supervisor. I do this before the auditor has had a chance to make a decision which may be against the taxpayer.

In a recent audit of one of my clients at an IRS branch office, I dealt with a field auditor who appeared to be quite inexperienced. There were several complicated areas of the tax code being questioned and I was fairly certain that my interpretation was correct in each of these areas.

The first question she raised was on the propriety of handling OEX options as commodities, i.e., marking them to market at year end and reporting them as Section 1256 transactions. I was quite experienced in this area and could tell that she did not know what I was talking about.

I was very respectful and did not take the attitude "I know more than you so why don't you go check it out," but rather "I believe I am correct and perhaps we should discuss this with someone more knowledgeable on this subject, just to be sure." This was my tactful way of requesting additional input from a higher level official. Her supervisor intervened and ruled in my favor as I thought he would.

The next level, beyond the supervisor, you can contact is the **Problem Resolution Office**. The Problem Resolution Office was set up to keep the IRS from going to court if possible. They have the power to compromise on issues and to resolve any dispute you may have with an agent or supervisor. Each local district of the IRS should have its own PRO. It is easy to obtain the phone number by either requesting it at your branch or by looking it up in the phone book under the United States Government, Internal Revenue Service, Problem Resolution Office.

Many times I have contacted the PRO to help resolve issues which could not be settled at the local office level. I have found them to be particularly helpful in cases involving more than one district office where I could not pin down the center of authority on an issue.

The next step, should you need it, is to take the IRS to court. The big dollar settlements can only be made in **Tax Court**, and you would be required to have an attorney to present your side of the argument. This is often a very costly and time consuming endeavor and should only be done in cases which warrant such expense. The IRS publications on appeals and review procedures outline this process in greater detail.

I have recently read that cases with under $10,000 at issue can be settled in **Small Claims Tax Court**. The judgement is final here, and appeals are not permitted. But the cost for pursuing this avenue is very little, so it is a trade–off.

This section has presented a summary of ideas on how to deal with the IRS at various stages. The strategies provided here will facilitate your interaction with them before, during, and after the audit process.

The next three sections will go on to examine several general tax strategies and the various concepts associated with each. In the following chapters I will discuss methods for sheltering your wealth and legally reducing your tax liability through:

(A) Retirement planning;

(B) Transferring Wealth to Future Generations; and

(C) Creating a Trading Business.

Chapter 11

Retirement Plans

Individual Retirement Accounts (IRAs)

Retirement planning is one of the few straightforward tax strategies left at our disposal for sheltering taxable income. There is nothing complicated or tricky about retirement planning, it's all laid out for you in the law. If you take the time to learn the regulations, requirements, and restrictions involved with this section of the tax code, it will surely be worth the time spent in terms of tax dollars saved. It is for this reason that I refer to retirement plans as being one of the last remaining "tax shelters."

Individual Retirement Accounts or IRAs are the most widely known type of retirement plan. Contrary to what some people believe, IRAs were not eliminated with the Tax Reform Act of 1986. But, there have been restrictions put on the amounts of money allowed as **deductible** contributions to an IRA each year. These restrictions do not affect everybody and even those affected can still contribute to an IRA, although not necessarily deduct the entire contribution from their taxable income.

The equity, however, will still accrue without tax liability in a non–deductible IRA, and it may be worth making contributions to such a plan for this reason only. If you recall in the section on True Yield, I showed that Total Return Investment Planning (TRIP) required that tax liability be factored into the calculation of yield on any investment. I demonstrated the significant difference in return over the years when the tax factor was included.

Difference in Return of 30–Year Investment With and Without the Tax Factor

The following table represents the growth of a 15% investment over a 30–year period with and without taxes being taken out. As you will see, even a non–deductible IRA contribution of $2,000 per year will be worth considerably more after 30 years. This calculation does not take into account the tax savings you would attain by making the same $2,000 contribution per year, as tax deductible. We will discuss the significance of making a tax deductible versus a non–deductible contribution shortly.

TAXABLE VERSUS TAX–FREE INVESTING
$2,000 per Year Available to Invest Before Taxes

End of Year	With Tax Protection	Without Tax Protection
5	$15,500	$13,047
10	46,699	33,121
15	109,435	64,007
20	235,620	111,529
25	489,424	184,648
30	999,914	297,150

$4,000 per Year Available to Invest Before Taxes

End of Year	With Tax Protection	Without Tax Protection
5	$31,015	$26,093
10	93,397	66,241
15	218,870	128,014
20	471,240	223,058
25	978,848	369,296
30	1,999,828	594,301

$10,000 per Year Available to Invest Before Taxes

End of Year	With Tax Protection	Without Tax Protection
5	$77,537	$65,233
10	233,492	165,603
15	547,175	320,034
20	1,178,101	557,645
25	2,447,120	923,240
30	4,999,569	1,485,752

The assumptions made here are as follows: a 30–year investment, paying 15% per annum, compounded annually, tax rate of 40% federal and state. This could be the typical scenario of somebody putting away $2,000 per year, $4,000 per year, and $10,000 per year, for their retirement in 30 years.

As you can see, the difference between a taxable investment versus putting it in a tax deferred investment, such as an IRA is significant. The difference over 30 years in return on investment is:

a) For a $2,000 per year investment–an additional
$702,764
b) For a $4,000 per year investment–an additional
$1,405,527
c) For a $10,000 per year investment–an additional
$3,513,817

These numbers represent total earnings, which in each case represents a 337% increase in return on investment! That is simply the difference between letting your retirement money grow in an IRA versus letting it grow outside an IRA in a taxable investment. Now that you have some idea of just what is in involved, let us examine the specifics of IRAs.

Specific Characteristics of an IRA

IRAs were established as part of the Employee Retirement Income Security Act of 1974 (ERISA) as a way for workers to supplement their social security retirement income. The provisions allow for a deductible contribution to be made up to 100% of salary or $2,000 per wage earner, whichever is lower, with certain restrictions to these limits. In addition, a **non–working** spouse can contribute $250 to such a plan.

The deductibility depends on several variables. If you are not covered by another retirement plan, there are no income limitations on your ability to contribute, other than earned income, as discussed above. If, however, you belong to another retirement plan, such as a SEP or a KEOGH, you must have income under a certain level. If you are single and have such a plan, you must phase out your deductible contributions when you have income of $25,000, up to a maximum of $35,000, at which point you can deduct **no** amount of an IRA contribution.

If you are married, filing jointly, and either spouse is covered by another retirement plan, the following restrictions apply: your phase out of deductible IRA contributions begins at $40,000 of gross income and ends at $50,000, at which point **none** of your IRA contribution will be deductible.

Form 8606 (Exhibit 11A) is used to determine your non–deductible amount. It must be filed each year if a non–deductible contribution is made. It is up to the taxpayer to determine deductibility of an IRA contribution as financial institutions are not responsible for doing this. You should consult with a tax advisor as to your own status if in doubt.

Contributions may be made to an IRA up until the due date for filing the federal tax return without extensions–April 15th. The opening of new IRA accounts are also subject to this deadline. When the contribution is made you must be certain that the institution correctly indicates the year to which it applies as this information is transmitted to the IRS. During the period from January 1st to April 15th, contributions can be made for either the current or prior tax year.

Contributions are reported to the IRS on Form 5498, issued on May 31st of each year. Contributions do not have to be made each year and individuals can revoke a new IRA contribution, without penalty, within seven days of opening the account.

Distributions, or payment made from an IRA to the owner of the account, can occur at any time. The tax consequences vary, depending upon the age, health, and form of pay out. In general, pay outs made before the taxpayer reaches age 59 1/2 will be subject to a 10% premature distribution penalty, in addition to the regular income tax on this amount. There may also be fees or penalties charged by the institution which holds the IRA.

There are certain exceptions to this penalty, including death or disability. A taxpayer may designate anyone he chooses as a beneficiary. Multiple beneficiaries can be made to split the IRA, with the percentages indicated in the IRA. In the case of disability, a pay out is generally made in one payment to the owner of the IRA if there is a permanent incapacitation.

Other general information about IRAs consists of such items as:

a. Owner must receive annual statement showing fair market value on December 31st each year.

Form **8606**

Department of the Treasury
Internal Revenue Service

**Nondeductible IRA Contributions,
IRA Basis, and Nontaxable IRA Distributions**
► Please see Recordkeeping Requirements on the back.
► Attach to Form 1040, Form 1040A, or Form 1040NR.

OMB No. 1545-1007

1990

Attachment
Sequence No. **47**

Name (If married, file a separate Form 8606 for each spouse. See instructions.)

Your social security number

**Fill In Your Address Only
If You Are Filing This
Form by Itself and Not
with Your Tax Return**

Home address (number and street, or P.O. box if mail is not delivered to your home) | Apt. no.

City, town or post office, state, and ZIP code

1	Enter the total value of **ALL** your IRAs as of 12/31/90. (See instructions.)	**1**
2	Enter your IRA contributions for 1990 that you choose to be nondeductible. Include those made during 1/1/91–4/15/91 that were for 1990. (See instructions.)	**2**
3	Enter your total IRA basis for 1989 and prior years. (See instructions.)	**3**
4	Add lines 2 and 3 and enter the total. If you did not receive any IRA distributions (withdrawals) in 1990, skip lines 5 through 13 and enter this amount on line 14	**4**
5	Enter only those contributions included on line 2 that were made during 1/1/91–4/15/91. (This amount will be the same as line 2 if all of your nondeductible contributions for 1990 were made in 1991 by 4/15/91.) (See instructions.)	**5**
6	Subtract line 5 from line 4 and enter the result	**6**
7	Enter the amount from line 1 plus any outstanding rollovers. (See instructions.)	**7**
8	Enter the total IRA distributions received during 1990. Do not include amounts rolled over before 1/1/91. (See instructions.)	**8**
9	Add lines 7 and 8 and enter the total	**9**
10	Divide line 6 by line 9 and enter the result as a decimal (to at least two places)	**10**
11	Multiply line 8 by the decimal amount on line 10 and enter the result. This is the amount of your **nontaxable distributions for 1990.** (See instructions.) ►	**11**
12	Subtract line 11 from line 6 and enter the result. This is the **basis in your IRA(s) as of 12/31/90**	**12**
13	Enter the amount, if any, from line 5	**13**
14	Add lines 12 and 13. This is your **total IRA basis for 1990 and prior years** ►	**14**

**Sign Here Only If You
Are Filing This Form
by Itself and Not with
Your Tax Return**

Under penalties of perjury, I declare that I have examined this form, including accompanying attachments, and to the best of my knowledge and belief, it is true, correct, and complete.

►

Your signature   Date

Paperwork Reduction Act Notice.—We ask for the information on this form to carry out the Internal Revenue laws of the United States. You are required to give us this information. We need it to ensure that you are complying with these laws and to allow us to figure and collect the right amount of tax.

The time needed to complete and file this form will vary depending on individual circumstances. The estimated average time is:

Recordkeeping . . . . . 26 minutes

**Learning about the law
or the form** . . . . 7 minutes

Preparing the form . . . . 22 minutes

**Copying, assembling, and
sending the form to IRS** . . 20 minutes

If you have comments concerning the accuracy of these time estimates or suggestions for making this form more simple, we would be happy to hear from you. You can write to both the **Internal Revenue Service**, Washington, DC 20224, Attention: IRS Reports Clearance Officer,

T:FP; and the **Office of Management and Budget**, Paperwork Reduction Project (1545-1007), Washington, DC 20503. **DO NOT** send this form to either of these offices. Instead, see **When and Where to File**, below.

General Instructions

Purpose of Form.—You must use Form 8606 to report the amount of your IRA contributions that you choose to be nondeductible. You may wish to make nondeductible contributions, for example, if all or part of your contributions are not deductible because of the income limitations for IRAs. First, figure the amount of your deductible contributions using the Instructions for Form 1040 or Form 1040A, whichever apply to you. Report the deductible contributions on Form 1040, Form 1040A, or Form 1040NR. Then enter on line 2 of Form 8606 the amount you choose to be nondeductible.

The part of any distributions you receive attributable to nondeductible contributions will not be taxable. If you have at any time made nondeductible contributions, also use Form 8606 to figure the nontaxable part of

any IRA distributions you received in 1990. Line 11 will show the amount that is not taxable.

Who Must File.—You must file Form 8606 for 1990 if you do not have to file an income tax return because you do not meet the
• You made nondeductible contributions to your IRA for 1990, or
• You received IRA distributions in 1990 and you have at any time made nondeductible contributions to any of your IRA(s).

When and Where To File.—Attach Form 8606 to your 1990 Form 1040, Form 1040A, or Form 1040NR.

If you are required to complete Form 8606, but do not have to file an income tax return because you do not meet the requirements for filing a return, you still have to file a Form 8606 with the Internal Revenue Service at the time and place you would be required to file Form 1040, Form 1040A, or Form 1040NR.

Name and Social Security Number.— Enter your name and social security number on Form 8606. If you file a joint return on Form 1040 or Form 1040A, show the name and social security number of the spouse whose IRA information is shown.

Form **8606** (1990)

Exhibit 11A

    b. IRAs can be awarded in divorce settlements and do not have to be probated as part of a will if beneficiaries are named in the document.

    c. IRAs are not protected from creditors in most states.

    d. The owner of an IRA is responsible for verifying the accuracy of contributions, deductions, and distributions being reported.

    e. Rollovers from an IRA are a means of maintaining the tax deferral on the money in the plan. It is also a way of moving money from one IRA to another. Certain criteria must be met to keep the integrity of the tax deferral:

        1. The same money can only be rolled over once in the same 365–day period, and

        2. The rollover must be completed within 60 days.

    f. The taxpayer must reflect this rollover on his tax return as a non–taxable item as the financial institution reports this withdrawal to the IRS. Any part of the withdrawal not rolled over within 60 days will be subject to tax and penalties in most cases as discussed above.

    g. Loans are not permitted from most IRAs.

    h. Rollovers are permitted for people aged 70 1/2; however, mandatory distributions must begin at this age and must be made prior to the rollover.

More specific strategies on how to utilize IRAs to their fullest potential will be presented in the last section of this book, "50 Tax Reduction Strategies–Read My Tips."

Simplified Employee Pension Plans (SEPs)

The SEP was developed in the late 1970s as a way for an employee to have a retirement plan without having to deal with all the administrative issues. A SEP is an IRA or annuity that must meet special requirements for participants.

    If an employer establishes the SEP, the maximum amount that can be contributed is 15% of each employee's compensation or $30,000, whichever is less. A participant in a SEP is considered to be an active participant in a retirement plan when evaluating eligibility for an IRA deduction.

General rules regarding a SEP are as follows:

1. Minimum age of 21;
2. Perform services for the employer in at least three of the five preceding calendar years;
3. Received at least $342 of compensation (to be indexed annually for inflation); and
4. All eligible employees must participate in the plan except employees who fall into the following categories:
   a. Employees who have not met minimum service requirements for the plan;
   b. Employees whose retirement benefits are the subject of collective bargaining;
   c. Nonresident aliens with no U.S. source income; or
   d. Employees earning less than minimum annual compensation.

Unlike qualified retirement plans, which will be discussed next, an employer does not have the complicated filing requirements such as an annual Form 5500 with a SEP or an IRA (see Exhibits 11B, 11C, 11D ,11E, 11F, and 11G). Disclosure of the plan must be made to all employees outlining such areas as eligibility, contribution formula and limits, plan administrator, terms and rules of the IRA, participants' rights and withdrawal provisions, tax treatment and rollover provisions, and financial disclosures.

Both incorporated and unincorporated businesses can establish SEP plans but employers who establish Defined Benefit Retirement Plans cannot establish a SEP plan. These plans are frequently used by self–employed persons who are considered employees of their own business. This effectively raises the maximum limitation on IRA deductible contributions from $2,000 to the maximum for a SEP as described previously in this chapter.

Unlike a regular IRA, the deadline for contributing to a SEP plan can extend beyond the April 15th due date. You are allowed to contribute to a SEP plan up until the final extension date, October 15th, if you extend your return through that date. In addition, you can even start a new SEP account through that date and contribute to it for the prior year. This is a tremendous advantage for people who need to do some "prior year tax planning."

179

Form **5500**	**Annual Return/Report of Employee Benefit Plan**	OMB No. 1210-0016
Department of the Treasury Internal Revenue Service Department of Labor Pension and Welfare Benefits Administration Pension Benefit Guaranty Corporation	**(With 100 or more participants)** This form is required to be filed under sections 104 and 4065 of the Employee Retirement Income Security Act of 1974 and sections 6039D, 6057(b), and 6058(a) of the Internal Revenue Code, referred to as the Code. ▶ See separate instructions	**1991** This Form Is Open to Public Inspection.

For the calendar plan year 1991 or fiscal plan year beginning , 1991, **and ending** , 19

		For IRS Use Only
A	If (1) through (4) do not apply to this year's return/report, leave the boxes unmarked. This return/report is:	EP-ID

(1) ☐ the first return/report filed for the plan;   (3) ☐ the final return/report filed for the plan; or

(2) ☐ an amended return/report;   (4) ☐ a short plan year return/report (less than 12 months).

Information in 1a through 6b is used to identify your employee benefit plan. Check it for accuracy and make any necessary corrections. Also complete any incomplete items in 1a through 6b. This page must accompany your completed return/report.

B   IF YOU MADE ANY CHANGES TO THE PREPRINTED INFORMATION OR FILLED IN ANY INCOMPLETE INFORMATION IN 1a THROUGH 6b BELOW, CHECK HERE . ▶ ☐

C   If your plan year changed since the last return/report, check this box . . . . ▶ ☐

D   If you filed for an extension of time to file this return/report, check this box and attach a copy of the extension . . . . ▶ ☐

1a Name and address of plan sponsor (employer, if for a single-employer plan) (address should include room or suite no.)	**1b** Employer identification number
	1c Sponsor's telephone number
	1d Business code (see instructions, page 19)
	1e CUSIP issuer number
2a Name and address of plan administrator (if same as plan sponsor, enter "Same")	**2b** Administrator's employer identification no.
	2c Administrator's telephone number

3   If you are not filing a page one with the historical plan information preprinted and the name, address and EIN of the plan sponsor or plan administrator is different than that on the last return/report filed for this plan, enter the information from the last return/report in a and/or b and complete c.

a   Sponsor . . . . EIN . . . . Plan number . . . .

b   Administrator . . . . EIN . . . .

c   If a indicates a change in the sponsor's name, address and EIN, is this a change in sponsorship only? (See instruction 3c for definition of sponsorship.) Enter "Yes" or "No."

4   Enter the applicable plan entity code listed in the instructions for line 4 on page 8. ▶

5a(1) Name of plan ▶	**5b** Effective date of plan (mo., day. yr.)
	5c Enter three-digit plan number ▶
(2) Does this plan cover self-employed individuals? (Enter "Yes" or "No.") ▶	

All filers must complete 6a, 6b, and 6c as applicable.

6a(1) Welfare or fringe benefit plan (Enter the applicable codes from page 8 of the instructions in the boxes.) ▶

(2) If you entered a code M, N, or O is the plan funded? (see instructions) . . . . ▶ ☐ Yes ☐ No

6b Pension benefit plan (Enter the applicable pension codes from page 8 of the instructions.) ▶

Be sure to include all required schedules and attachments. This page must accompany your completed return/report.

Caution: A penalty for the late or incomplete filing of this return/report will be assessed unless reasonable cause is established.

Under penalties of perjury and other penalties set forth in the instructions, I declare that I have examined this return/report, including accompanying schedules and statements, and to the best of my knowledge and belief, it is true, correct, and complete.

Signature of employer/plan sponsor ▶ . . . . Date ▶ . . . .

Type or print name of individual signing for the employer/plan sponsor . . . .

Signature of plan administrator ▶ . . . . Date ▶ . . . .

Type or print name of individual signing for the plan administrator

For Paperwork Reduction Act Notice, see page 1 of the instructions.	Cat. No. 13500F	Form **5500** (1991)

12/30/91   Published by Tax Management Inc., a Subsidiary of The Bureau of National Affairs, Inc.   5500.1

Exhibit 11B

6c Other plan features (if you check box *(1)* or *(2)*, attach Schedule E (Form 5500)):   *(1)* ☐ ESOP   *(2)* ☐ Leveraged ESOP
  (3) ☐ Participant-directed account plan   *(4)* ☐ Pension plan maintained outside the United States
  (5) ☐ Master trust (see instructions)   *(6)* ☐ 103-12 investment entity (see instructions)
  (7) ☐ Common/collective trust   *(8)* ☐ Pooled separate account

		Yes	No
d	Single-employer plans enter the tax year end of the employer in which this plan year ends ▶ Month..... Day ..... Year.....		
e	Is the employer a member of an affiliated service group?		
f	Does this plan contain a cash or deferred arrangement described in Code section 401(k)?		

7 Number of participants as of the end of the plan year (welfare plans complete only a(4), b, c, and d):
  a Active participants:*(1)* Number fully vested. — **a(1)**
    (2) Number partially vested — **a(2)**
    (3) Number nonvested — **a(3)**
    (4) Total — **a(4)**
  b Retired or separated participants receiving benefits — **b**
  c Retired or separated participants entitled to future benefits — **c**
  d Subtotal (add a(4), b, and c). — **d**
  e Deceased participants whose beneficiaries are receiving or are entitled to receive benefits. — **e**
  f Total (add d and e). — **f**
  g Number of participants with account balances (Defined benefit plans do not complete this line item.) — **g**

		Yes	No
h *(1)*	Was any participant(s) separated from service with a deferred vested benefit for which a Schedule SSA (Form 5500) is required to be attached to this form? (See instructions.) **h(1)**		
(2)	If "Yes," enter the number of separated participants required to be reported ▶		
8a	Was this plan amended in this plan year or any prior plan year? If "No," go to item 9a		
b	If a is "Yes," enter the date the most recent amendment was adopted. ▶ Month....... Day........ Year..... If the date in b is in the plan year for which this return/report is filed, complete c through f		
c	Did any amendment during the current plan year result in the retroactive reduction of accrued benefits for any participants?		
d	Did any amendment during the current plan year provide former employees with an additional allocation or accrual this year?		
e	During this plan year did any amendment change the information contained in the latest summary plan descriptions or summary description of modifications available at the time of amendment?		
f	If e is "Yes," has a summary plan description or summary description of modifications that reflects the plan amendments referred to in e been both furnished to participants and filed with the Department of Labor?		
9a	Was this plan terminated during this plan year or any prior plan year? If "Yes," enter the year ▶		
b	Were all plan assets either distributed to participants or beneficiaries, transferred to another plan, or brought under the control of PBGC?		
c	Was a resolution to terminate this plan adopted during this plan year or any prior plan year?		
d	If a or c is "Yes," have you received a favorable determination letter from IRS for the termination?		
e	If d is "No," has a determination letter been requested from IRS?		
f	If a or c is "Yes," have participants and beneficiaries been notified of the termination or the proposed termination?		
g	If a is "Yes" and the plan is covered by PBGC, is the plan continuing to file a PBGC Form 1 and pay premiums until the end of the plan year in which assets are distributed or brought under the control of PBGC?		
h	During this plan year, did any trust assets revert to the employer for which the Code section 4980 excise tax is due?		
i	If h is "Yes," enter the amount of tax paid with your Form 5330 ▶ $		

10a In this plan year, was this plan merged or consolidated into another plan(s), or were assets or liabilities transferred to another plan(s)? If "No," go to item 11 .... ☐ Yes ☐No
  If "Yes," identify other plan(s)   **c** Employer identification number(s)   **d** Plan number(s)
  b Name of plan(s) ▶..................................

  e Has Form 5310 or 5310-A been filed? .... ☐ Yes ☐No

11 Enter the plan funding arrangement code from page 9 of the instructions . . . . . ▶   **12** Enter the plan benefit arrangement code from page 9 of the instructions ▶ | Yes | No |

13a Is this a plan established or maintained pursuant to one or more collective bargaining agreements?. . . **13a**
  b If a is "Yes," enter the appropriate six-digit LM number(s) of the sponsoring labor organization(s) (see instructions):
  (1)   *(2)*   *(3)*

14 If any benefits are provided by an insurance company, insurance service, or similar organization, enter the number of **Schedules A (Form 5500)**, Insurance Information, that are attached. If none, enter "-0-." ▶

Exhibit 11C

Form 5500 (1991)			Page 3

Welfare Plans Do Not Complete Items 15 Through 27. Go To Item 28. Fringe Benefit Plans see page 5 of the instructions.

			Yes	No
15a	If this is a defined benefit plan, subject to the minimum funding standards for this plan year, is **Schedule B** (Form 5500) required to be attached? (If this is a defined contribution plan leave blank.)	15a		
b	If this is a defined contribution plan, i.e., money purchase or target benefit, is it subject to the minimum funding standards? (If a waiver was granted, see instructions.) (If this is a defined benefit plan leave blank.)	b		
	If "Yes," complete (1), (2), and (3) below:			
	(1) Amount of employer contribution required for the plan year under Code section 412 **b(1)** $			
	(2) Amount of contribution paid by the employer for the plan year **b(2)** $			
	Enter date of last payment by employer ▶ Month........ Day....... Year......			
	(3) If (1) is greater than (2), subtract (2) from (1) and enter the funding deficiency here; otherwise, enter zero. (If you have a funding deficiency, file Form 5330.) **b(3)** $			
16	Has the plan been top-heavy at any time beginning with the 1984 plan year?	16		
17	Has the annual compensation of each participant taken into account under the current plan year been limited to $222,220?	17		
18a	(1) Did the plan distribute any annuity contracts this year? (See instructions.)	a(1)		
	(2) If (1) is "Yes," did these contracts contain a requirement that the spouse consent before any distributions under the contract are made in a form other than a qualified joint and survivor annuity?	a(2)		
b	Did the plan make distributions to participants or spouses in a form other than a qualified joint and survivor annuity (a life annuity if a single person) or qualified preretirement survivor annuity (exclude deferred annuity contracts)?	b		
c	Did the plan make distributions or loans to married participants and beneficiaries without the required consent of the participant's spouse?	c		
d	Upon plan amendment or termination, do the accrued benefits of every participant include the subsidized benefits that the participant may become entitled to receive subsequent to the plan amendment or termination?	d		
19	Were distributions, if any, made in accordance with the requirements under Code sections 411(a)(11) and 417(e)?	19		
20	Have any contributions been made or benefits accrued in excess of the Code section 415 limits, as amended by the Tax Reform Act of 1986?	20		
21	Has the plan made the required distributions in 1991 under Code section 401(a)(9)? (See instructions.)	21		
22a	Does the employer apply the separate line of business rules of Code section 414(r) when testing to see if this plan satisfies the coverage and discrimination tests of Code sections 410(b) and 401(a)(4)?	22a		
b	If a is "Yes," enter the total number of separate lines of business claimed by the employer ▶ .... If more than one separate line of business, see instructions for additional information to attach.			
c	Does the plan consist of more than one part that is mandatorily disaggregated under Income Tax Regulations section 1.410(b)-7(c)?	c		
	If "Yes," see instructions for additional information to attach.			
d	In testing whether this plan satisfies the coverage and discrimination tests of Code sections 410(b) and 401(a), does the employer aggregate plans?	d		
e	Does the employer restructure the plan into component plans to satisfy the coverage and discrimination tests of Code sections 410(b) and 401(a)(4)?	e		
f	If you meet either of the following exceptions, check the applicable box to tell us which exception you meet and do NOT complete the rest of question **22:**			
	(1) ☐ No highly compensated employee benefited under the plan at any time during the plan year;			
	(2) ☐ This is a collectively bargained plan that benefits only employees covered under a collective bargaining agreement, and no more than 2 percent of the employees who are covered under the collectively bargained agreement are professional employees.			
g	Did any leased employee perform services for the employer at any time during the plan year?	g		

			Number
h	Enter the total number of employees of the employer. Employer includes entities aggregated with the employer under Code sections 414(b), (c), or (m). The number of employees includes leased employees and self-employed individuals.	h	
i	Enter the total number of employees excludable because of: (1) failure to meet requirements for minimum age and years of service; (2) coverage under a collective bargaining agreement; (3) nonresident aliens who receive no earned income from U. S. sources; and (4) the 500 hours of service/last day rule	i	
j	Enter the number of nonexcludable employees (subtract line i from line h)	j	
k	Do 100 percent of the nonexcludable employees entered on line j benefit under the plan? . ☐ Yes ☐ No If line k is "Yes," do NOT complete lines 22l through 22o.	k	
l	Enter the number of nonexcludable employees (line j) who are highly compensated employees	l	
m	Enter the number of nonexcludable employees (line j) who benefit under the plan.	m	
n	Enter the number of employees entered on line m who are highly compensated employees	n	
o	This plan satisfies the coverage requirements on the basis of (check one):		
	(1) ☐ The average benefits test		
	(2) ☐ The ratio percentage test—Enter value ▶		

Exhibit 11D

Form 5500 (1991)

Page **4**

		Yes	No

23a Is it intended that this plan qualify under Code section 401(a)? . . . . **| 23a |**

If "Yes," complete **b** and **c** .

b Enter the date of the most recent IRS determination letter. . . . . ▶ Month .... Year ....

c Is a determination letter request pending with IRS? . . . . **| c |**

24a If this is a plan with Employee Stock Ownership (ESOP) features, was a current appraisal of the value of the stock made immediately before any contribution of stock or the purchase of the stock by the trust for the plan year covered by this return/report? . . **| 24a |**

(If this plan has NO ESOP features leave blank and go to item 25.)

b If **a** is "Yes," was the appraisal made by an unrelated third party? . . . . **| b |**

c If dividends paid on employer securities held by the ESOP were used to make payments on ESOP loans enter the amount of the dividends used to make the payments . . . . . . **| 24c |**

25 Does the plan provide for permitted disparity? See Code sections 401(a)(5) and 401(l) . . . . . . **| 25 |**

26 Does the employer/sponsor listed in **1a** of this form maintain other qualified pension benefit plans?. . . **| 26 |**

If "Yes," enter the total number of plans, including this plan ▶

27 If this plan is an adoption of a master, prototype, or regional prototype plan, indicate which type by checking the appropriate box: **a** ☐ Master   **b** ☐ Prototype   **c** ☐ Regional Prototype

28a Did any person who rendered services to the plan receive directly or indirectly $5,000 or more in compensation from the plan during the plan year (except for employees of the plan who were paid less than $1,000 in each month)? . . **| 28a |**

If "Yes," complete Part I of **Schedule C** (Form 5500).

b Did the plan have any trustees who must be listed in Part II of **Schedule C** (Form 5500)? . . . . . . **| b |**

c Has there been a termination in the appointment of any person listed in **d** below? . . . . **| c |**

d If **c** is "Yes," check the appropriate box(es), answer **e** and **f**, and complete Part III of **Schedule C** (Form 5500):

    (1) ☐ Accountant   *(2)* ☐ Enrolled actuary   *(3)* ☐ Insurance carrier   *(4)* ☐ Custodian

    (5) ☐ Administrator *(6)* ☐ Investment manager   *(7)* ☐ Trustee

e Have there been any outstanding material disputes or matters of disagreement concerning the above termination? **| e |**

f If an accountant or enrolled actuary has been terminated during the plan year, has the terminated accountant/actuary been provided a copy of the explanation required by Part III of **Schedule C** (Form 5500) with a notice advising them of their opportunity to submit comments on the explanation directly to DOL?. . **| f |**

g Enter the number of **Schedules C** (Form 5500) that are attached. If none, enter -0- ▶

29a Is this plan exempt from the requirement to engage an independent qualified public accountant? . . . **| 29a |**

b If **a** is "No," attach the accountant's opinion to this return/report and check the appropriate box. This opinion is:

    (1) ☐ Unqualified

    (2) ☐ Qualified/disclaimer per Department of Labor Regulations 29 CFR 2520.103-8 and/or 2520.103-12(d)

    (3) ☐ Qualified/disclaimer other   *(4)* ☐ Adverse *(5)* ☐ Other (explain) ....

....

....

c If **a** is "No," does the accountant's report, including the financial statements and/or notes required to be attached to this return/report disclose (1) errors or irregularities; (2) illegal acts; (3) material internal control weaknesses; (4) a loss contingency indicating that assets are impaired or a liability incurred; (5) significant real estate or other transactions in which the plan and (A) the sponsor, (B) the plan administrator, (C) the employer(s), or (D) the employee organization(s) are jointly involved; (6) that the plan has participated in any related party transactions, or (7) any unusual or infrequent events or transactions occurring subsequent to the plan year end that might significantly affect the usefulness of the financial statements in assessing the plan's present or future ability to pay benefits? **| c |**

d If **c** is "Yes," provide the total amount involved in such disclosure ▶

30 If **29a** is "No," complete the following questions. (You may NOT use "N/A" in response to item 30): If **a, b, c, d, e,** or **f** is checked "Yes," schedules of these items in the format set forth in the instructions are required to be attached to this return/report.

During the plan year:

a Did the plan have assets held for investment?. **| 30a |**

b Were any loans by the plan or fixed income obligations due the plan in default as of the close of the plan year or classified during the year as uncollectible? . . . . **| b |**

c Were any leases to which the plan was a party in default or classified during the year as uncollectible? . **| c |**

d Were any plan transactions or series of transactions in excess of 5% of the current value of plan assets? **| d |**

e Do the notes to the financial statements accompanying the accountant's opinion disclose any nonexempt transactions with parties-in-interest?. . . . . **| e |**

f Did the plan engage in any nonexempt transactions with parties-in-interest not reported in **e** ? . . . . **| f |**

g Did the plan hold qualifying employer securities that are not publicly traded? . . . . **| g |**

h Did the plan purchase or receive any nonpublicly traded securities that were not appraised in writing by an unrelated third party within 3 months prior to their receipt? . . . . **| h |**

i Did any person manage plan assets who had a financial interest worth more than 10% in any party providing services to the plan or receive anything of value from any party providing services to the plan? . . . **| i |**

31 Did the plan acquire individual whole life insurance contracts during the plan year? . . . . **| 31 |**

5500-4   Published by Tax Management Inc., a Subsidiary of The Bureau of National Affairs, Inc.   12/30/91

Exhibit 11E

Form 5500 (1991)   Page 5

32	During the plan year:		Yes	No
a	**(1)** Was this plan covered by a fidelity bond? If "Yes," complete a(2) and a(3)	32a(1)		
	(2) Enter amount of bond ▶ $			
	(3) Enter the name of the surety company ▶			
b	**(1)** Was there any loss to the plan, whether or not reimbursed, caused by fraud or dishonesty? . . .	b(1)		
	(2) If **(1)** is "Yes," enter amount of loss ▶ $			

33a Is the plan covered under the Pension Benefit Guaranty Corporation termination insurance program?

☐ Yes   ☐ No   ☐ Not determined

b If a is "Yes" or "Not determined," enter the employer identification number and the plan number used to identify it.
Employer identification number ▶   Plan number ▶

34 Current value of plan assets and liabilities at the beginning and end of the plan year. Combine the value of plan assets held in more than one trust. Allocate the value of the plan's interest in a commingled trust containing the assets of more than one plan on a line-by-line basis unless the trust meets one of the specific exceptions described in the instructions. Do not enter the value of that portion of an insurance contract which guarantees, during this plan year, to pay a specific dollar benefit at a future date. **Round off amounts to the nearest dollar; any other amounts are subject to rejection.** Plans with no assets at the beginning and the end of the plan year, enter zero on line f.

Assets		(a) Beginning of year	(b) End of Year
a	Total noninterest-bearing cash	a		
b	Receivables: **(1)** Employer contributions	b(1)		
	(2) Participant contributions	(2)		
	(3) Income	(3)		
	(4) Other	(4)		
	(5) Less allowance for doubtful accounts	(5)		
	(6) Total. Add b(1) through (4) and subtract (5) . . . . ▶	(6)		
c	General Investments: **(1)** Interest-bearing cash (including money market funds) . .	c(1)		
	(2) Certificates of deposit	(2)		
	(3) U.S. Government securities	(3)		
	(4) Corporate debt instruments: **(A)** Preferred	(4)(A)		
	(B) All other	(4)(B)		
	(5) Corporate stocks: **(A)** Preferred	(5)(A)		
	(B) Common	(5)(B)		
	(6) Partnership/joint venture interests	(6)		
	(7) Real estate: **(A)** Income-producing	(7)(A)		
	(B) Nonincome-producing	(7)(B)		
	(8) Loans (other than to participants) secured by mortgages: **(A)** Residential	(8)(A)		
	(B) Commercial	(8)(B)		
	(9) Loans to participants: **(A)** Mortgages	(9)(A)		
	(B) Other	(9)(B)		
	(10) Other loans	(10)		
	(11) Value of interest in common/collective trusts	(11)		
	(12) Value of interest in pooled separate accounts	(12)		
	(13) Value of interest in master trusts	(13)		
	(14) Value of interest in 103-12 investment entities	(14)		
	(15) Value of interest in registered investment companies	(15)		
	(16) Value of funds held in insurance company general account (unallocated contracts)	(16)		
	(17) Other	(17)		
	(18) Total. Add c(1) through c(17) . . . . ▶	(18)		
d	Employer-related investments: **(1)** Employer securities	d(1)		
	(2) Employer real property	(2)		
e	Buildings and other property used in plan operation	e		
f	**Total assets. Add a, b(6), c(18), d(1), d(2), and e** . . . . ▶	f		
	Liabilities			
g	Benefit claims payable	g		
h	Operating payables	h		
I	Acquisition indebtedness	I		
j	Other liabilities	j		
k	**Total liabilities. Add g through j** . . . . ▶	k		
	Net Assets			
l	Line f minus line k . . . . ▶	l		

Exhibit 11F

Form 5500 (1991)   Page 6

35 Plan income, expenses, and changes in net assets for the plan year. *Include all income and expenses of the plan, including any trust(s) or separately maintained fund(s), and any payments/receipts to/from insurance carriers.* **Round off amounts to the nearest dollar; any other amounts are subject to rejection.**

Income		(a) Amount	(b) Total
a Contributions:			
(1) Received or receivable from:			
(A) Employers	a(1)(A)		
(B) Participants	(B)		
(C) Others	(C)		
(2) Noncash contributions	(2)		
(3) Total contributions. Add a(1)(A), (B), (C) and a(2) ▶	(3)		
b Earnings on investments:			
(1) Interest			
(A) Interest-bearing cash (including money market funds)	b(1)(A)		
(B) Certificates of deposit	(B)		
(C) U.S. Government securities	(C)		
(D) Corporate debt instruments	(D)		
(E) Mortgage loans	(E)		
(F) Other loans	(F)		
(G) Other interest	(G)		
(H) Total interest. Add b(1)(A) through (G) ▶	(H)		
(2) Dividends: (A) Preferred stock	b(2)(A)		
(B) Common stock	(B)		
(C) Total dividends. Add b(2)(A) and (B) ▶	(C)		
(3) Rents	(3)		
(4) Net gain (loss) on sale of assets: (A) Aggregate proceeds	(4)(A)		
(B) Aggregate carrying amount (see instructions)	(B)		
(C) Subtract (B) from (A) and enter result	(C)		
(5) Unrealized appreciation (depreciation) of assets	(5)		
(6) Net investment gain (loss) from common/collective trusts	(6)		
(7) Net investment gain (loss) from pooled separate accounts	(7)		
(8) Net investment gain (loss) from master trusts	(8)		
(9) Net investment gain (loss) from 103-12 investment entities	(9)		
(10) Net investment gain (loss) from registered investment companies	(10)		
c Other income	c		
d Total income. Add all amounts in column (b) and enter total ▶	d		
Expenses			
e Benefit payment and payments to provide benefits:			
(1) Directly to participants or beneficiaries	e(1)		
(2) To insurance carriers for the provision of benefits	(2)		
(3) Other	(3)		
(4) Total payments. Add e(1) through (3) ▶	(4)		
f Interest expense	f		
g Administrative expenses: (1)*Salaries and allowances*	g(1)		
(2) Accounting fees	(2)		
(3) Actuarial fees	(3)		
(4) Contract administrator fees	(4)		
(5) Investment advisory and management fees	(5)		
(6) Legal fees	(6)		
(7) Valuation/appraisal fees	(7)		
(8) Trustees fees/expenses (including travel, seminars, meetings, etc.)	(8)		
(9) Other	(9)		
(10) Total administrative expenses. Add g(1) through (9)	(10)		
h Total expenses. Add e(4), f and g(10) ▶	h		
i Net income (loss). Subtract h from d	i		
j Transfers to (from) the plan (see instructions)	j		
k Net assets at beginning of year (Item 34, line I, column (a))	k		
l Net assets at end of year (Item 34, line I, column (b)) ▶	l		

	Yes	No
36 Did any employer sponsoring the plan pay any of the administrative expenses of the plan that were not reported in line 35g?		

5500.6   Published by Tax Management Inc., a Subsidiary of The Bureau of National Affairs, Inc.   12/30/91

Exhibit 11G

For example, let us presume that I am a trader with $100,000 net income on my Schedule C and no retirement plan for 1992. In April of 1993, I realize that I need to come up with a good way to shelter some income from the prior year to avoid an excessive tax liability. One way is to extend my 1992 tax return prior to April 15, 1993, paying the amount which would be due in taxes net of a 15% contribution (up to the maximum $30,000) to my SEP plan which I would not have to contribute to until the date I file my return, up through October 15, 1993. I could use the tax savings, from a future contribution, to earn money throughout that year and to add to the funds I would have to contribute to the plan by the deadline.

Qualified Retirement plans (KEOGHs)

Qualified retirement plans are simply retirement plans which have been sanctioned by the IRS and are commonly referred to as KEOGH plans. When approved, these plans may be used by an employer, and contributions to them will qualify as deductions from income. Self–employed persons may also establish these types of plans for themselves, as they are considered to be employees of their own businesses.

There are two major categories of qualified plans:
1. Defined Benefit – where the amount of benefits received is regulated.
2. Defined Contribution – where the amount of con-tribution is regulated;

1. A **Defined Benefit Plan** will provide for a set return in retirement as a percentage of salary or flat monthly amount. Actuaries will determine the amount of contribution necessary each year for the employees covered by such a plan. The determinants which influence this annual contribution depend on factors such as the amount to be distributed during retirement, the ages of the employees covered by the plan, and the growth of the plan over the past year. This amount is adjusted annually.

The actuary uses certain assumptions for mortality, interest, turnover, etc., to establish how much the employer must put into the plan to ensure that there are sufficient funds to provide for the promised benefit. These plans are most beneficial to self–employed persons or employers with very few or very young employees, with the employer being over age 50. This will allow for a maximum contribution for the employer and a minimum contribution for other employees. The objectives of the employer setting up this plan is to fund as much of the plan as possible in current and future years to generate as large a tax deduction for himself as possible. I will demonstrate the effectiveness of such a plan shortly, with an example of some recent retirement planning I have done.

2. A **Defined Contribution Plan** is the opposite of a Defined Benefit Plan in that it does not have a fixed benefit formula, but rather the contributions are the variables.

a. A **Money Purchase Plan** has a fixed contribution formula, such as 10% or 15% of income. This percentage, however, must be fixed from year to year, although the amount of contribution may vary depending on the income earned. It is limited to the lower of a 25% or $30,000 deductible contribution per year.

b. A **Profit Sharing Plan** is established to provide participation in the profit of a company by the employees. The overall percentage of contribution based on profit can vary from year to year; however, it must have a definite formula for allocating contributions among employees.

General rules governing qualified plans are as follows:

a. They must not discriminate among employees;
b. They must be in writing;
c. They must be of a long and indeterminate term;
d. There must be specific rules and regulations that govern eligibility, funding, and benefits. To maintain qualification, a plan must meet and maintain certain requirements.

Individuals can be excluded only for the following reasons:

a. Age – individuals under age 21 may be excluded; and
b. Service – plans may require up to three years of service for participation.

Vesting is when a participating employee's rights to the contributions are fully owned. The law permits the following two types of vesting in qualified plans.

The first of these is called the **Five–Year Cliff**. It requires that the employee be 100% vested after five years of service. The second method in which an employee can be vested is called the **Seven–Year Graded**. Under this type of vesting arrangement an employee must be partially vested after three years of service and fully vested after seven years. The schedule for vesting is 20% in the third year, and

187

an additional 20% in each year up through the seventh year when the employee will be 100% vested.

Defined Contribution Profit Sharing Plans allow a maximum contribution of 15% for one plan and 25% for two plans based on compensation, up to a maximum of $30,000. Like a SEP plan, contributions may be made to the plan up to the deadline for the tax return of the business or the personal return in the case of sole proprietor, including extensions. Unlike a SEP plan, the plan must be established by the end of the employer's fiscal year or December 31st in the case of a personal tax return.

Distributions from a qualified plan can be made for the following reasons:

      a. Separation from service: prior to age 59 1/2, there is a 10% premature distribution penalty plus tax on the amount unless the pay out is at age 55 of the participant or due to disability or death. In addition, a penalty can be avoided with a rollover as previously discussed.

      b. Disability: or physical impairment that prevents the individual from performing their job indefinitely.

      c. Death: payout to the beneficiary as in the case of an IRA.

      d. Normal distributions: may begin at age 59 1/2. The 10% excise tax is waived. Pay outs are taxable when received and are subject to voluntary withholding. Individuals can elect to have up to 10% withheld from their pay out to pay the income tax. Distributions must begin at age 70 1/2. **Note:** Starting January 1993 there will be a 20% withholding tax taken out of all retirement plan distributions paid to individuals.

Annuities

Annuities are another way to tax defer money for retirement. Annuities have often been characterized as "umbrellas" over investments that protect profits from taxes. As long as you leave your money invested in any annuity, your money compounds tax free. When you withdraw part or all of the money, the amount you withdraw becomes taxable income for that year.

Annuities can be qualified if they are employer–related. In such a case they would be subject to similar restrictions as other qualified plans.

Annuities which are not employment–related are nonqualified and can be self–directed. A self–directed annuity is a tax–sheltered mutual fund family in which you have a choice of investments. There are many annuities which have only one investment choice or a fixed interest account. But all self–directed annuities offer at least three investment choices – stock, bond, and money market funds. Because the money is tax deferred, you can move from one fund to the next with no tax liability. Also, in most annuities you can withdraw up to 10% of your money each year for whatever purpose you have without any penalty or commission. You would, nonetheless, be subject to income tax on this amount.

Annuities as originally started before IRAs were established were intended to help people provide for their retirements. At that time, before they were formally approved by Congress, insurance companies claimed that income taxes should be deferred on the interest earned until the money was withdrawn at retirement. At the time there was no provision for this in the IRS code, yet Congress allowed the tax deferred status by not specifically denying it. This provision was formally passed as part of the Economic Recovery Act of the 1980s which legitimized the concept of a tax–deferred annuity. Because of its tax deferred status, there is now a penalty of 10% on all amounts withdrawn from the annuity before age 59 1/2. This penalty should not deter you from contributing as it is more than made up for in several years of tax–free growth and compounding interest.

Unlike IRAs, SEPs, or KEOGHs, there is no deduction for a contribution to the annuity. However, similar to those vehicles, the earnings within the annuity are tax deferred. For that reason I would recommend contributing to a tax deferred annuity only after you have reached your full IRA, SEP, or KEOGH limitation.

You may contribute to some annuities as long as you wish, and unlike most retirement plans you are not necessarily required to start your withdrawals at the mandatory age of 70 1/2. When you do withdraw, you will be given several options of receiving distributions – cash, periodic payments, or allowing the account to annuitize (which means that the company will guarantee to pay you a monthly income for a specified number of years).

189

For those interested in self–directed annuities several sources are available. Some of the more well known self–directed annuities are offered by insurance companies such as Nationwide, Guardian, Anchor National, Keyport, Security Benefit, Kilico, and Golden America. You can probably find a local listing for them in your telephone directory.

A Case Study

Let us look at a hypothetical situation. Assume you are an investment/tax consultant now fully experienced in investment and retirement planning. A client comes to you needing to know what to do with $150,000. He thinks it best to put the money into a tax–free investment, and is leaning towards a tax free municipal bond.

Upon further discussion, it comes to your attention that this taxpayer has his own business (let us assume for instance that he is a full time trader and commodities advisor), has virtually no retirement plan, is making good income in his business, has no employees, and is currently 55 years old.

First of all, it should be clear to you that a tax–free municipal bond is not the best investment vehicle for a person in this situation. The primary tip off should be that he has no retirement plan in place and is relatively close to retirement. The type of retirement plan will then be determined by the more specific circumstances.

You would first advise him of the disadvantages of purchasing a municipal bond for such a large investment. In terms of the investment itself:

1. He would be locked into a fixed rate of return for a period of time significantly greater than would be available to him through other investments.

2. This fixed rate of return will drastically affect the value of the investment over time. Although he would be able to redeem the municipal bond at the due date for face value (assuming the liquidity of the issuer), the investor very well might be locked into this investment until that time. If interest rates increase from the current historically low levels as they are apt to, the investment, with a fixed rate of return, would be worth considerably less in the open market.

3. Given the current level of extremely low interest rates, and the prospect of a likely increase in rates in the near future, I would not advise the purchase of anything but very short–term fixed rate

investments (one to two years at the most). Chances are that a longer term fixed rate investment would decline in value significantly at some point soon.

4. Municipalities have been having trouble lately, and the future holds more of the same. Cities and states are being given less financial assistance from the federal government. Before investing in a municipal bond, one should consider the security of the investment in the event of a potential default by the municipality.

Secondly we should of advise the investor of the disadvantages of purchasing a municipal bond for such a large investment, in terms of the tax related issues:

c. Not all municipal bonds are 100% tax–free of federal taxes. Due to the expansion of the alternative minimum tax this year, many types of municipal bonds are taxable in varying degrees through the AMT. Namely, Private Activity Bonds are semi–taxable. The investor must monitor and evaluate his ongoing tax situation with regard to potential alternative minimum tax liability.

b. Municipal bonds are fully taxable to the state if the municipality issuing them is outside the investor's resident state. In other words, a New Jersey municipal bond, although tax–free on the federal tax return, would be 100% taxable on a New York State and New York City tax return. If the investor lived in New Jersey and purchased New York State municipal bonds the same situation would be true.

c. Most importantly, municipal bonds offer tax relief only on the income they produce. There are much better ways to invest for a greater tax benefit. This is especially true for the taxpayer who is in business for himself, not working for a salary, and who does not already have an extensive retirement plan.

When people consider retirement planning they are often intimidated by the prospect of tying up their money for a long period of time. This does not have to be the case. In addition, many people are under the misconception that they are severely limited in their choice of investments and types of planning.

This concern is not a valid one as there is a huge array of retirement plan options available. If the investor cannot find one that suits his specific needs, he can have one drafted for a relatively small fee. These plans would make available virtually any investment vehicle, any amount of contribution, and a very flexible distribution schedule to meet cash flow needs in the future.

This is particularly true of a taxpayer over age 55 who can make withdrawals from the plan without penalty for premature distribution at any age after 59 1/2.

Lastly, I would briefly explain the types of plans available, as discussed earlier in this section, and put forth both the advantages and disadvantages to tne investor of each type of plan. Basically, for someone in his particular situation, a defined benefit plan would be optimal. The reason is that it can be funded to provide for a set return per year after a certain retirement age as selected in the plan. For maximum benefit I would suggest five–year funding for someone who is aged 55 1/2 or so.

The annual contribution would be precisely determined by an actuary and would be dependent on factors such as age, projected retirement age, and the projected annual distributions. We would be able to allow for much greater flexibility in the design of this plan than in a defined contribution plan. For the taxpayer who is self–employed, in his late 50s, with no other employees, and with no significant retirement plan, the tax savings of doing this would be a real bonanza.

The way this retirement plan works is to give the taxpayer a dollar–for–dollar deduction from taxable income for every contribution made to this plan. In addition, all income earned within the plan would be tax deferred until it is withdrawn. This concept can be thought of as creating "double duty retirement dollars."

Let us examine more specifically the way this works. Let us further assume that in 1992 this taxpayer had $150,000 in earned income. Also, let us assume that we have set up a defined benefit KEOGH plan which allowed him to contribute $100,000 in 1992 to fund his retirement. Looking at this example with the taxpayer in the 35% tax bracket (federal and state combined) the tax savings would be calculated as follows:

	Without KEOGH	**With KEOGH**
Net Income	$150,000	$150,000
Less:Contribution	0	100,000
Taxable Income	150,000	50,000
Tax Rate	.35	.35
Tax Due	$52,500	$17,500

Summary:

Tax Due without KEOGH	$52,500
Tax Due with KEOGH	−17,500
Tax Savings	$35,000

As you can see, the taxpayer would save approximately $35,000 in taxes per $100,000 contributed to the fund. The following year he would be able to do the same thing, using some of these tax savings to fund the plan. As we have seen in the table on page 176 that compares the growth of a $2,000, $4,000, and $10,000 investment over 30 years, the thing just keeps on growing. In addition to earning tax deferred income on the investment, the investor would actually get a free gift from the government for whatever his tax rate is multiplied by the amount of contribution. In this case, $100,000 times 35% equals $35,000.

The best part of this is that as a taxpayer who makes a living from trading and providing investment–related services, he would be able to do most of his trading within the plan. Retirement plans can now be set up to accommodate commodity trading or virtually any other type of investment. By doing this, he would be able to generate a tax deferred profit from trading. The only income he would then have to shelter from taxes would be the income earned from his other line of work, investment advisory services. This can easily be accomplished within the structure of the plan.

By sheltering income this way, tax reduction would not be done through any form of tax loophole or other such scam, but rather through a legitimate strategy utilizing one of the last few remaining "tax shelters" under current law. There is nothing wrong with or illegal about tax avoidance if it is accomplished by knowledgeable tax and investment planning, combined with a well thought out retirement plan.

There are several more techniques I would relate to the near retirement aged investor in drawing out a potential retirement plan strategy. I will not go into detail on any of them here, but rather will discuss them more fully in the final section of this book entitled "50 Tax Reduction Strategies–Read My Tips."

Conclusion

The lesson of this section, I believe, should be that retirement planning is one of the most significant forms of tax reduction available to the taxpayer. Furthermore, at this point, retirement plans are quite flexible and can be tailored to meet your own particular needs.

If you cannot find a "prefabricated" standard plan which permits you to direct your investment in the vehicle you wish, an alternative to this would be to have your own plan written by an attorney or a CPA and submitted to the IRS for approval. I have done this many times, particularly for traders of a wide range of ages who would like to earn tax deferred income within the plan and use that money to trade a wide array of investment vehicles.

I have created plans which allow for the purchase and sale of options, both equity and index, the writing and purchase of covered puts and calls, the trading of all types of commodities, and virtually any other type of investment which is not specifically excluded by law.

The tax rules present you with an almost unlimited assortment of investments acceptable for your KEOGH or IRA. In fact, the only things specifically excluded are:

1. Collectibles – such as art, Persian rugs, and precious coins, except for the exceptions mentioned later in "50 Tax Reduction Strategies–Read My Tips."

2. Mortgaged rental property – or any investment in which your account would be used as collateral or security for a loan. The IRS treats an IRA used as security in such a manner as if you had withdrawn the money.

3. A business in which you own more than a 5% interest.

A self–directed retirement plan is one of the best ways to shelter your income from taxes and provide for your retirement.

Never invest in a **tax–free** vehicle with your retirement money. Tax–free vehicles generally have a lower rate of return because they are tax–free and that factor has been calculated into their yield. Since the income within the plan is tax–free until it is withdrawn because of the retirement plan status, why get a lower yield from such items as municipals, U.S. Treasuries, or other such tax exempts?

It would not be prudent for you to invest in such tax exempt items because you can earn a higher rate of return in other invest-

194

ments like mutual funds, discount mortgages, or other growth items. As we have demonstrated over and over again in this book, the fact that these investments can grow and compound tax free over the years increases their true yield significantly.

We will now discuss another strategy for sheltering your wealth in the next section entitled "Transferring Your Wealth To Future Generations."

Chapter 12

Transferring Your Wealth to Future Generations

They Don't Make Hearses With Luggage Racks

You can't take it with you so you had better decide what to do with all the wealth you've accumulated by following the tax strategies of this book before the government does it for you.

As Charles J. Givens puts it:

> "While you are alive, the IRS will attempt to take what you've made. When you are not, the IRS will attempt to take what it missed."[39]

There are two phases to transferring wealth. The first phase is how to transfer as much of your assets to future generations while you are still alive, and the second is how to keep as much of your wealth as possible out of your taxable estate upon your death. The first phase is commonly referred to as **gifting** and has several benefits. In addition to contributing to the second goal of bypassing estate taxes in the future, it can be used in and of itself to transfer income to relatives in lower tax brackets than yours. In this way, less overall tax will get paid on the income the investment generates.

Many people put off the second phase, **estate tax planning,** because thinking about dying, especially thinking about your own death, is not very pleasant. In addition, it is a very complicated area and one which is too often misunderstood. Many people are misinformed and assume that estate tax planning is no longer necessary. They are under the false impression that the estate tax has been repealed, that there is no longer a need to plan an estate, and that under current laws everything will automatically go to their spouse and/or heirs without any problem anyway.

Good estate planning is directly related to a policy of annual gifting to your family. A good estate plan must also consider taxes, probate, insurance, investing, charitable contributions, and family wealth distribution. It is much more involved than simply avoiding taxes; it also involves determining the manner in which you want your property distributed and how this can be done with a minimum of administrative and legal expenses.

In his book, *Tax Liberty*, Robert C. Carlson, J.D., C.P.A., states the following:

> [This discussion of estate tax planning will] point you toward the biggest tax saving opportunities of your life. Why the biggest? Because estate taxes are your final tax bill, and can be the largest taxes your family will have to face. You still have to plan to ensure that the assets will go to your heirs, not the tax collector or lawyer. What's more, good estate planning can help cut taxes **during** your lifetime.[40]

Using The Annual Gift Tax Exemption

The easiest way to reduce your gross estate is to set up a program of gifting your assets annually to your heirs while you are still alive. The law provides for up to $10,000 of property per year to be given from any one person to any other person without gift tax being incurred except with regard to the Generation Skipping Transfer Tax (I will explain The Generation Skipping Transfer Tax further in the next section). If a married couple is making the gift together, regardless of whose property or cash is being gifted, the annual exclusion from gift taxes is $20,000 to any other person. There is no limit on how many different people you can give gifts to each year using the $20,000 per couple exclusion. There is also no limit on the amount of cash or property which can be given to your spouse.

There is never any gift tax due from the person receiving the gift. It is only the person making the gift who may be subject to gift taxes. There are two further exemptions from gift tax, one for education and one for medical expense. In addition to the $10,000 per person per recipient per year limit, you can give away or receive any amount of money for education paid directly to an educational institution and/or for medical expenses paid to a healthcare provider.

Money given to minor children under a gifting program should not be used for necessities such as food, clothing, shelter, or medical care. A parent is legally obligated to provide these items, and because of that they do not qualify for the annual gift exclusion.

When your gifts to any one beneficiary exceed the $20,000 per couple exclusion, you can start to utilize your unified credit, which, as I will explain more fully, is $600,000 per person per lifetime. Any amount of this credit is used up while making gifts during a person's lifetime cannot be used to offset the estate tax upon his death.

If your policy of gifting is well planned, you can entirely avoid using up any unified credit. It then will be fully available to offset the estate tax on the first $600,000 of taxable estate upon your death. Meanwhile, throughout your lifetime you will be transferring your wealth to your heirs, tax–free.

If in any year you generate a taxable gift (above the limits just discussed) you must file a Form 709, Federal Gift Tax Return (see Exhibits 12A, 12B, 12C, and 12D). On this tax return you report the amount of the gift, the beneficiary of the gift, and you calculate the amount of unified credit used in making the gift. Once you exceed this lifetime exclusion, you calculate the tax on the gift as if it were a taxable estate item. All gifts are valued at fair market value at the date the gift is made. If it is a publicly traded stock or similar type item, you determine **mean valuation** by taking an average of the high and low price for the day.

Consideration: Generation Skipping Transfer Tax

If a transfer is made between generations out of sequence, there is an additional surtax on the transfer regardless of whether or not it exceeds the annual gift tax exclusion. In other words, if as a grandparent, you transfer an asset to your grandchild, without first gifting it to your child and then having your child gift it to the grandchild, you will be subject to this surtax. There is a $1,000,000 lifetime exemption per person making the gift (giftor).

Essentially, the government does not want to bypass one level of taxation on the transfer of wealth between generations.

Consideration: Basis When Making Gifts

Don't give away property that shows an unrealized loss. When a recipient receives property as a gift, his or her basis will be the lower of the properties' fair market value or the giftor's basis at the time of the gift.

199

The Serious Investor's Tax Survival Guide

Form **709**

United States Gift (and Generation-Skipping Transfer) Tax Return

(Rev. November 1991)

(Section 6019 of the Internal Revenue Code) (For gifts made after October 8, 1990, and before January 1, 1993)

Department of the Treasury
Internal Revenue Service

Calendar year 19 ....

▶ See separate instructions. For Privacy Act Notice, see the Instructions for Form 1040.

OMB No. 1545-0020
Expires 8-31-93

Part 1.—General Information

1 Donor's first name and middle initial	2 Donor's last name	3 Social security number
4 Address (number, street, and apartment number)		5 Legal residence (Domicile)
6 City, state, and ZIP code		7 Citizenship

		Yes	No
8	If the donor died during the year, check here ▶ ☐ and enter date of death........................... 19		
9	If you received an extension of time to file this Form 709, check here ▶ ☐ and attach the Form 4868, 2688, 2350, or extension letter		
10	Enter the total number of separate donees listed on Schedule A—count each person only once .... ☐		
11a	Have you (the donor) previously filed a Form 709 (or 709-A) for any other year? If the answer is "No," do not complete line 11b.		
11b	If the answer to line 11a is "Yes," has your address changed since you last filed Form 709 (or 709-A)?		
12	Gifts by husband or wife to third parties.—Do you consent to have the gifts (including generation-skipping transfers) made by you and by your spouse to third parties during the calendar year considered as made one-half by each of you? (See instructions.) (If the answer is "Yes," the following information must be furnished and your spouse must sign the consent shown below. If the answer is "No," skip lines 13–18 and go to Schedule A.)		
13	Name of consenting spouse	14 SSN		
15	Were you married to one another during the entire calendar year? (See instructions.)		
16	If the answer to 15 is "No," check whether ☐ married ☐ divorced or ☐ widowed, and give date (see instructions) ▶		
17	Will a gift tax return for this calendar year be filed by your spouse?		
18	Consent of Spouse—I consent to have the gifts (and generation-skipping transfers) made by me and by my spouse to third parties during the calendar year considered as made one-half by each of us. We are both aware of the joint and several liability for tax created by the execution of this consent.		

Consenting spouse's signature ▶   Date ▶

Part 2.—Tax Computation

1	Enter the amount from Schedule A, Part 3, line 15	1	
2	Enter the amount from Schedule B, line 3	2	
3	Total taxable gifts (add lines 1 and 2)	3	
4	Tax computed on amount on line 3 (see Table for Computing Tax in separate instructions)	4	
5	Tax computed on amount on line 2 (see Table for Computing Tax in separate instructions)	5	
6	Balance (subtract line 5 from line 4)	6	
7	Maximum unified credit (nonresident aliens, see instructions)	7	192,800 00
8	Enter the unified credit against tax allowable for all prior periods (from Sch. B, line 1, col. C)	8	
9	Balance (subtract line 8 from line 7)	9	
10	Enter 20% (.20) of the amount allowed as a specific exemption for gifts made after September 8, 1976, and before January 1, 1977 (see instructions)	10	
11	Balance (subtract line 10 from line 9)	11	
12	Unified credit (enter the smaller of line 6 or line 11)	12	
13	Credit for foreign gift taxes (see instructions)	13	
14	Total credits (add lines 12 and 13)	14	
15	Balance (subtract line 14 from line 6) (do not enter less than zero)	15	
16	Generation-skipping transfer taxes (from Schedule C, Part 3, col. H, total)	16	
17	Total tax (add lines 15 and 16)	17	
18	Gift and generation-skipping transfer taxes prepaid with extension of time to file	18	
19	If line 18 is less than line 17, enter BALANCE DUE (see instructions)	19	
20	If line 18 is greater than line 17, enter AMOUNT TO BE REFUNDED	20	

Please attach check or money order here.

Under penalties of perjury, I declare that I have examined this return, including any accompanying schedules and statements, and to the best of my knowledge and belief it is true, correct, and complete. Declaration of preparer (other than donor) is based on all information of which preparer has any knowledge.

Donor's signature ▶   Date ▶

Preparer's signature (other than donor) ▶   Date ▶

Preparer's address (other than donor) ▶

For Paperwork Reduction Act Notice, see page 1 of the separate instructions for this form.   Cat. No. 16783M   Form **709** (Rev. 11-91)

Exhibit 12A

Form 709 (Rev. 11-91)   Page **2**

SCHEDULE A   Computation of Taxable Gifts

Part 1.—Gifts Subject Only to Gift Tax. *Gifts less political organization, medical, and educational exclusions—see instructions*

A Item number	B Donee's name, relationship to donor (if any), and address and description of gift. If the gift was made by means of a trust, enter trust's identifying number below and attach a copy of the trust instrument. If the gift was securities, enter the CUSIP number(s), if available.	C Donor's adjusted basis of gift	D Date of gift	E Value at date of gift
1				

Part 2.—Gifts Which are Direct Skips and are Subject to Both Gift Tax and Generation-Skipping Transfer Tax. You must list the gifts in chronological order. *Gifts less political organization, medical, and educational exclusions—see instructions. (Also list here direct skips that are subject only to the GST tax at this time as the result of the termination of an "estate tax inclusion period." See instructions.)*

A Item number	B Donee's name, relationship to donor (if any), and address and description of gift. If the gift was made by means of a trust, enter trust's identifying number below and attach a copy of the trust instrument. If the gift was securities, enter the CUSIP number(s), if available.	C Donor's adjusted basis of gift	D Date of gift	E Value at date of gift
1				

Part 3.—Gift Tax Reconciliation

1	Total value of gifts of donor (add column E of Parts 1 and 2)	1
2	One-half of items ....attributable to spouse (see instructions)	2
3	Balance (subtract line 2 from line 1)	3
4	Gifts of spouse to be included (from Schedule A, Part 3, line 2 of spouse's return—see instructions) . .	4
	If any of the gifts included on this line are also subject to the generation-skipping transfer tax, check here ▶ ☐ and enter those gifts also on Schedule C, Part 1.	
5	Total gifts (add lines 3 and 4)	5
6	Total annual exclusions for gifts listed on Schedule A (including line 4, above) (see instructions) . . .	6
7	Total included amount of gifts (subtract line 6 from line 5)	7
Deductions (see instructions)		
8	Gifts of interests to spouse for which a marital deduction will be claimed, based on items ....of Schedule A	8	
9	Exclusions attributable to gifts on line 8	9	
10	Marital deduction—subtract line 9 from line 8	10	
11	Charitable deduction, based on items ....to ....less exclusions .	11	
12	Total deductions—add lines 10 and 11	12
13	Subtract line 12 from line 7	13
14	Generation-skipping transfer taxes payable with this Form 709 (from Schedule C, Part 3, col. H, Total) .	14
15	Taxable gifts (add lines 13 and 14). Enter here and on line 1 of the Tax Computation on page 1 . . .	15

(If more space is needed, attach additional sheets of same size.)

709.2   Published by Tax Management Inc., a Subsidiary of The Bureau of National Affairs, Inc.   12/30/91

Exhibit 12B

Form 709 (Rev. 11-91)   Page **3**

| **SCHEDULE A** | Computation of Taxable Gifts *(continued)* |

16 Terminable Interest (QTIP) Marital Deduction. (See instructions.)

If a trust (or other property) meets the requirements of qualified terminable interest property under section 2523(f), and

   a. the trust (or other property) is listed on Schedule A, and

   b. the value of the trust (or other property) is entered in whole or in part as a deduction on line 8, Part 3 of Schedule A,

then the donor shall be deemed to have made an election to have such trust (or other property) treated as qualified terminable interest property under section 2523(f).

   If less than the entire value of the trust (or other property) that the donor has included in Part 1 of Schedule A is entered as a deduction on line 8, the donor shall be considered to have made an election only as to a fraction of the trust (or other property). The numerator of this fraction is equal to the amount of the trust (or other property) deducted on line 10 of Part 3. The denominator is equal to the total value of the trust (or other property) listed in Part 1 of Schedule A.

   If you make the QTIP election (see instructions for line 8 of Schedule A), the terminable interest property involved will be included in your spouse's gross estate upon his or her death (section 2044). If your spouse disposes (by gift or otherwise) of all or part of the qualifying life income interest, he or she will be considered to have made a transfer of the entire property that is subject to the gift tax (see Transfer of Certain Life Estates on page 3 of the instructions).

17 Election out of QTIP Treatment of Annuities

☐ ◄ Check here if you elect under section 2523(f)(6) **NOT** to treat as qualified terminable interest property any joint and survivor annuities that are reported on Schedule A and would otherwise be treated as qualified terminable interest property under section 2523(f). (See instructions.) Enter the item numbers (from Schedule A) for the annuities for which you are making this election ►

| **SCHEDULE B** | Gifts From Prior Periods |

If you answered "Yes" on line 11a of Page 1, Part 1, **see the instructions for completing Schedule B. If your answer is "No," skip to the Tax Computation on Page 1 (or Schedule C, if applicable).**

A Calendar year or calendar quarter (see instructions)	B Internal Revenue office where prior return was filed	C Amount of unified credit against gift tax for periods after December 31, 1976	D Amount of specific exemption for prior periods ending before January 1, 1977	E Amount of taxable gifts

1 Totals for prior periods (without adjustment for reduced specific exemption)	**1**		
2 Amount, if any, by which total specific exemption, line 1, column D, is more than $30,000	**2**		
3 Total amount of taxable gifts for prior periods (add amount, column E, line 1, and amount, if any, on line 2) (Enter here and on line 2 of the Tax Computation on page 1.)	**3**		

(If more space is needed, attach additional sheets of same size.)

12/30/91   Published by Tax Management Inc., a Subsidiary of The Bureau of National Affairs, Inc.   709.3

Exhibit 12C

Form 709 (Rev. 11-91)   Page **4**

SCHEDULE C   Computation of Generation-Skipping Transfer Tax

Note: *Inter vivos direct skips which are completely excluded by the GST exemption must still be fully reported (including value and exemptions claimed) on Schedule C.*

Part 1.—Generation-Skipping Transfers

A Item No. (from Schedule A, Part 2, col. A)	B Value (from Schedule A, Part 2, col. E)	C Split Gifts (enter ½ of col. B) (see instructions)	D Subtract col. C from col. B	E Nontaxable portion of transfer	F Net Transfer (subtract col. E from col. D)
1					
2					
3					
4					
5					
6					

	Split gifts from spouse's Form 709 (enter item number)	Value included from spouse's Form 709	Nontaxable portion of transfer	Net transfer (subtract col. E from col. D)
If you elected gift splitting and your spouse was required to file a separate Form 709 (see the instructions for "Split Gifts"), you must enter all of the gifts shown on Schedule A, Part 2, of your spouse's Form 709 here.	S-			
In column C, enter the item number of each gift in the order it appears in column A of your spouse's Schedule A, Part 2. We have preprinted the prefix "S-" to distinguish your spouse's item numbers from your own when you complete column A of Schedule C, Part 3.	S- S- S- S-			
In column D, for each gift, enter the amount reported in column C, Schedule C, Part 1, of your spouse's Form 709.	S- S- S- S-			

Part 2.—GST Exemption Reconciliation (Code section 2631) and Section 2652(a)(3) Election

Check box ▶ ☐ if you are making a section 2652(a)(3) (special QTIP) election (see instructions)

Enter the item numbers (from Schedule A) of the gifts for which you are making this election ▶ ....

1	Maximum allowable exemption	1	$1,000,000
2	Total exemption used for periods before filing this return	2	
3	Exemption available for this return (subtract line 2 from line 1)	3	
4	Exemption claimed on this return (from Part 3, col. C total, below)	4	
5	Exemption allocated to transfers not shown on Part 3, below. You must attach a Notice of Allocation. (See instructions.)	5	
6	Add lines 4 and 5	6	
7	Exemption available for future transfers (subtract line 6 from line 3)	7	

Part 3.—Tax Computation

A Item No. (from Schedule C, Part 1)	B Net transfer (from Schedule C, Part 1, col. F)	C GST Exemption Allocated	D Divide col. C by col. B	E Inclusion Ratio (subtract col. D from 1.000)	F Maximum Estate Tax Rate	G Applicable Rate (multiply col. E by col. F)	H Generation-Skipping Transfer Tax (multiply col. B by col. G)
1					55% (.55)		
2					55% (.55)		
3					55% (.55)		
4					55% (.55)		
5					55% (.55)		
6					55% (.55)		
					55% (.55)		
					55% (.55)		
					55% (.55)		
					55% (.55)		

| Total exemption claimed. Enter here and on line 4, Part 2, above. May not exceed line 3, Part 2, above . . . . . | | **Total generation-skipping transfer tax.** Enter here, on line 14 of Schedule A, Part 3, and on line 16 of the Tax Computation on page 1 . . . . | | |

(If more space is needed, attach additional sheets of same size.)

Exhibit 12D

If you give away property that has an unrealized loss or, in other words, the fair market value is lower than the price you paid for the property, no one gets to take the unrealized loss as a deduction. The loss is gone forever as a tax deduction.

But, if you sell the property first, you get to deduct the loss. Then you can give away the cash you receive from the sale of the property and there will still be money left over because of the tax savings for deducting the loss.

Consideration: Property Size When Making Gifts

You can give away any type of property, in any size you wish, in order to remain within the limits of your $20,000 per couple, per person gift tax exemption. If you own a large portfolio of stocks, your spouse and you, jointly, can give away $20,000 worth of shares each year.

Any real estate you have can be divided into $10,000 pieces each year, although legal and title expenses involved could be prohibitive. With real estate one technique used is to sell the property to the person you will be gifting it to and take back a 100% mortgage from them. Then your spouse and you can forgive $20,000 worth of the principal each year as is covered by the annual exclusion.

Using Estate Tax Planning Strategies

Good estate tax planning is a very sophisticated area and should not be attempted alone. This section is meant to familiarize you with the basic concepts, not to make you an expert. You should still consult with a competent estate tax planner to finalize your blueprint.

There are several basic ways to approach estate tax planning:

1. A strategy which focuses on **keeping property out of your gross estate**. One way to achieve this would be, again, to gift as much of your property to your heirs while you are still alive. The point here is to try to move as much of your wealth to your heirs without using up the unified credit. Basically, the **unified credit** is a $600,000 tax credit on transferred assets either through your estate or through gifting above and beyond the amount allowed to be gifted tax free each year. Transfers to a spouse, however, can be unlimited since they are not subject to gift and estate taxation and do not use up the unified credit.

2. A strategy which focuses on **maximizing estate tax deductions**. For example, you could set up a provision to pay your son a salary as executor of your estate upon your death. The salary would be an administrative deduction from the estate which would be deductible against taxable estate income at, perhaps, the maximum rate of 55%. The amount that he received would have to be reported as taxable income on his personal tax return at whatever tax rate he was in, which in 1992 would be a maximum of 31%. This is still considerably less than the 55% maximum estate tax rate.

On the other hand, you could have your son be the executor without any salary. In which case, however, he could still receive the money, however it would now be taxed at the estate tax rate, maximum 55%.

3. A strategy which focuses on **maximizing tax credits**, such as for donations to charity or credit for state taxes paid.

4. A strategy which focuses on carrying adequate **estate insurance** to meet all of the tax liabilities. Under this strategy you do not focus on the amount of estate taxes as long as there is enough insurance outside your estate to cover the tax bill.

Other specific strategies for reducing estate taxes using the four methods above will be included in the section, "50 Tax Reduction Strategies–Read My Tips."

The estate tax is levied on the entire estate before the assets are passed down to the heirs. It is not an inheritance tax to be paid by the beneficiary when they received an inheritance. The estate is liable for the entire tax before anything is distributed. Beneficiaries of a will do not have to pay federal estate taxes on property received.

The gross estate is all of the property you owned, valued at its fair market value at the time of your death. There is another way to value a gross estate. Called the **alternate valuation**, it is the value of all the assets six months after the date of death. From the gross estate, deductions are subtracted such as marital, administrative, charitable, and the unified credit. This leaves your taxable estate, against which the estate tax rate is applied to produce the estate tax due (see the estate tax table to follow for current rates).

Other considerations in addressing estate tax planning are as follows:

1. **Be Certain Your Property is Fairly Valued.**

Since the estate tax is based on the value of your property, it is critical that you determine an accurate estimate of how much your property is worth before doing any estate tax planning.

Most people either underestimate or overestimate the value of their estates. Some people don't realize that inflation has increased the value of their assets. An estate worth more than $600,000 is not that unusual when you consider items such as a home, pension, investments, insurance, and possibly a business, in addition to the usual personal assets. In this case you will need to plan your estate rigorously to avoid paying most of it to the government and attorneys.

On the other hand, your assets, such as real estate, might have lost a substantial amount of their value during the 1980s, in which case you need only a very simple estate plan. You should use the services of a reputable appraiser in determining your estate valuation. The benefit of estate planning is directly related to the accuracy of your estimate of the estate's value.

2. **Property You Control is also Considered to be Property You Own**.

The government did not want you to be able to avoid paying estate tax by keeping control of property while putting the title in someone else's name. You cannot reduce estate taxes by putting property into a living trust which pays you income for life, but gives the remainder to a beneficiary after your death. You will still be considered the owner of the property you put into a trust if you retain the right to amend or revoke the trust.

3. **Check Your Estate for Any Hidden Assets**.

If you have given away property in the past, but retained power or some other interest in the property, it could be included in your estate. Sometimes you may have received a seemingly small, contingent interest in an estate from either a parent or a spouse. This might cause this entire property to be valued in your estate at your time of death.

Sometimes, in someone else's will, you are given the power to determine who gets a particular piece of property after their death. This power could cause the property to be included in your estate, even if you do not exercise the power.

4. **Be On the Lookout For Situations Where a Person Does Not Have Enough Property**.

In some cases a person may not have enough property to take full advantage of the $600,000 estate tax exemption. If this is the case you should consider making what is known as a reverse gift to this person even if he is elderly or ill and possibly on the verge of dying.

Property that passes through a descendant's estate gets what is known as a stepped up basis. That is, the person who inherits it is treated for income tax purposes as if he bought it and paid what it is worth on the date of death (or six months subsequent, if alternate valuation is used).

For example, Mrs. Z, a cancer patient, has $50,000 worth of assets. Her husband has a large estate including $500,000 worth of stock with a basis of $100,000. That means he has $400,000 worth of taxable gain built into the stock. Mr. Z gives the stock to his wife. There is no tax on gifts between spouses. Mrs. X sets up a revocable living trust and leaves the stock to the children. The children inherit the stock with the basis stepped up to $500,000. Thus, if they turn around and sell it for $500,000 there is no taxable gain.

With these shares Mrs. Z's estate is still $550,000 and under the exempt amount of $600,000. The stepped up basis is achieved without paying estate tax and the property is taken out of Mr. Z's estate where it might be taxed due to additional property he might have over the $600,000 exclusion.

5. **Married Individuals Can Leave All of Their Assets to Their Spouse Free of Any Estate Tax**.

This sounds like a real bonanza, however, unless a careful plan is drawn up, the overall tax burden on a married couple could end up being more than it should.

If property passes entirely to the spouse, it must be included in the surviving spouse's taxable estate. Assuming the survivor dies without depleting the estate, that second estate will be subject to tax on the full inherited amount plus its appreciated value. A better policy is to allow part of the property to be passed on through the lifetime $600,000 exclusion to a son or a daughter through a revocable living trust. More will be discussed on this method in point #9.

6. **Life Insurance is a Significant Part of Your Wealth and Should be Kept Out of Your Estate**.

Life insurance proceeds will not be considered part of your estate if you did not own the policy. A simple way to arrive at this is to have your spouse own the policy and pay the premiums. You can give your spouse the money to make the payments as long as the money is kept separate from your account and the spouse writes a separate check for each premium payment.

You can do the same thing with a child. Alternatively you can also create an irrevocable life insurance trust. The trust owns the insurance policy but you can make a gift to the trust each year that is used to pay the premium. When you die the proceeds are paid to the trust which in turn pays them to the beneficiaries according to stipulations set up in the trust.

   7. **Types of Assets Which Comprise Most Estates Fall into Six Categories**:

   a. Your residence;
   b. Tangible personal property, such as furniture, jewelry, paintings, cars, boats, etc.;
   c. Investment real estate, such as houses or buildings not occupied by their owners but rented to tenants;
   d. Your closely–held business whether its a sole proprietorship, an interest in a partnership, or an interest in a controlled corporation;
   e. Checking accounts, savings accounts, certificates of deposit, stocks and bonds, the sum of your liquid assets except for insurance proceeds; and
   f. Proceeds of life insurance.

   See Exhibits 12E, 12F, and 12G for the estate tax return Form 706 to examine how they should be precisely listed on this form.

   8. **The Estate Tax Table**.

   The estate tax table, with the current rates of taxation is as follows:

ESTATE TAX TABLE[41]

Size of **Taxable** Estate	Amount of Tax	Plus % of Excess
$100,000	$18,200	28%
150,000	23,800	30
250,000	38,800	32
500,000	70,800	34
1,000,000	248,300	39
2,500,000	780,800	45
3,000,000	1,025,800	55

   Although the tax law gives everyone a $600,000 exemption from estate taxes, they consider a married couple to be the same as **one person** for the purposes of determining this exemption! In order not to be confined to only one exemption, a couple must take specific action to separate and identify their assets by creating a revocable living trust.

Form **706** (Rev. October 1991) Department of the Treasury Internal Revenue Service	**United States Estate (and Generation-Skipping Transfer) Tax Return** Estate of a citizen or resident of the United States (see separate instructions). To be filed for decedents dying after October 8, 1990, and before January 1, 1993. For Paperwork Reduction Act Notice, see page 1 of the instructions.	OMB No. 1545-0015 Expires 6-30-93

Part 1.—Decedent and Executor

1a Decedent's first name and middle initial (and maiden name, if any)	1b Decedent's last name		2 Decedent's social security no.
3a Domicile at time of death (county and state, or foreign country)	3b Year domicile established	4 Date of birth	5 Date of death
6a Name of executor (see instructions)	6b Executor's address (number and street including apartment or suite no. or rural route; city, town, or post office; state; and ZIP code)		
6c Executor's social security number (see instructions)			
7a Name and location of court where will was probated or estate administered			7b Case number
8 If decedent died testate, check here ▶ ☐ and attach a certified copy of the will.	9 If Form 4768 is attached, check here ▶ ☐		
10 If Schedule R-1 is attached, check here ▶ ☐			

Part 2.—Tax Computation

1	Total gross estate (from Part 5, Recapitulation, page 3, item 10)	**1**	
2	Total allowable deductions (from Part 5, Recapitulation, page 3, item 20)	**2**	
3	Taxable estate (subtract line 2 from line 1)	**3**	
4	Adjusted taxable gifts (total taxable gifts (within the meaning of section 2503) made by the decedent after December 31, 1976, other than gifts that are includible in decedent's gross estate (section 2001(b))	**4**	
5	Add lines 3 and 4	**5**	
6	Tentative tax on the amount on line 5 from Table A in the instructions	**6**	
7a	If line 5 exceeds $10,000,000, enter the lesser of line 5 or $21,040,000. If line 5 is $10,000,000 or less, skip lines 7a and 7b and enter -0- on line 7c . **7a**		
b	Subtract $10,000,000 from line 7a **7b**		
c	Enter 5% (.05) of line 7b	**7c**	
8	Total tentative tax (add lines 6 and 7c)	**8**	
9	Total gift tax payable with respect to gifts made by the decedent after December 31, 1976. Include gift taxes by the decedent's spouse for such spouse's share of split gifts (section 2513) only if the decedent was the donor of these gifts and they are includible in the decedent's gross estate (see instructions)	**9**	
10	Gross estate tax (subtract line 9 from line 8)	**10**	
11	Maximum unified credit against estate tax **11** 192,800 00		
12	Adjustment to unified credit. (This adjustment may not exceed $6,000. See instructions.). **12**		
13	Allowable unified credit (subtract line 12 from line 11)	**13**	
14	Subtract line 13 from line 10 (but do not enter less than zero)	**14**	
15	Credit for state death taxes. Do not enter more than line 14. Compute the credit by using the amount on line 3 less $60,000. See Table B in the instructions and **attach credit evidence** (see instructions)	**15**	
16	Subtract line 15 from line 14	**16**	
17	Credit for Federal gift taxes on pre-1977 gifts (section 2012) (attach computation) **17**		
18	Credit for foreign death taxes (from Schedule P). (Attach Form(s) 706CE) **18**		
19	Credit for tax on prior transfers (from Schedule Q) **19**		
20	Total (add lines 17, 18, and 19)	**20**	
21	Net estate tax (subtract line 20 from line 16)	**21**	
22	Generation-skipping transfer taxes (from Schedule R, Part 2, line 10)	**22**	
23	Section 4980A increased estate tax (from Schedule S, Part I, line 17) (see instructions)	**23**	
24	Total transfer taxes (add lines 21, 22, and 23)	**24**	
25	Prior payments. Explain in an attached statement **25**		
26	United States Treasury bonds redeemed in payment of estate tax . . **26**		
27	Total (add lines 25 and 26)	**27**	
28	Balance due (or overpayment) (subtract line 27 from line 24)	**28**	

Under penalties of perjury, I declare that I have examined this return, including accompanying schedules and statements, and to the best of my knowledge and belief, it is true, correct, and complete. Declaration of preparer other than the executor is based on all information of which preparer has any knowledge.

Signature(s) of executor(s)   Date

Signature of preparer other than executor   Address (and ZIP code)   Date

Cat. No. 20548R

Exhibit 12E

Form 706 (Rev. 10-91)

Estate of:

Part 3.—Elections by the Executor

Please check the "Yes" or "No" box for each question.	Yes	No
1 Do you elect alternate valuation?		
2 Do you elect special use valuation? . . . . If "Yes," you must complete and attach Schedule A–1	/////	/////
3 Do you elect to pay the taxes in installments as described in section 6166? . . . . If "Yes," you must attach the additional information described in the instructions.	/////	/////
4 Do you elect to postpone the part of the taxes attributable to a reversionary or remainder interest as described in section 6163?		

Part 4.—General Information (Note: *Please attach the necessary supplemental documents.* **You must attach the death certificate.**)

Authorization to receive confidential tax information under Regulations section 601.502(c)(3)(ii), to act as the estate's representative before the Internal Revenue Service, and to make written or oral presentations on behalf of the estate if return prepared by an attorney, accountant, or enrolled agent for the executor:

Name of representative (print or type)	State	Address (number, street, and room or suite no., city, state, and ZIP code)

I declare that I am the ☐ attorney/ ☐ accountant/ ☐ enrolled agent (you must check the applicable box) for the executor and prepared this return for the executor. I am not under suspension or disbarment from practice before the Internal Revenue Service and am qualified to practice in the state shown above.

Signature	CAF number	Date	Telephone number

1   Death certificate number and issuing authority (attach a copy of the death certificate to this return).

2   Decedent's business or occupation. If retired, check here ► ☐ and state decedent's former business or occupation.

3   Marital status of the decedent at time of death:
   ☐ Married
   ☐ Widow or widower—Name, SSN, and date of death of deceased spouse ► ....
   ....
   ☐ Single
   ☐ Legally separated
   ☐ Divorced—Date divorce decree became final ►

4a Surviving spouse's name	4b Social security number	4c Amount received (see instructions)

5   Individuals (other than the surviving spouse), trusts, or other estates who receive benefits from the estate (do not include charitable beneficiaries shown in Schedule O) (see instructions). For Privacy Act Notice (applicable to individual beneficiaries only), see the Instructions for Form 1040.

Name of individual, trust, or estate receiving $5,000 or more	Identifying number	Relationship to decedent	Amount (see instructions)

All unascertainable beneficiaries and those who receive less than $5,000 . . . . ►

Total . . . .

(Continued on next page)   **Page 2**

Exhibit 12F

Form 706 (Rev. 10-91)

Part 4.—General Information *(continued)*

Please check the "Yes" or "No" box for each question.		Yes	No
6	Does the gross estate contain any section 2044 property (qualified terminable interest property (QTIP) from a prior gift or estate)? (see instructions)?		
7a	Have Federal gift tax returns ever been filed?		
	If "Yes," please attach copies of the returns, if available, and furnish the following information:		
7b Period(s) covered	7c Internal Revenue office(s) where filed		
If you answer "Yes" to any of questions 8–16, you must attach additional information as described in the instructions.			
8a	Was there any insurance on the decedent's life that is not included on the return as part of the gross estate?		
b	Did the decedent own any insurance on the life of another that is not included in the gross estate?		
9	Did the decedent at the time of death own any property as a joint tenant with right of survivorship in which (a) one or more of the other joint tenants was someone other than the decedent's spouse, and (b) less than the full value of the property is included on the return as part of the gross estate? If "Yes," you must complete and attach Schedule E		
10	Did the decedent, at the time of death, own any interest in a partnership or unincorporated business or any stock in an inactive or closely held corporation?		
11	Did the decedent make any transfer described in section 2035, 2036, 2037, or 2038 (see the instructions for Schedule G)? If "Yes," you must complete and attach Schedule G		
12	Were there in existence at the time of the decedent's death:		
a	Any trusts created by the decedent during his or her lifetime?		
b	Any trusts not created by the decedent under which the decedent possessed any power, beneficial interest, or trusteeship?		
13	Did the decedent ever possess, exercise, or release any general power of appointment? If "Yes," you must complete and attach Schedule H		
14	Was the marital deduction computed under the transitional rule of Public Law 97-34, section 403(e)(3) (Economic Recovery Tax Act of 1981)?		
	If "Yes," attach a separate computation of the marital deduction, enter the amount on item 18 of the Recapitulation, and note on item 18 "computation attached."		
15	Was the decedent, immediately before death, receiving an annuity described in the "General" paragraph of the instructions for Schedule I? If "Yes," you must complete and attach Schedule I		
16	Did the decedent have a total "excess retirement accumulation" (as defined in section 4980A(d)) in qualified employer plans and individual retirement plans? If "Yes," you must complete and attach Schedule S		

Part 5.—Recapitulation

Item number	Gross estate	Alternate value	Value at date of death
1	Schedule A—Real Estate		
2	Schedule B—Stocks and Bonds		
3	Schedule C—Mortgages, Notes, and Cash		
4	Schedule D—Insurance on the Decedent's Life (attach Form(s) 712)		
5	Schedule E—Jointly Owned Property (attach Form(s) 712 for life insurance)		
6	Schedule F—Other Miscellaneous Property (attach Form(s) 712 for life insurance)		
7	Schedule G—Transfers During Decedent's Life (attach Form(s) 712 for life insurance)		
8	Schedule H—Powers of Appointment		
9	Schedule I—Annuities		
10	Total gross estate (add items 1 through 9). Enter here and on line 1 of the Tax Computation		

Item number	Deductions	Amount
11	Schedule J—Funeral Expenses and Expenses Incurred in Administering Property Subject to Claims	
12	Schedule K—Debts of the Decedent	
13	Schedule K—Mortgages and Liens	
14	Total of items 11 through 13	
15	Allowable amount of deductions from item 14 (see the instructions for item 15 of the Recapitulation)	
16	Schedule L—Net Losses During Administration	
17	Schedule L—Expenses Incurred in Administering Property Not Subject to Claims	
18	Schedule M—Bequests, etc., to Surviving Spouse	
19	Schedule O—Charitable, Public, and Similar Gifts and Bequests	
20	Total allowable deductions (add items 15 through 19). Enter here and on line 2 of the Tax Computation	

Page 3

Exhibit 12G

9. **Create a Revocable Living Trust to Separate the Assets of a Married Couple**.

The way to accomplish this is as follows: it would be written in the living trust documents that upon the death of the first spouse the estate would be separated into two parts. The first part would represent exactly $600,000 of property, the amount exempt from estate taxes. This $600,000 can be handled in two ways:

    a. It can be given directly to your heirs upon the death of the first spouse, with the balance of the estate going to the surviving spouse; or

    b. It can be put into another living trust so that the heirs will have title to the assets but cannot touch them while your spouse is still living. Thus, your spouse can receive income from the investments while alive. In addition, the home could be included in this living trust so that the spouse could continue to live in it.

The second part of the first estate is the balance beyond $600,000. This can represent any amount of money, be it $5,000 or $1,000,000. The point, though, is that because you have set up a revocable living trust and separated the assets of the two spouses before the death of either spouse, you have essentially created an additional $600,000 unified credit exemption.

If you had not created this revocable living trust and you had allowed all of the assets to be transferred to your spouse as part of the unlimited marital deduction, then you (the couple) would be considered to be one person for the sake of the exemption. The unlimited marital deduction rule simply means that the government will defer tax on a couple's estate until the death of the second spouse. The government then collects on what are now the combined remaining assets of the couple before anything goes to the heirs.

With the formation of this type of trust, $600,000, the initial part of the first deceased spouse's assets has already been removed from the combined assets with no estate tax.

Upon the later death of the second spouse an additional $600,000 will become exempt from estate taxes. What this has effectively done is to have created a unified credit of $1,200,000 as opposed to simply $600,000.

This is a perfectly legal and very simple strategy which can save you up to $192,800 in unnecessary estate taxes. It is not common knowledge that this strategy is necessary or available, and

212

furthermore, those who are aware of it often will not want to pay the expense of setting up a trust such as this. Yet when you compare the tremendous tax savings which can be achieved from the establishment of a revocable living trust and equate this savings with the money it costs to set one up, there is no comparison.

I would suggest that you utilize all that is available to you under the current tax law for planning your estate tax strategy.

10. **Considerations for Unmarried Taxpayers**.

Unmarried taxpayers need an estate plan more so than do married couples. Most single people prefer to distribute assets among a number of beneficiaries, while married people generally leave property to the surviving spouse and children.

Additionally, if you are unmarried, you will not get the benefit of the marital deduction to reduce estate taxes. Therefore, estate planning is vital to ensure that the bulk of your property goes to beneficiaries and not to the government or to the administration of your estate.

Cohabitation presents a special set of problems when most of the estate is left to the cohabitant. A lawsuit by family members could consume most of the estate's assets. A solution to this, if you expect hostility from family members, is to have a lawyer draft a will that disinherits anyone who contests the will. You should also prepare evidence that you were not subject to undue influence or duress when writing the will. This is particularly important when you are significantly older than your cohabitant or if you were ill at the time the will was drawn.

A better solution to this problem would be to create an irrevocable lifetime trust and to make use of your $10,000 per year per person gift tax exclusion while you are still alive.

I will close this section with a true story about estate tax planning, or rather the lack of estate tax planning. Robert S. Kerr, Senator from Oklahoma, was a wealthy member of the establishment. As a member of the U.S. Senate he supported and voted for estate tax legislation that grabbed up to 70% of people's assets upon their death.

In 1978, Senator Kerr died suddenly. His estate at the time of death was worth approximately $20,000,000. Unfortunately, and quite ironically, he died without the most basic estate planning tool, a will. His heirs had to deal with many difficult problems, although none were as great as the $9,000,000 bill they got from the IRS. The bill being a direct result of estate tax legislation supported by Senator Kerr.

213

His family had the problem, as do most surviving families, raising that kind of cash to satisfy the IRS in such a short period of time. Some of Senator Kerr's estate was liquid, however the rest was in family real estate, which was not liquid. They did not want to have to sell the family property in a tremendous bargain basement sale, so they were forced to take out a $6,000,000 loan to supplement the $3,000,000 available to them in cash.

The interest rates then were somewhere in the 20% range and they were forced to pay an outrageous amount of interest on the borrowed money simply to satisfy their estate tax obligation. This was a nightmare for them.

The same situation could happen to you, even if you have a will. Federal estate taxes are levied on any estate beyond the $600,000 unified credit amount. The tax rate quickly rises from a low of 37% to the maximum 55% rate.

In this chapter I have given you a basic background on estate planning and the considerations involved. It is up to you to protect your assets from the IRS and the attorneys in the event of your death. To ensure that the maximum wealth is passed down to future generations, it is necessary for you to seek professional counseling in this area more than any other.

As I stated at the beginning of this section, the estate tax is one of the most severe taxes in existence today. I will fill you in on more specific solutions to deal with this problem in the section entitled, "50 Tax Reduction Strategies–Read my Tips."

Chapter 13

This Business of Trading

Creating a Trading Business

For those who qualify, one of the best tax reduction strategies is to be setup as a **trader**. I have related some of the advantages of this strategy previously and will recap them once again in this section.

The major advantage of this strategy is that you are able to deduct, dollar–for–dollar, the expenses incurred in your trading business. If you do not establish yourself as a "Schedule C – Trader," you will be forced to deduct your investment expenses as miscellaneous itemized deductions on Schedule A–assuming you have enough deductions to itemize.

As mentioned earlier, the major downside to this treatment is that before any expenses can be deducted against your income, you must exceed a base amount commonly referred to as the "2% floor." This amount is equal to 2% of your adjusted gross income before itemized deductions.

In addition, starting in 1991, there is another amount deductible from all your itemized deductions before they are subtracted from income. This amount is currently equal to 3% of your adjusted gross income above the $100,000 level ($105,250 for 1992 tax returns) and is likely to be increased in the near future. It has been my experience that once a floor is set, the government quickly builds upon it.

Please refer back to the third section of this book, "Changes For the Investor: Now You See It, Now You Don't." Point 4 of Part B of this section addresses this particular aspect of the Tax Reform Act in detail. The overall result, however, is that the investor has lost a good part of his deductions for expenses associated with the production of investment income.

An Investor, A Trader, or A Dealer (Market Maker)

One of the areas of the tax law discussed for several years among tax practitioners involved in investment taxation is the **classification** of the investor.

Up until the Tax Reform Act of 1986, the only significance this distinction had to the taxpayer was on the question of how much investment interest expense was deductible as an itemized deduction. The rule, prior to tax reform, was that an investor could deduct all of his of his investment interest expense, or margin interest, up to his investment income. Beyond this amount he was allowed to deduct only $10,000 in margin interest.

For example, if an investor had $30,000 in interest, dividends, and net capital gains, and had margin interest of $50,000, he would be able to deduct only $40,000 in that year as investment interest expense. The remainder, $10,000, would have to be carried over to future years in order to be deductible.

With the Tax Reform Act of 1986, as you will recall, this has now been changed so that the $10,000 deduction beyond investment income has been eliminated. Under the current law, only $30,000 of investment interest can be deducted against $30,000 of investment income. The $20,000 balance will have to be carried to future years when it can be deducted against future investment income.

If, on the other hand, an investor were to be classified as more than just a **passive investor**, indeed, if he could be classified as an **active trader**, then investment interest expense would no longer have to be considered simply investment interest expense. It could more accurately be classified as a **business-related** interest expense. Thus, it would be **fully** deductible as an expense of doing business as a **trader**.

The tax code makes a distinction between three types of individual investors: the **investor**, the **trader**, and the **dealer**. Never before has this distinction been so important.

A Dealer (Market Maker)

The law is quite clear on the distinction of **dealer** or **market maker**.

216

> A 'dealer' in securities – that is, one who is a merchant of securities with an established place of business who regularly engages in the purchase of securities and their resale to customers with the intent of making a profit – may treat the securities held as inventory (Reg. Section 1.471–5). A dealer may be an individual, a partnership, or a corporation. Unlike securities held by investors, securities held for sale to customers in the ordinary course of business are not capital assets. See paragraph 1760.[42]

What this section of the code addresses is a very specific type of activity. It is describing a **market maker**, or one who does business with the intent of facilitating trade for one or more of the major exchanges. A market maker is a legal distinction. It is a designation and must be bestowed upon that individual with the fulfillment of certain criteria established by the various stock exchanges.

This designation grants certain privileges which go beyond the ones we have been considering. Not only can a market maker deduct dollar–for–dollar any amount of any type of expense he incurs in conducting the business of his profession, he also gets another break which neither a trader nor investor is eligible for. A market maker gets to consider any stock, option, or other investment vehicle he buys or sells as a "non–capital asset," or an inventory item.

This means that such a dealer in securities would not be limited to the $3,000 per year capital loss limitation to which other taxpayers are subject. The law states specifically that these items, since they are being purchased and sold as business items, and are not being traded for a dealer's own account, should be treated as business inventory. If such a dealer lost $100,000 in the market as a market maker he would be able to take the entire loss, plus any expenses incurred in generating this loss, as a business loss on his tax return. This would not be considered a capital loss, and is quite different than the way other taxpayers would be required to report capital transactions (limited to a net $3,000 loss per year).

An Investor

In contrast, an **investor** is defined by the tax law as:

> a person who buys and sells securities for his own account...however, a person can be a dealer in securities and still trade for his own account. Thus, if the business of being a dealer is simply a branch of the trading activities carried on by such person, the securities inventoried may include only those held for the purpose of resale and not for investment (Code Section 263A).[43]

Basically, an investor is clearly defined as one who "invests" in securities for his own account. A dealer in securities may also be an investor and, if he is, each activity must be treated differently for tax purposes.

Furthermore, all expenses incurred in the activity of investing are considered to be **investment expenses**. These expenses would be deducted as miscellaneous itemized deductions on Schedule A of the investors's tax return.

A Trader

The tax law makes a third distinction as follows:

> Because a trader, as distinguished from a dealer, in securities is subject to the capital gain and loss limitations, it is important to distinguish between a securities "dealer" and a securities "trader." A securities dealer is comparable to a merchant in that he purchases stock in trade (securities) with the expectation of reselling at a profit. Such profit is based on hopes of merely finding a market of buyers who will purchase the securities from him at a price in excess of their cost.

On the other hand, a securities trader buys and sells securities for his own account. A trader's expectation of making a profit depends upon such circumstances as a rise in value or an advantageous purchase to enable him to sell at a price in excess of cost.[44]

You May Have a Trader in Your Midst

In the August 1992 issue of *The Tax Advisor*, there is an article by Scott P. Murphy a CPA from Akron, Ohio. The article addresses the question of how one distinguishes between the three classifications just discussed. In this article Mr. Murphy states that ever since the Revenue Act of 1934 it has been well known that there are three types of individuals or entities that have transactions with respect to stocks or securities: dealers, investors, and traders.

He goes on to advise that by far the largest number of taxpayers are considered to be investors. For these taxpayers, gains and losses on transactions in stocks and securities are treated as capital gains or losses. Individual taxpayers who are investors may deduct portfolio and investment management expenses as only 2% floor itemized deductions. Thus, many of these expenses become non–deductible. In addition, the deductibility of investment interest expense by an investor may be limited, particularly in years of low investment income.

Dealers, such as Wall Street brokerage houses or market makers on the floors of the various exchanges, are entities that hold stocks or securities primarily for sale to customers in the ordinary course of business. These taxpayers recognize ordinary gains and losses on transactions in securities and they're able to deduct, in full, all costs relative to these investments as ordinary business expenses.

He goes on to discuss the third designation, that of a trader:

A **trader** is an investor who speculates and trades securities on his own account. He does not hold securities for resale to customers. **However, the trader's stock activity is of the na-**

ture that rises to a level of being a trade or business. If a taxpayer is classified as a trader, gains or losses on securities transactions give rise to capital gains or losses under Section 1221. However, portfolio and investment management expenses and investment interest expenses become deductible without limitation under Section 162 in arriving at adjusted gross income. This can be a significant benefit to many taxpayers who have lost deductions as a result of severe limitations imposed by recent tax law changes.[45]

This is quite a significant distinction, and one which has become even more important with the passage of the Tax Reform Act of 1986. To qualify as a trader, there are no fixed requirements in the tax code. It is agreed that the taxpayer must trade in stock or securities on a relatively short–term basis. If there is a preponderance of frequent trades, short–term in nature, relative to long–term positions, this would be an indication of his status as a trader.

In addition, the taxpayer must be involved in tracking daily market movements in order to be in position to profit on a short–term basis. Therefore, technical analysts, or those who analyze the market on a predominantly short–term bias, based on chart and volume formations, are more likely to be considered traders than fundamental analysts.

Since fundamental analyst looks beyond short–term chart formations to decide which direction a security or the market in general will most likely go, they are more inclined to take longer term positions, and less likely to be viewed as traders. In addition, a trader must be able to show that he spends a great deal of time managing the buying and selling of securities or other trading vehicles.

While the number of trades is not the exclusive factor, certainly a taxpayer with a large number of short–term transactions will be in a better position to demonstrate that he qualifies as a trader. However, the length of the trades and the nature of the type of trading are generally the determining factors rather than purely the number of trades.

As dealer status would be beneficial when losses are realized on stock transactions, there are very few individuals or entities who would be able to qualify for such status. However, there are probably a great many taxpayers who qualify for trader status. In some cases this may be as beneficial or even more beneficial than being a dealer.

The case of the **Estate of Louis Yaeger** and the court decision on it is an excellent example of this situation. For those of you who are interested, there has been other caselaw which elaborates on how these factors are viewed. They include the following: **Kemon**, 16 TC 1026 (1951), **Huebschman**, TC Memo 1980–537, **King**, 89 TC 445 (1987), **Reinarch**, USTC par. 9274 (1967), **Fuld**, USTC par. 9123(1943), and **Whipple**, USTC par. 9466(1963).

Was Louis Yaeger A Trader?

A Case For Consideration

A most significant case relevant to this discussion is that of the **Estate of Louis Yaeger versus the Commissioner**. The specifics, for those who wish to review the case are as follows:

> U.S. Court of Appeals, 2nd Circuit;
> 89–4045, 89–4059, 11/7/89. Affirm-
> ing in part, reversing and remanding
> in part a Tax Court decision, 55 TCM
> 1101, Dec. 44,843(M), T.C. Memo.
> 1988–264.

The issue in question here was whether or not margin interest expense (investment interest) should be subject to the limitations provided in the law. At the time the case went to court, the annual deduction for investment interest expense was limited to $10,000 in excess of investment income. Anything more than that amount would have to be carried over to another year.

Louis Yaeger was a full time "investor/trader." The issue in question, though, was which of the two designations most accurately fit the type of activity he participated in. If he were to be considered a trader, then all interest generated from his trading activities could be deducted as a general business expense. If, on the other hand, he was considered an investor, he would be subject to the investment interest expense limitation.

The importance of this issue increased tenfold due to the fact that he was no longer either one of those two designations. He was,

221

in fact, dead. This meant that on his final tax return the amount of investment interest expense allowed to be deducted would be final. Since there would be no more investment income, there'd be no way to carry forward any disallowed investment interest expense for use in future years.

When the estate filed the posthumous personal tax return for Mr. Yaeger they took the position that he was a trader and consequently deducted all investment interest expense as a cost of doing business. This was disallowed by the IRS under audit examination, and was contested in the Tax Court by the estate.

The decision was made **against** the estate and **declined** the late Mr. Yaeger the status of trader.

> Interest expense: Trade or business expense: investment interest expense. Interest expense incurred by the taxpayer when buying and selling securities was determined to be investment interest expense since the taxpayer was found to be an investor rather than a trader. The two fundamental criteria that distinguish traders from investors in securities are the length of their holding period and the source of their profit. Most of the taxpayer's sales were of securities held for over a year and most of his profit came from holding stock until its market improved. His emphasis on capital growth and profit from resale indicated that his activity was investment motivated. Back references: Paragraphs 1332.1475 and 1425.50.[46]

Before exploring the court decision in detail, let's examine the background of Mr. Yaeger and the nature of his "investing/trading" activities.

Louis Yaeger graduated from Columbia University School of Business and Finance. Upon graduation he went to work as an accountant and subsequently became employed as an audit agent for the IRS. After several years he left the IRS to become a bond salesman and investment counselor.

He then began actively trading stocks and bonds for his own account, in addition to his investment consulting business. Twenty years later Mr. Yaeger gave up his investment consulting business because the management of his own account had grown so demanding and time consuming. Thereafter he devoted himself exclusively to trading his own account, which he did as his sole occupation until the day he died.

Mr. Yaeger maintained a handful of accounts with several brokerage firms including his largest at H. Hentz and Co. At that time this was the largest account the firm had ever maintained for a U.S. citizen.

Yaeger maintained an office at H. Hentz and Co. where he spent most of his working day and conducted most of his trading activity. The firm provided Yaeger with a private office, an assistant, a telephone, use of the secretarial pool, and access to the research staff and facilities of the firm.

Mr. Yaeger spent a full day at his office researching investment opportunities and placing orders. He would then go home to read more financial reports late into the night. He worked every day of the week, and when he was out of town he maintained continual telephone contact with the brokers who handled his account. Yaeger was actively trading his own account in the stock market the day he died.

The tax returns in question were for two years, 1979 and 1980. During these years, the activities of his account, which were viewed as evidence for the classification of activity were as follows:

	1979	**1980**
Purchase transactions	1,176	1,088
Sales transactions	86	39
Number of shares bought	1,453,555	1,658,841
Number of shares sold	822,955	173,165

As you can see, Louis Yaeger did quite a bit of "investing/ trading." He subscribed to a distinct investment strategy. His strategy was to buy the stock of undervalued companies. He would then hold the stock until it reached a price that reflected the underlying value of the company.

He hardly ever purchased blue chip stocks, and most of the stocks he held paid no dividends. Instead, Mr. Yaeger looked for companies that were experiencing financial trouble but whose underlying value was not reflected in the stock price.

The strategy he employed was extremely successful and required extensive research which went beyond the study of popular publications. He would spend much time reviewing annual reports and brokerage house reports. Once Yaeger determined his target he would begin buying the stock of the company in small quantities to avoid attracting attention from other investors. When he obtained a sizable amount of stock, he would let his position be known and would take whatever steps he felt were necessary to improve the position of the company. He often supplied managers with unsolicited business advice, and even went so far as to attempt to arrange mergers or acquisitions for them.

In addition to selecting these types of companies, Yaeger increased the gain on his investments by extensively using margin debt. He financed his purchases using the maximum allowable margin, generally 50%. If the value of his holdings increased, he would use that increase in value as equity to support more debt.

From time to time Yaeger shifted accounts from one brokerage house to another in order to maximize the amount of margin debt he could carry. Several times during his career Yaeger was over leveraged and suffered substantial losses when he was forced to sell enough stock to cover his margin debt.

During 1979 and 1980 the amounts reported on Yaeger's tax returns were as follows:

Character of Income	1979	1980
Long–term capital gain	$13,839,658	$1,099,921
Short–term capital gain	184,354	728,404
Dividends	2,339,080	3,648,441
Interest	57,958	91,717
Director's fees	0	10,600
	$16,421,050	$5,579,083

Clearly, Louis Yaeger made a great deal of money from these activities. In addition, it is also apparent that interest and dividends comprised a relatively small part of his overall income. However, the percentage of total sales of securities he held for 12 months or more was 88% and 91% in 1979 and 1980 respectively. The purchase dates of the securities sold in 1980 ranged from March 1970 to December 1979.

In 1979, Yaeger did not sell any security that he had held for less than three months, and in 1980, he did not sell any security that he had held for less than six months. On Schedule C of his tax returns, Yaeger deducted interest expense in 1979 and 1980 of $5,865,833 and $7,995,010, respectively.

The sole issue considered by the Tax Court was whether the claimed deductions for interest Yaeger incurred in purchasing securities on margin were subject to the limitation of deductibility of investment interest as described in Section 163(d) of the Code.

This issue boiled down to whether or not Yaeger's stock market activities constituted investment activity or trading in securities as a trade or business. **According to the Tax Court, the main question was whether Yaeger was interested in deriving income from capital appreciation or from short–term trading**.

The Court determined that Yaeger was an investor, not a trader, because he held stocks and bonds for lengthy periods of time anticipating that they would appreciate in value. Thus, the interest expense he had incurred was investment **interest** within the scope of Section 163(d) and subject to the restrictions of that section.

What This All Means

The IRS Code does not define trade or business as it applies to trading activities. In another case, **Higgins v. Commissioner**, the following determination was made:

> The Internal Revenue Code does not define 'trade or business.' Determining whether a taxpayer's trading activities rise to the level of carrying on a trade or business turns on the facts and circumstances of each case.[47]

A 1984 decision in the case of **Moller v. Commissioner**, it was put forth that:

> In determining whether taxpayers who manage their own investments are traders, 'relevant considerations are

> the taxpayer's investment intent, the
> nature of the income to be derived
> from the activity, and the frequency,
> extent, and regularity of the taxpayer's
> securities transactions.'[48]

Furthermore, the "Federal Tax Report" states that traders' profits are derived from the direct management of purchasing and selling. Investors, though, derive profit from interest, dividends, and capital appreciation of securities. They are primarily interested in the longer term growth potential of their stocks.

Traders, in contrast, buy and sell securities with reasonable frequency in an endeavor to catch the swings in the daily market movements and profit thereby on a short–term basis.

Thus, the two fundamental criteria that distinguish traders from investors is the **length of the holding period** and the **source of the profit**. The activity of holding securities for a length of time to produce interest, dividends, and capital gains fits the definition of an investor.

It is true that Louis Yaeger initiated over 2,000 securities transactions in 1979 and 1980 and pursued his security activities vigorously on a full–time basis. And, there is no doubt as the Tax Court stated that Yaeger:

> maintained a margin of debt which
> would have caused a more faint
> hearted investor to quail. However, no
> matter how large the estate or how
> continuous or extended the work re-
> quired may be, the management of
> securities investments is **not** the trade
> or business of a trader.[49]

More importantly, most of his sales were of securities held for more than a year. He did not sell any security held for less than three months, and he realized a profit on the securities through both dividends and interest, as well as capital gain.

Most of this profit came from the holding of undervalued stock until its market improved. This emphasis on capital growth and the profit from resale indicates an investment motivated activity.

The distinction between a trader and an investor should be relatively clear. A trader is one who is in the business of trading his holdings for the purpose of generating a short–term profit as a result of frequent market swings. Because of this he is able to deduct all of his trading expenses, including interest, as well as other trading expenses as part of the cost of doing business.

An investor, on the other hand, cannot, and is subject to the restrictions as outlined above.

The Schedule C – Born to Be Filed

Once you have determined that you qualify as a trader, it's a whole new ballgame. Expenses such as computer programs and equipment, on–line data retrieval services, investment advisory fees, and other such related expenses now are directly deductible from your trading income.

The question, however, becomes "How do I set this whole thing up?"

The way to do it is the way in which any sole proprietor in business would report income and expenses, on the Schedule C. It is obvious that expenses should be reported on the Schedule C, however the question has been raised "Since the income for a trader still consists of capital transactions, shouldn't it be reported on a Schedule D?" (see Exhibits 3C and 3D).

The answer is yes. The transactions are basically transactions as defined in Section 1221 of the Code. In fact, Form 1099B is often generated showing total year end gross proceeds from securities transactions (see Exhibit 13A).

Another question usually asked goes something like this: "Since the income generated is **not** really investment income, but rather is considered as active business income, shouldn't it be subject to self–employment tax?" In this case, wouldn't it then be reported on Schedule C, as well as Schedule SE, Form for Calculating Self–Employment Tax (see Exhibit 7C)?

The answer to all of these questions is probably "Yes." The income is considered to be capital gain income (or loss), but since we are considering it to be business income, it should most likely be subject to self–employment tax too. It is really a question of how to properly report it on the tax return.

Since this is a relatively new area, there is no one correct answer given in the code. I have seen it done two ways, and, in fact, have reported it differently myself, depending on the taxpayer's circumstances. Both methods start out with reporting the income on the Schedule D and the expenses on the Schedule C.

```
                                                      - 1991 **
  PAYER S name, street address, city, state, and ZIP code

  NB CLEARING CORP                       ☐ CORRECTED                    PAGE
  67 WALL STREET
  NEW YORK NY   10005          CONSOLIDATED 1099-INT-DIV-MISC-OID-1099B


                                          RECIPIENT S name, street address, city, state, and ZIP code
  THIS IS IMPORTANT TAX INFORMATION AND IS BEING FURNISHED TO THE
  INTERNAL REVENUE SERVICE. IF YOU ARE REQUIRED TO FILE A RETURN A        MR. N. VESTOR
  NEGLIGENCE PENALTY WILL BE IMPOSED ON YOU IF ANY OF THIS INCOME IS      401 KAY ST.
  TAXABLE AND THE IRS DETERMINES THAT IT HAS NOT BEEN REPORTED.
  BROKER FEDERAL ID        RECIPIENT S ID NUMBER                          DOLLAS
      123.456                012.34-5678                                  TAXES'
  ACCOUNT NUMBER           RR NUMBER


  FOR INQUIRIES PLEASE CONTACT YOUR  SERVICE REPRESENTATIVE IMMEDIATELY.
  NOTICE OF CORRECTIONS MUST BE      RECEIVED BY MARCH 15, 1992 TO INSUR
  PROCESSING PRIOR TO IRS REPORTING
  ================================================================================
  INTEREST INCOME (1099-INT)        OMB NO. 1545-0112            AMOUNT
  1. INTEREST INCOME NOT INCLUDED IN LINE 3..........           67.64
  2. EARLY WITHDRAWAL PENALTY.......................            0.00
  3. INTEREST ON US SAVINGS BONDS & TREAS. OBLIGATIONS          0.00
  4. FEDERAL INCOME TAX WITHHELD....................            0.00
  5. FOREIGN TAX PAID...............................            0.00
  ================================================================================
  DIVIDEND DISTRIBUTIONS (1099-DIV)   *** NO INFORMATION REPORTED TO IRS ***
  ================================================================================
  MISCELLANEOUS INCOME (1099-MISC)    *** NO INFORMATION REPORTED TO IRS ***
  ================================================================================
  GROSS PROCEEDS (1099-B)           OMB NO. 1545-0715
  DATE (1A)      DESCRIPTION (5)    CUSIP (1B)  PROCEEDS (2)  WITHHELD (4)
  08/06 MIRAGE RESORTS INC          60462E10     74,969.50      0.00

            1 ITEMS TOTAL                        74,969.50      0.00
  ================================================================================
  ORIGINAL ISSUE DISCOUNT (1099-OID) *** NO INFORMATION REPORTED TO IRS ***
  ================================================== END OF 1099 STATEMENT FORM ======
```

Exhibit 13A

The next step, however, is open to some interpretation and is, in fact, handled quite differently by different tax practitioners. Some believe that the income should completely bypass the Schedule C and go straight from the Schedule D to the front of the return. In this manner, it is reported as a capital item, bypassing the self–employment tax.

The problem with this method, however, is that in doing so, you must also carry forward a significant loss (trading expenses) to the front of the return, on Schedule C. If this is the method you choose, be sure to include an explanatory note on the return that the income which corresponds to these expenses is reported on the Schedule D. This will reduce the chance of the IRS disallowing it as a "hobby loss" after two years.

Another problem with this method is that you can not realistically expect to deduct a retirement plan from any income on which you have avoided paying self–employment tax. You can't say, on one hand, that you are considering it self–employment income for the purpose of setting up a Keogh, but on the other hand, that it is not!

The way I handle this, in most cases, is to first report it on the Schedule D, but not carry the income directly to page one of the return. Rather, I flow the income to the Schedule C and put a note at the bottom of the Schedule D stating that "Taxpayer qualifies for trader status. Income from securities transactions being reported on Schedule C."

In other words, I carry the total from the Schedule D to line 1 of the Schedule C as I would any other business income. I then come up with my expense figure, subtract it from the income, and carry the net business income to line 2 of the Schedule SE to calculate self–employment tax on this income (see Exhibits 5A and 7C).

I subscribe to the belief that if you are claiming that you are in the business of trading securities, you cannot claim an exemption from paying self–employment tax on this net income. It is my feeling that a more conservative approach is generally worth taking here, especially in an area which may be scrutinized in the near future–or at least until a legal precedent is established.

If I am telling the IRS that a client is entitled to claim all business expenses associated with his business, I cannot sit on the other side of the fence and tell the IRS, "No, this is not a business in terms of self–employment tax." Besides, by setting it up this way, you

229

are now in a better position to justify taking the maximum Keogh deduction on this income. And **that**, in and of itself, **may be worth the price**!

Other Benefits of Claiming Trader Status

As Robert Frost once said:

> By working hard eight hours a day,
> you may eventually get to be boss
> and be able to work hard twelve
> hours a day.

The first experience I ever had in business was at a very young age. When I was 11 years old my good friend Scott Pollowitz and I decided we would like to have a little extra money to supplement our allowances. We put our collective brain trust together along with several more of our neighborhood buddies and started to explore all the possibilities which could generate this income.

After several hours we had it figured out. We decided that since everybody in our suburban neighborhood drove automobiles, the most needed service we could provide at our age would be to clean them. So our business conglomerate embarked upon what we hoped would be a very successful enterprise.

It seemed quite easy to start. All we would need is a bucket of soapy water, some sponges, and a few towels (or rags) to dry the cars. It was assumed that since everybody in suburbia had houses with lawns, it would be easy enough to use their hoses and water to wash away the soap from the cars before drying them.

After going door to door and handing out flyers for several hours we got a bite and we landed our first job. It was a fancy new white Cadillac!

The five of us gathered eagerly around the car after negotiating the price with the owner. We each grabbed a sponge and started soaping away. Within minutes the layer of dirt around the white paint was gone. It was replaced with our soapy bubbles we had scrubbed hard to clean the car. At this point Scott told me to run up to the house and ask the lady where her hose was so that we could wash away the product of our hard work, the soap.

I remember how I felt when she told me, "But we don't have a hose, and our water's not hooked up outside yet!" It was almost like having eaten a pound of candy corn and drinking two hot chocolates. I felt it in my stomach.

When I started down to inform Scott and the others that there was no way of washing the soap off the car, I was already fumbling in my mind for a solution to the problem. By the time I reached them I had it. We'd just use the towels to dry off the soap and hopefully that would do the trick. I informed Scott and the gang that we were going to have to do a "drycleaning" job.

I passed out the towels and we all began to wipe the soap off the car. It looked pretty good. In fact, most of the dirt came off with the soap, and one could hardly tell we didn't use water to rinse it off.

That is, until the next day. Our car wash group had just finished drying off the car of the lady next door to our first client, and we were being paid when it began to rain. Hard.

Our first client came cruising out of her driveway in her gleaming white cadillac. And, for some reason unbeknownst to her, it appeared as if the Lawrence Welk Orchestra was performing. She backed down her driveway to a myriad of little soap bubbles floating in the air from all parts of her car. We grabbed the money and left quickly, before anyone else could figure out what had happened.

The moral of this story for Scott and I was that before we started a business job we had to plan ahead thoroughly. We had to make sure that every last detail was taken care of, even in cases where we had assumed it was. That served as a lesson to me that the most important component of a successful business plan is just that, the plan.

In translating this down to a trading business, it is equally as important that you consider every contingency in planning ahead. That means that you want to make absolutely certain that you qualify as a trader, and that you provide adequate documentation for the IRS, in case you are questioned.

You must make absolutely certain that you fit the criteria of a trader as outlined previously and that you keep a set of books and records so as to document the business nature of your trading.

Furthermore, all of your deductible trading expenses should be well supported and documented, including:

1. Accounting fees;
2. Automobile expenses;
3. Books and audio/video tape courses on investing;
4. Brokerage fees;

231

5. Calculators, adding machines, cassette tape recorders, and typewriters;
6. Costs of collecting interest and dividends;
7. Costs of managing investments for a minor;
8. Financial advice on audio/video tapes;
9. Tax advice (such as the cost of *The Serious Investor's Tax Survival Guide*, by Ted Tesser);
10. Home computer and software;
11. Data retrieval service;
12. Investment advice;
13. Investment interest expense;
14. Legal fees;
15. Entertainment and meals during which business is conducted;
16. Safe deposit box rental for storage of investment documents;
17. Salary of bookkeepers, accountants, or others who keep your investment records;
18. Subscriptions to investment publications;
19. Trips to look after investments (such as real estate, or for visits with investment advisors or money managers);
20. Cost of trading seminars attended;
21. Video tape recorder used for education; and
22. A portion of your home expenses which qualify as home/office deductions.

Any item such as a VCR, home computer, or cassette tape recorder which is used for both business and pleasure can be assigned a percentage of business use. That percentage of its cost can be deducted as a business expense as we discussed in a prior section. You should review the section of "Dauntless Doug, the Duke of Deductions" for a complete discussion of the types of business expenses which are allowable for sole proprietors.

You Pay For It Anyway, Why Not Deduct It?

When you have a business, almost every related business activity becomes legally tax deductible. If the business generates income, it may still generate thousands of dollars of tax deductions which can be used to shelter other income from tax.

In fact, a small business, and in particular for readers of this book, a small trading business is one of the few true tax shelters left.

232

After the Tax Reform Act, there aren't many activities left which allow the use of tax deductions from one source, your business, to offset taxable income from other sources, such as your job. The business becomes a tax shelter when it shows a "paper loss." Taxable income is actually reduced by the amount of deductions legitimately associated with the business which are in excess of business income. These deductions can be used to offset income from other sources.

In a business many of the personal things you own become fully or partially tax deductible when you can show that the items or activities are connected to your small business.

Chapter 14

The Portfolio Revisited

At this time, let me reference you back to Chapter 4 where I listed ten investment practices and their effect on the tax situation of the investor, both before and after tax reform. I will now provide the third piece of information to this analysis–an alternative way of investing to produce a more beneficial tax outcome, post–Tax Reform Act of 1986.

1. **Practice**: Investment in smaller, high risk growth stocks and venture capital funds.

Outcome and Effect: Increased risk for a lower potential reward, with the increase in capital gains tax rate to come.

Change in Portfolio: Because of the relative increase in capital gains tax rate, it no longer made sense for my clients to risk their money on lower priced growth stocks which generally paid off, if they paid off, in capital gains appreciation. I invested a larger percentage of their portfolio in higher dividend producing stocks since dividends were now taxed at the same rate as capital gains. This shifted a large portion of the portfolio from smaller, riskier NASDAQ stocks to larger, more stable blue chips.

2. **Practice**: Investment in real estate and other passive activities generating passive activity losses.

Outcome and Effect: Loss of deduction against other investment income and consequently less tax benefit from the investment.

Change in Portfolio: I looked to invest in some passive income generating investments (PIGS). Some of the investments I picked for them were income producing apartment complexes. I could then use the passive activity losses generated by some of the passive investments my clients already had to offset this new income, reestablishing the tax benefits of the PALS (Passive Activity Losses).

3. **Practice**: Investment in passive activity bonds and other partially taxable municipals.

Outcome and Effect: Loss of tax–exempt status on future purchases and some prior holdings under newly revised alternative minimum tax.

Change in Portfolio: For those clients who were close to or in the alternative minimum tax bracket, I got rid of a part of their private activity bonds. For these taxpayers I purchased non–private activity bonds.

4. **Practice**: Investment in U.S. Treasuries by those living in low tax bracket states or states with no income tax at all.

Outcome and Effect: Lower yielding investment as a trade–off for no state tax benefit.

Change in Portfolio: For those taxpayers living in lower tax bracket states or states with no tax bracket at all, I exchanged U.S. Treasuries for comparably safe and higher yielding AAA rated "blue chip," corporate bonds.

5. **Practice**: Charitable contributions being made with low cost basis, highly appreciated assets.

Outcome and Effect: Loss of substantial part of deduction through alternative minimum tax.

Change in Portfolio: I made the charitable contributions using the highest basis stocks in the portfolio if there was a chance of triggering the alternative minimum tax. Those taxpayers who were not in danger of AMT donated the lowest basis stocks to charity. In other words, before a gift of appreciated capital stock was donated, a tax projection was done to determine which item to donate.

6. **Practice**: Investment accounts being highly margined.

Outcome and Effect: Loss, or partial loss, of investment interest expense deduction.

Change in Portfolio: For those taxpayers where the trader status applied, I allowed full margining of accounts without other considerations. When it was time to file the personal returns, I set up a Schedule C and deducted the entire amount of interest as a business interest expense. In those cases where the client was not earning enough investment income to allow the full investment interest expense deduction, the accounts were margined at less than their maximum potential to avoid generating interest expenses which were not fully deductible in that year.

7. **Practice**: Large miscellaneous expenses relating to investments being taken as itemized deductions.

Outcome and Effect: Disallowance of significant portion of these expenses due to 2% (of AGI) exclusion.

Change in Portfolio: For those taxpayers where the status of trader applied, I allowed these expenses to be incurred with no modification then deducted them in full on the Schedule C as discussed in the last section. For those taxpayers who were not able to establish trader status, I made them aware of potential non–deductible expenses which had to be closely monitored throughout the year.

8. **Practice**: Gifts not being made to younger family members on an annual basis.

Outcome and Effect: Loss of $20,000 per couple, per year, per recipient tax–free gift allowance.

Change in Portfolio: I established an annual gifting program which provided for the regular passing down of wealth from one generation to the next. This process was more fully addressed in Chapter 11.

9. **Practice**: High income producing gifts being made to children under the age of 14.

Outcome and Effect: Children being taxed on investment income of over $1,000 at maximum parental tax rates.

Change in Portfolio: The nature of gifting from one generation to the next was changed to favor the lower priced, higher potential appreciation stocks. I tried to avoid having parents pass down blue chip stocks which produced higher current income with less growth potential. This was a good match to fit in with the Change in Portfolio Strategy #1, where the parents needed to get rid of the lower priced, higher risk, growth potential stocks and to keep the higher income producers. In addition to selling many of these NASDAQ stocks, I simply began a program of gifting them to their children.

10. **Practice**: Gifts being made from grandparents to grandchildren with the direct skip of the middle generation.

Outcome and Effect: Such transfers above and beyond the initial $2,000,000 per grandchild exclusions would now be subject to "generation skipping transfer tax."

Change in Portfolio: There was a one time exclusion set up in 1986 which allowed for certain skips in generations to take place without the surtax. I took full advantage of these exemptions since they were being phased out shortly, and passed as much of the wealth down as I could at that time. Later, I made people aware of the effect of these types of transfers which were then avoided when possible.

These are the strategies I employed but they are not the only ones which could have been pursued. The next section of this book provides other potential solutions to tax problems. Hopefully it will further educate you on the strategies most suitable for the optimum tax management of your own investment portfolios.

Chapter 15

50 Tax Reduction Strategies for Investors

1988 – No New Taxes – "Read My Lips"

The 1990 tax hike was put through in spite of President Bush's campaign promise not to raise taxes under any circumstances. Although it wasn't complicated, a significant tax increase occurred nonetheless. I have heard some talk of this being the second largest tax increase in history. I'm not certain this is correct, but it is clear that many taxpayers are paying thousands of dollars more now than in 1986.

The highlights of the 1990 Omnibus Budget Reconciliation Act (OBRA) are as follows: Any individual with an adjusted gross income of $100,000 or more loses itemized deductions equivalent to the lesser of:

1) 3% of income over $100,000; or
2) 80% of itemized deductions excluding medical, casualty loss, and investment interest expenses.

If history is any indication of what is to come next, this 3% subtraction will increase very shortly to 5%, 10%, and possibly more.

In addition, the OBRA raised limits on part of social security from deductions payroll of high income individuals. The medicare payroll tax now covers the first $125,000 of income. For salaried people the percentage is 1.45% and for self–employed people the percentage is 2.9%. This amount of money is more than double last year's limit of $53,000. For people who are successfully self–employed, that's approximately $2,000 of additional taxes which will be paid as a result of just this one provision.

1990s – The New Taxes – "Read My Tips"

As part of my plan to combat this 1990 increase and to help neutralize the devastating effect on investors of the 1986 Tax Reform Act, I have put together a compilation of 50 of my favorite strategies for reducing tax liability. All of these strategies, if correctly applied, can help reduce your tax burden. Actually, they are more than simply pointers, they are part of an overall strategy for tax reduction. For this reason I call them strategies as well as "tips," because in this context, the two words are synonymous. Regardless of what they are called, you should use the ones which most appropriately fit your tax situation, and in doing so, they will allow you to increase your investment yield through implementing a maximization of total return investment planning (TRIP).

So now, on to the 50 tax reduction strategies for investors, or "Read My Tips."

Tax Tip #1: Establish a trading business. If you qualify as a trader, report your trading income on Schedule C along with your expenses (as was specified in Chapter 13). Don't forget to calculate any self–employment tax on your net profits. Aside from bypassing the 2% and 3% floors for itemized deductions, you will be able to deduct many expenses which you are presently incurring but haven't deducted.

Tax Tip #2: Hire your son or daughter to work for you as either a salaried employee or a consultant. Any service they may provide for you, relating to your business, will qualify them to receive deductible compensation from you for this service. Jobs such as straightening up your desk, sweeping the room, carrying out your trash, and servicing and updating your computers, etc., can be valuable services to your business. In setting the situation up like this, you can legally deduct allowance payments you may already be making to them but are not able to deduct. They will, of course, have to declare this money as income, but chances are it will be taxed at a lower rate. And, unless they have income above a certain level, they will not be taxed on it at all. This is a good method of shifting income among your family members to lower tax brackets. There may be some payroll tax due, so have someone familiar with this statute help you set it up.

242

Tax Tip #3: Always review your investments periodically to determine which, if any, can be written off. Keep all documentation relating to the potential worthlessness of an investment, such as an attorney's letter, news article, etc., in a special tax folder as backup. There are no specific standards which the IRS will look towards as a precondition for worthlessness of an investment. Discretion is reserved for each situation. An investment deemed worthless can be taken as a short–term capital loss, subject to the same capital loss restrictions as other types of capital losses per Section 1221. The tax law allows you to write off an investment in the year that it becomes completely worthless (Code Section 165(g)). Bankruptcy of a company is not a precondition if worthlessness is evidenced through other substantiation.

Tax Tip #4: Always review your portfolio towards year end to determine if sales of securities will be beneficial to your tax situation. Should you have a realized loss on the sale of stock during the year exceeding $3,000, you may want to sell another investment which has an unrealized gain at that time. You might want to invest in something else, or simply reinvest in the same stock, but wish a higher tax basis for gifting or contribution purposes. "Wash sale" rules do not prohibit you from selling your stock at a gain and then repurchasing it within 30 days. This is only true if there is a loss on the sale of the stock (Code Section 1091(a)).

Tax Tip #5: Instead of selling a stock at year end to protect a gain, you may consider the alternative of buying puts to protect against erosion in your position while you avoid paying capital gains tax on it. By purchasing a put on stock or an OEX put, you would be able to assure that a loss in value could not go beyond a certain amount while still owning the stock.

For instance, say you purchased General Grits for $80 in November, and the stock goes up to $100 by December 31st. You believe the stock is basically worth holding, but feel the market is due for a correction. You may do the following: purchase the January, $95 puts for approximately $2 per put, guaranteeing you receive no less than $95 per share for your "Grits," or $15 per share profit. Even in the event of a serious market decline, the premium of $2 per share, or $200 per 100 shares, would protect you against any erosion in value beyond $5 per share.

243

Tax Tip #6: If you feel that the market is **not** in for a serious decline, but rather a very minor pullback, you can sell the January calls on your stock to protect against the erosion in value of only several points. You would not have to declare income on these calls until they expired next year. Another somewhat more advanced strategy would be to put on an OEX January call credit spread. This might be preferable due to the tax considerations and could actually be managed more aggressively to result in your taking out some profit even in a sideways move.

Tax Tip #7: If you are expecting a severe market decline, and you have a similar situation as tax strategy #5 above, another course of action would be to "short General Grits against the box." When you short against the box you are basically borrowing somebody else's stock to sell in the market, instead of selling yours. This will allow you to postpone the gain until the following year when you can use your stock to pay back the borrowed shares and complete the transaction. At this point you would report the gain or loss from the shorting of the stock as well as the gain or loss from your original purchase.

Tax Tip #8: Earmark shares of stock and mutual fund purchases so as to maximize your tax advantage when these items are sold. When shares are purchased over a period of time they are purchased at different prices. At the time shares are sold you can control which shares are considered to have been sold.

You can earmark shares sold to have either the highest or lowest cost basis, depending on whether or not you want to recognize more or less income in the year of the sale. For example, suppose you bought 1,000 shares of a stock at $20 per share and later bought another 1,000 shares at $30 per share. In the future, if the price goes up to $35 per share and you want to sell half of your position, you have a choice of which 1000 lot share to sell.

If you tell your broker to sell the second thousand shares, your gain is $5 per share. But, if you do not designate which shares you want sold, the IRS will treat it as if the first shares purchased were the first shares sold (Code Section 1012–1(c)).

The gain would be $15 per share, or in this case $15,000 as opposed to $5,000. Your broker should be notified in writing with instructions for selling specific lots of stock. A copy of this letter should be kept in your tax file.

Tax Tip #9: Get the IRS to absorb some of the cost of the sales load when you buy into a mutual fund. The way to work this is to first put your money into a fund you do not want to stay in, say, the money market fund. In most fund families, there is no load for switching between funds, only in or out of the group.

If this is the case, after three months, switch your investment to the fund you want to invest in, for example the growth fund. When you sell out of the money market, you will have realized a small loss, which is the load you were charged for the original purchase. When you report this transaction on your tax return, the result will be a loss equal to the amount of the load. In this manner, you get to deduct the sales fee from your tax return immediately.

In a recent ruling the IRS made this process more difficult by claiming that it was a "step transaction" and disallowed the loss. However, the way it stands, if you wait 90 days you should have no problem.

Tax Tip #10: Use tax swapping to defer gains on exchanges of capital assets. The tax swap is an action which generates paper losses. The way it works is the investor finds in his portfolio that some securities have decreased in value since being acquired. He sells these securities to generate the loss and then immediately reinvests the sale proceeds to purchase **similar** securities. The sale generates a capital loss that can be used to offset any capital gains received during the year, plus up to an additional $3,000 loss against ordinary income.

But the loss is really only a paper loss, since the value of the investor's portfolio remains approximately the same.

By similar, I mean **similar and not identical**. If a bond were to be sold, a similar bond might be one of a different company with the same coupon, maturity date, and credit rating. When a stock is sold a similar stock might be that of a different company in the same type of industry. Be certain not to invest in the same exact item unless you wait a full 31 days before doing so. Otherwise, the loss will be disqualified due to the "wash sale" rule.

Tax Tip #11: Make a tax deferred exchange of real estate or insurance policies. If you would like to sell real property on which you have a gain, or you would like to get out of an insurance policy, but don't want to recognize the gain, you may be able to use what is known as a deferred tax swap of like kind property. The rules for doing this are rather complicated, but many people can meet these criteria. No tax will be paid regardless of the amount of gain involved if you qualify. You should consult with your investment–tax advisor as to what is necessary to qualify for this tax treatment.

Tax Tip #12: Make use of the installment sale method of selling certain types of capital gain items. The installment sale rules have been modified significantly with the Tax Reform Act. Publicly traded items such as stock cannot be sold on installment. However, there still is the opportunity to use such a method of recognizing your gain over a longer period of time than simply when the sale is made for other capital items such as real estate. Check into the opportunities for availing yourself of this treatment before you make a large sale of property.

Tax Tip #13: Prepay your state estimated taxes prior to the end of the year. Although the fourth quarter estimated tax payment is not due until January 15th of the following year, if you mail it out prior to Dec. 31st, you may deduct it on that year's tax return.

A caveat here is that you have to be aware of potential alternative minimum tax liability if the payment is very large or if you have a great many "preference" items. The deduction for state taxes paid is now an AMT addback. Also, do not **overpay** your state taxes just to get the deduction. If you do, the IRS can penalize you for overpaying and deducting an unreasonable amount.

Tax Tip #14: If you own vacation property, consider renting it out for two weeks or less per year to collect income which does not have to be reported on your tax return. Code section 280A specifically states that if a property is rented for less than 15 days a year, no rental income needs to be reported.

Tax Tip #15: Instead of having one or two retirement plans which contain the bulk of your funds, consider breaking them up into 12 different smaller ones. If this is done properly, you can roll over a plan each month, and, in effect, have a tax free, interest free, permanent 60–day loan from your retirement plans.

A taxpayer is allowed to withdraw money from an IRA for up to 60 days once every 365 days (Code section 402(A)(5)). This provision is designed to let you move funds from one IRA sponsor to another. But there is no restriction on what you do with the money during the 60–day period, as long as you redeposit it to an IRA within that time period.

Tax Tip #16: Gift assets with low current income streams to children under the age of 14. This would be done to keep them from having investment income above $1,000, which would subject them to the kiddie tax. This method of shifting assets should be done on an annual basis to provide for maximum passage of tax–free wealth from one generation to the next.

Tax Tip #17: Gift assets with the lowest cost basis to the youngest heirs. This strategy is similar to strategy #16 in purpose. By transferring the lowest cost basis stocks and other assets to the youngest heirs, you are, in essence, gifting those assets with the highest potential appreciation to them.

Tax Tip #18: Avoid tax on dividends by selling mutual funds before dividends are declared and repurchase them afterwards. Most mutual funds declare dividends only once a year, in late December. You can usually determine when these dividends will be declared by calling the fund and asking them. You can then sell the fund and transfer the proceeds to a money market fund shortly before the dividend is declared. After the dividend is declared, repurchase the fund immediately. You will have to consider the advantages and disadvantages of such a strategy depending on your capital gain or loss situation for the year.

Such a sale is a capital transaction in most cases and consequently will generate a capital gain or a capital loss. But if you are in a tax situation where you have a capital loss in another investment not fully being used and a capital gain in the fund, this strategy can save you considerable tax dollars. Instead of having to recognize a taxable dividend from this fund, you can convert it into a capital gain which can then be offset by the capital loss which you otherwise may not have been able to utilize that year.

Tax Tip #19: If you have contributed the maximum deductible contribution to your retirement plan for the year, consider investing in a tax deferred annuity.

247

Tax Tip #20: If you have a business or can start one, hire your spouse and create a deductible IRA. No matter what you do, you can hire a non–working spouse, pay them, and create a $2,000 tax deduction from your total income. This is assuming that you qualify for a deductible IRA contribution as outlined in the chapter on retirement plans.

You can also hire elderly parents or other family members to work for you. In addition to the benefits of putting away deductible money for them, you can provide such items as company paid life insurance, health insurance, tuition for job–related education, travel, and entertainment, which will be deductions to your business. As in Tip #2, there may be payroll tax considerations and possible compliance with various statutes, so have a CPA or someone knowledgeable in this area assist you in setting it up initially.

Tax Tip #21: Parents should consider reporting their children's investment income on their own tax return. If your child is under age fourteen and has investment income over $1,000, you can avoid the hassle and expense of filing a separate tax return and kiddie tax form for the child by including their income on your tax return.

Tax Tip #22: Use the long form to file your tax return, even if you do not itemize your deductions. Some deductions are taken as "adjustments" to income and are known as above the line deductions. These are available even if you do not itemize your expenses. They are not available to those who file a short form.

Such subtractions you may be entitled to are: retirement plan contributions, penalties on early withdrawal of savings, alimony payments, deduction for self–employment tax and health insurance, and disability income exclusion.

Tax Tip #23: Sometimes you can save money by not filing a joint tax return if you are married. As we have explained throughout this book, several types of expenses are deductible only when they exceed a percentage of adjusted gross income. If one spouse has a high amount of these expenses and a lower gross income, it might make sense for the couple to file separate returns.

Tax Tip #24: The IRS allows a deduction of 27 1/2 cents per mile for business related automobile use (for the 1991 tax year). This

248

would include actual business travel, as well as trips for the purpose of business promotion. Mileage associated with a business–related move is also deductible, but at a rate of $.09 per mile.

There is one caveat regarding the above deduction. You must maintain detailed and accurate records of all such automobile use with reference to purpose, location, and actual mileage.

Tax Tip #25: If you are holding bonds which have increased in value since you purchased them, use that gain to offset a realized loss you may have on another item. Many investors may have bonds with a higher interest rate than the newer ones offered today. If this is the case, they will be worth a premium over their face value.

Sell your bonds and realize the gain. Then buy the same bonds back at a premium. The law allows you to amortize the premium over the life of the bond so you get an annual deduction from the interest earned. The wash sale rules do not apply here, even if you purchase the same bonds back the day you sold them, because you have a **gain.**

Tax Tip #26: Create a revocable living trust to avoid huge costs of probate. In addition, as described in Chapter 12, you will increase your unified credit per married couple from $600,000 of assets to $1,200,000 of assets.

Tax Tip #27: Open an IRA and/or KEOGH. Even if your income is too high to qualify for the IRA deduction you will still benefit by making non–deductible contributions. Interest, dividends, and capital gains grow and compound tax–free inside the retirement plan. See Section 11 on the added wealth you will accumulate within such a tax–free plan as opposed to investing in a taxable instrument.

One particularly good no–load fund I use for this is the SIT "New Beginnings" Mutual Fund Group. They are headed up by Eugene Sit, a Harvard–trained economist who personally manages the funds. They offer a wide range of funds and are still small enough to be managed properly. They have several different options available for retirement planning and can arrange to have an amount of money automatically transferred to your account each month. This makes for an easy and disciplined method of contributing to your retirement plan.

Tax Tip #28: Deduct the full contribution to an IRA even though you have not yet contributed. The full amount must be deposited by April 15th of the following year. If you file early enough in the year to receive a refund by the date the contribution is due, you can use this refund to partially fund the IRA.

For example, suppose you have an IRA and are eligible for a fully deductible contribution of $2,000. You file your 1992 tax return in early January of 1993, deducting $2,000 for an IRA contribution which you have not yet made. Assuming you live in New York City, where the combined federal and state tax rate can be in excess of 40%, the tax saving on such a contribution would be approximately $800. When you receive your refund, assuming it is prior to April 15, 1993, you use this $800 to partially fund the IRA.

Thus, the government essentially contributes $800 for every $1200 you contribute towards your retirement. This is a gift from your Uncle Sam and should be accepted graciously.

Tax Tip #29: You can get an instant deduction on a stock you are carrying at a loss without giving up the stock. Under most circumstances, the wash sale rules would deter you from selling a stock for a loss and then buying it back again within 30 days.

However, you could sell it out of your regular portfolio for a loss (which you could take as a capital loss on your tax return) and contribute the cash to your retirement plan. If you then repurchase it in your retirement plan, it is treated as a new purchase by another entity and the wash sale rules do not apply.

Tax Tip #30: Make use of the new gold and silver bullion coins minted by the United States Treasury as investments for your retirement plan. As was discussed in the section on retirement planning, most collectibles are not permitted as investments for retirement plans. The exception to this rule are these bullion coins, and although you cannot put other forms of gold or silver into your IRA, these coins are now permitted as investments.

Tax Tip #31: If your child or grandchild is of college–age, consider purchasing a small apartment building or multi–bedroom house in the college town. It would serve as an investment for you and could provide additional tax benefits and help pay for tuition.

Assuming your son or daughter goes away to college, the proper way to handle this from a tax point of view would be to have them live in the apartment and serve as manager. They would live in the apartment rent free, and be paid a salary for doing this. The salary, as well as the building upkeep and the depreciation would be deductible. In return, they would mow the lawn, collect the rent, supervise any repairs and maintenance of the property, and so on. Of course, they would have to pay income tax on the salary, but the first $3,400 of compensation escapes federal taxation, and the remainder, net of deductions, would probably be taxed at a 15% tax rate. This is a lower tax rate than you would pay on the same money and they could use it to pay for their tuition.

Tax Tip #32: Establish an annual gifting program to family members. To cut down on estate taxes, make use of the $10,000 per year ($20,000 per couple), per recipient gift tax exclusion. Evaluate the basis of the asset before making the gift. When the gift is made, it takes on the lower of the market value or the original basis of the gift. When the asset passes through an estate at the time of the one's death, it gets a "stepped up basis" to either the fair market value or the alternate valuation, six months after death. Give away the highest basis assets first.

Tax Tip #33: Assets you are holding at a loss should never be gifted. In doing so, the loss could never be recognized by either person. The asset would take on the market value at the time of the gift since it is lower than the cost. Rather, a person should sell the asset, recognize the loss on his tax return, and then gift the money from the sale of the asset. The value given away would be the same, only the giftor would get the benefit of a tax loss.

Tax Tip #34: Give appreciated assets away to charity. Suppose you wanted to give $10,000 to your favorite charity: consider making the gift in the form of appreciated property you have. In this fashion, you avoid paying the capital gains tax on the appreciation. However, because the appreciation may be subject to alternative minimum tax, you would have to do a projection to determine if this would affect you. Most people are not subject to AMT. If you are, you would chose to give away an asset with a high rather than low basis.

Tax Tip #35: If the end of the year has arrived and you have not made any provision for retirement planning, it's not too late. Assuming you meet the criteria, you can still establish an SEP for

last year. Even if you do not have the available cash to currently fund it, you could extend your tax return until October 15th. If you make the contribution by then, it can still be deducted on what is essentially last year's tax return.

Tax Tip #36: Invest in Series EE savings bonds to save for a child's college expenses. The interest on such bonds issued after 1989 will be tax–free when it is used to pay for college. The requirements are addressed more fully in Section 5.

Tax Tip #37: Use margin accounts only to purchase taxable investments. If the investment you purchase on margin is tax–free, the margin interest you pay is not tax deductible.

Tax Tip 38: Never purchase tax–free instruments in a retirement account. The return on a tax–free instrument reflects its tax–free status, and it usually pays a much lower yield. If you are purchasing an asset for your retirement plan, there is no further benefit to purchasing one that is tax–free. Everything earned within the plan is tax deferred; thus, yield should not be sacrificed for favorable tax status.

Tax Tip #39: Move to a lower tax state to save substantial state taxes. The range of state income tax rates goes from a high of approximately 15% to a low of 0. The larger municipalities such as Washington, D.C. and New York City have the highest state income tax rates, while states such as Texas and Florida have none.

January 1992, *Money* magazine published a survey of the tax burden of all 50 states. The "tax" consisted of a composite tax on income, sales tax, gasoline tax, and real estate taxes. They found that state taxes rose an average of 116% since 1980–almost twice the federal increase. And, in fact, state taxes rose $17 billion in 1991 alone, according to the article.

The difference between states is significant. A two–wage earner family of four, earning $69,275 (median *Money* household) would pay over twice the state and local tax in New York City ($8,841) compared to the same family in New Hampshire ($4,345).

Tax Tip #40: Never apply an overpayment to the next year's tax return or you will be giving the government a tax–free loan.

Regardless of how low the rate of return on that money would be in your hands, it is greater than getting absolutely nothing by letting the government hold it for a year.

Tax Tip #41: Establish a Charitable Remainder Trust (CRT) to generate a charitable contribution deduction and avoid capital gains tax on appreciated assets. By transferring growth stocks to a CRT you get an upfront charitable deduction, avoid capital gains on the sale of the assets, and avoid estate taxes. In addition, you can switch the beneficiary to any charity you choose should your preference change.

With this type of trust you continue to get the income from the investment for the duration of your life, and when you die, the assets go to charity. Furthermore, you can replace any asset with a higher yielding investment by selling it within the trust. You do not have to pay capital gains on the sale of this appreciated capital asset. The goal would be to sell whatever you donate and replace it with the highest current yielding investment available, such as a high income mutual fund.

Tax Tip #42: If you establish a Charitable Remainder Trust, you can still leave an amount equal to the donated property to your heirs, free of federal estate taxes. This is accomplished by the establishing of a Wealth Replacement Trust (Irrevocable Life Insurance Trust). You can use the additional income generated by the greater yielding investments purchased in the CRT to fund this trust.

The actual administration of these two trusts must be done by an attorney as it is somewhat complex. The benefits are, however, well worth the effort.

Tax Tip #43: Protect your estate from taxes by purchasing a "second–to–die" insurance plan. It would cost you approximately 1% of your total net worth to purchase a joint–last survivor insurance policy. The insurance company pays nothing until the second spouse dies. The unlimited marital deduction will pass all the assets to the surviving spouse and, upon his or her death, the insurance company provides cash to pay the estate taxes.

Tax Tip #44: Give property to a parent who does not have a large taxable estate. If you have an investment which has appreciated in value, gift it to your parents using the annual exclusion as previously described. When the parent dies, it will become part of their estate and get a stepped up basis. If the parent has an estate under $600,000, the property will pass through without any federal tax to anyone in the will with a higher tax basis.

Tax Tip #45: If you are self–employed and pay for your medical insurance, you receive an additional benefit. Aside from an itemized deduction (subject to a 7 1/2 % floor), you will be entitled to deduct one quarter of the cost directly from income. It is allowed as an "above the line" deduction as discussed in Tax Tip #22.

Tax Tip #46: Defer interest to subsequent years by the purchase of Treasury Bills. If you are in a high tax bracket currently but will be in a lower bracket the following year, you will want to postpone as much income as possible until then. One way of doing this is to purchase Treasury Bills with maturity dates in the next tax year.

With most regular bonds, you must recognize interest when it is accrued. With Treasuries, you do not have to recognize the income until the Bill comes due and you receive the cash. This would be in either three, six, or nine months, or a year, depending on how long a Treasury Bill you purchased.

Tax Tip #47: Defer interest to subsequent years by the purchase of a Certificate of Deposit. Another method of postponing income is through the purchase of a CD which allows you to elect to leave the interest with the bank until maturity. This type of arrangement will defer tax until the interest is received.

Tax Tip #48: If you have passive activities which are generating Passive Activity Losses (PALs) which can not be used, consider investing in a Passive Income Generator (PIG).

Explore the purchase of a parking lot or a partnership owning parking lots. They generally provide a steady source of income and there is no question as to their passive activities status. Also, a good real estate property or partnership which generates income is always considered to be passive, even if you participate in the management of it.

Tax Tip #49: If you have implemented the strategies reviewed in this book, your tax liability will decrease significantly.

Since you are legally allowed to increase the number of allowances you claim, you will reach a breakeven point with the IRS. Don't let your money sit with the government without earning interest.

Increase the number of allowances on your W–4 so that less withholding tax is taken out of your pay each week. You can do this anytime in the year by advising your employer. Do so in writing and he will be required to provide you with another W–4 to complete.

The number of allowances is not contingent entirely on your dependents. If you are in the 28% tax bracket, every allowance you add will increase your monthly take home by approximately $50. If you are in the 15% bracket, it will increase it by about $25. You should fine tune your withholding to the zero–tax–point level.

Tax Tip #50: **Write off this book!** It is both an investment and a tax guide, and consequently is a legitimate tax deduction. Most taxpayers would deduct it on the Schedule A, line 20, as a miscellaneous itemized deduction. If you qualify as a trader and file a Schedule C, it should be deducted on the Schedule C to avoid the 2% and 3% floors on miscellaneous itemized deductions.

In any event, this book has provided you with information which has increased your investment and tax expertise. Within this context, save your receipts, cancelled checks, and credit card statements, and remember to **WRITE IT OFF!**

1992–Election Postcript–"Read My Slips"

November 4, 1992: With the opportunity to do a bit of post–election reflection today, it becomes clear to me that the issues of this election boiled down to two major ones, the economy and the "T" word, taxes.

A discussion of **who** won is not as meaningful as **why** he did. Undoubtedly Mr. Clinton convinced the American Taxpayer that his economic plan and tax policy will contribute to recovery more effectively than that of Mr. Bush.

On the other hand, Mr. Bush apparently did more damage to his credibility than could be repaired after his infamous "read my lips" 1988 campaign promise and 1990 reversal. The final blow to this credibility was Mr. Bush's insistence that the economy was not really as bad as it seemed. The American Taxpayer, however, decided it was and basically used this election as a referendum of Bush's economic and tax policies.

255

As an example of the significance of these two issues on the campaign, and of the preoccupation each candidate had with them, we need only to review a slip of the tongue made by President Bush on the campaign trail. *The New York Times* reported,

> He [President Bush] accused Mr. Clinton of 'threatening 4.5 million jobs'...by proposing to raise taxes on foreign companies with American based plants...He warned repeatedly that Mr. Clinton was 'going right after your wallet,' with proposals for $150 billion in new Federal taxes...But the President inadvertently stepped on his anti–Clinton message–and perhaps betrayed his own concerns...He told a crowd of 15,000 that he appreciated their **lovely recession** rather than reception.*

George Bush suffered a tremendous defeat, especially in light of the enormous popularity he enjoyed earlier in 1992. *The New York Times* reported that as recently as March, 1991, his approval rating was an overwhelming 88%. They report a quote from prominent Republican J.R. West, who served under both Presidents Ford and Reagan,

> He was king of the mountain after the Persian Gulf War...He could have achieved almost anything. He was so popular that if he had drawn up a program, gone to Capital Hill and battled for it, Congress would not have dared defy him. But he didn't do anything at all.*

Now George Bush has suffered the fate of Jimmy Carter, William Taft, and Herbert Hoover, the only other presidents elected in the last century to lose a re–election bid. Those three others were also victims of recessions, weak economic policies, or both. And the American public has once again proven that when it comes right down to it they will sometimes vote their hearts, but will always vote their pocketbooks.

---

*Reprinted by permission of *New York Times*, ©1992, New York Times, Inc. All Rights Reserved Worldwide.

With Mr. Clinton getting something like two–thirds of the electorate, he will be hard pressed to turn this thing around, and to do it quickly. After an election triumph such as this, which also brought a Democratic Congress in on its coattails, there will be no excuse for him not producing the huge economic improvements he alluded to during the campaign.

It seems to me that if President Clinton wants to get off to a real good start, he might consider reinstating some of the tax breaks taken away from the investor. The Investment Tax Credit, for one, would be a nice start. Its omission was one of the big mistakes of the last tax bill.

If he truly wants GROWTH in the economy, he will need INVESTMENT, and in order to get this thing rolling he will need INVESTORS to do what they do best.

A favorable tax bill would be a good place to start. If this does happen, there is unlimited potential for economic growth and opportunity. With new markets opening all over the world, this could be the most favorable economic climate for investors since the turn of the century.

In any event, very shortly we shall see. "Clinton received a massive pro–change vote...to jumpstart this nation's stalled economy".* If he does, he earns my respect and I take my hat off to him. If not, he will probably just become number five.

Appendix
Summary of the Tax Treatment of Various Investment and Investment–Related Items

1) **Stock**: Generally a shareholder who sells or exchanges his stock for other property realizes a capital gain or loss. Whether or not the gain or loss is long–term or short–term depends on how long the investor held the stock before selling (or exchanging) it.

When shares are sold, the gain or loss is the difference between the investor's tax basis (the purchase price or adjusted purchase price) and the selling price. If stock is exchanged for similar stock in the same corporation, it is considered to be a like kind exchange and no gain or loss is required to be reported on the tax return.

When stock is all purchased in one lot, or purchased at the same time and cost as other lots of the same stock, there is no problem with establishing the date of acquisition. When holdings of the same stock have been acquired in several lots (at different dates and/or for different costs), the investor has to determine the date of acquisition and tax basis of the stock. This information is necessary to report the sale.

He can use a first–in first–out method, whereby the first lot purchased becomes the first lot sold. Or, he can use a method of specifically identifying the lot he wishes to consider sold. By using specific identification, an investor can sell a higher priced, subsequently purchased lot of stock first in order to postpone the potential recognition of a capital gain.

For example, an investor purchases 100 shares of IBM at $100 per share and a month later purchases another 100 lot at $110 per share. If he sells 100 shares (1/2 his holdings) two months later at $120 per share, he can determine his tax basis for the 100 shares sold in two ways.

Using the first–in first–out method, he would first sell the 100 shares he purchased at $100 per share. His gain would then be $20 per share, or $2,000. Using the second method of specific identification, he could specifically identify the lot he wishes to sell as being the second lot, purchased at $110 per share. In this case, his gain would be $10 per share ($120–$110), or $1,000. If, on the other hand, he purchased the first lot for more than the second, he could use the first–in first–out method to reduce the gain.

How To Report: Both gains and losses are reported on Schedule D. If the gain is short–term is it listed on Part I, line 1a and if the gain or loss is long–term, it is reported on Part II, line 8a.

2) **Equity Options**: If an option is not exercised, but rather sold before it expires, the tax treatment is the same as that of an ordinary equity. That is, the gain or loss is calculated based on purchase price (or tax basis, if different) and sales proceeds. Short– or long–term status is based on date of purchase and date of sale. There is no marking to market at year end for a holder of an equity option, as will be illustrated in the case in a non–equity option, to be discussed in #3, to follow.

For the holder of an option which expires worthless, a loss is recognized for the amount of premium. For the writer of an option which expires worthless, a gain is recognized for the amount of premium received (less commission costs). If the option is exercised, the tax treatment affecting the writer of the option and the purchaser of the option are different.

1) For the investor who has exercised the option, the cost of the option is not deductible, but rather affects the price of the stock. The following two scenarios can occur:

a) The option holder was long calls and exercises them to purchase a stock. In this case, the cost of the option is added to the cost basis of the security. Gain or loss will be calculated on the stock when it is sold.

b) The option holder was long puts and exercises them to sell stock. In this case, the cost of the put reduces the proceeds received for the stock.

2) For the writer (seller) of an option exercised before expiration, the proceeds from the sale of the option are not recognized alone as income, but rather affect the price of the stock being called or put. The following two scenarios can occur:

a) The writer of a call has the stock called away from him. In this case, the proceeds of the sale of the stock to the option holder are increased by the option premium received.

b) The writer of a put which has been exercised must now purchase the shares of stock for a certain price. In this case, the cost of the stock to him is reduced by the option premium he received for the put.

How To Report: Both gains and losses are considered short–term for options which expire worthless unless the person is in the business of equity options (market maker).

In cases where an option is exercised, a short– or long–term gain or loss is determined by the holding period of the stock, not the option.

The gain or loss is reported on Schedule D. If short–term it is listed on Part I, line 1a (if the transaction is reported to you on a 1099b, the most common way) or Part I, line 1d (if it is not reported to you on a 1099b).

If the gain or loss is long–term, it is reported on Part II, line 8a (if the transaction is reported to you on a 1099b, the most common way) or Part II, line 8d (if it is not reported to you on a 1099b).

3) **Index Options and Futures Contracts**: An index option, such as an OEX call or put, is treated as a commodity (futures contract) for tax purposes, not an equity. In this regard, it is marked to market at year end, and the purchase or sale is viewed as a complete transaction at that time (December 31st). The closing price on December 31st is considered to be the price received or paid to complete the transaction and is also used in calculating the new basis for the following year.

Other types of investment vehicles treated in this manner include Nikkei put warrants (see Chapter 1, and #8 below), foreign currency contracts, and dealer equity options.

How To Report: Any capital gains or losses arising from these transactions are treated as if they were 60% long–term and 40% short–term without regard to their holding period. They are reported on form 6781, part 1, line 1 (Exhibit B1). They are then carried to Schedule D, Part I, line 1d and Part II, line 8d. It does not matter how long the option or futures contract was actually held.

4) **U.S. T–Bills**: Interest taxable on the federal tax return, but usually tax–free on the state. If held to maturity, the interest is included in the proceeds received and is reported at the time of receipt for cash basis tax payers (99% of all individuals).

There is no capital gain or loss on a T–Bill held to maturity. The difference between the purchase price and the proceeds received is deemed to be interest.

261

Appendix

<table>
<tr><td colspan="2">Form 6781</td><td colspan="2">Gains and Losses From Section 1256 Contracts and Straddles
▶ See instructions on back.
▶ Attach to your tax return.</td><td>OMB No. 1545-0644
1991
Attachment Sequence No. 82</td></tr>
</table>

Department of the Treasury
Internal Revenue Service

Name(s) shown on tax return	Identifying number

A. ☐ Check here if you made the mixed straddle election under section 1256(d) this year or an earlier year.
B. ☐ Check here if you made the straddle-by-straddle identification election under section 1092(b).
C. ☐ Check here to make the mixed straddle account election under section 1092(b).
D. ☐ Check here if you elect to carry back a net section 1256 contracts loss.

Part I   Section 1256 Contracts Marked to Market

(a) Identification of account	(b) LOSS	(c) GAIN
1		

2 Add amounts on line 1 in columns (b) and (c) . . . . (   )
3 Net gain or (loss). Combine columns (b) and (c) of line 2 . . . .
4 Form 1099-B adjustments (see instructions and attach schedule) . . . .
5 Combine lines 3 and 4. (If a net gain, skip line 6 and enter the gain on line 7.) Partnerships and S corporations, see instructions
6 If you have a net section 1256 contracts loss and checked box D, enter the amount to be carried back . .
7 Subtract line 6 from line 5 . . . .
8 Multiply line 7 by 40%. Enter as a short-term capital gain or (loss) on Schedule D. Identify as Form 6781, Part I . .
9 Multiply line 7 by 60%. Enter as a long-term capital gain or (loss) on Schedule D. Identify as Form 6781, Part I

Part II   Gains and Losses From Straddles (Attach a separate schedule listing each straddle and its components.)

Section A.—Losses From Straddles

(a) Description of property	(b) Date entered into or acquired	(c) Date closed out or sold	(d) Gross sales price	(e) Cost or other basis plus expense of sale	(f) LOSS If column (e) is more than (d), enter difference. Otherwise, enter -0-.	(g) Unrecognized gain on offsetting positions	(h) RECOGNIZED LOSS. If column (f) is more than (g), enter difference. Otherwise, enter -0-.
10							

11a Enter short-term portion of line 10, column (h), here and on Schedule D. Identify as Form 6781, Part II . . . . . . (   )
  b Enter long-term portion of line 10, column (h), here and on Schedule D. Identify as Form 6781, Part II . . . . . . (   )

Section B.—Gains From Straddles

(a) Description of property	(b) Date entered into or acquired	(c) Date closed out or sold	(d) Gross sales price	(e) Cost or other basis plus expense of sale	(f) GAIN If column (d) is more than (e), enter difference. Otherwise, enter -0-.
12					

13a Enter short-term portion of line 12, column (f), here and on Schedule D. Identify as Form 6781, Part II . . .
  b Enter long-term portion of line 12, column (f), here and on Schedule D. Identify as Form 6781, Part II . . . .

Part III   Unrecognized Gains From Positions Held on Last Day of Tax Year (Memo Entry Only—See instructions)

(a) Description of property	(b) Date acquired	(c) Fair market value on last business day of tax year	(d) Cost or other basis as adjusted	(e) UNRECOGNIZED GAIN If column (c) is more than (d), enter difference. Otherwise, enter -0-.
14				

Instructions

(Section references are to the Internal Revenue Code unless otherwise noted.)

Paperwork Reduction Act Notice.—We ask for the information on this form to carry out the Internal Revenue laws of the United States. You are required to give us the information. We need it to ensure that you are complying with these laws and to allow us to figure and collect the right amount of tax.

The time needed to complete and file this form will vary depending on individual circumstances. The estimated average time is:

Recordkeeping	10 hrs., 17 min.
Learning about the law or the form	2 hrs., 28 min.
Preparing the form . . .	3 hrs., 40 min.
Copying, assembling, and sending the form to the IRS . . .	16 min.

If you have comments concerning the accuracy of these time estimates or suggestions for making this form more simple, we would be happy to hear from you. You can write to both the IRS and the Office of Management and Budget at the addresses listed in the instructions for the tax return with which this form is filed.

Purpose of Form.—Use Form 6781 to report:
● Any gain or loss on section 1256 contracts under the marked-to-market rules; and

Cat. No. 13715G   Form **6781** (1991)

Exhibit B1

If a T–Bill is sold before the maturity date, the proceeds must be split between interest and capital gain or capital loss. The amount of interest accrued to date of sale is calculated based on its original rate and reported as the interest (non–taxable to state) on the Schedule B if necessary or simply on line 8a, page 1 of the 1040. The cost plus this amount is used as your tax basis to calculate your gain or loss when subtracted from the proceeds received.

How To Report: Interest reported as federal interest on Schedule B (if total interest is over $400), or simply to line 8a (total interest $400 or less). On most state tax returns, you pick up the full amount of interest reported to the IRS, and put down "federal interest" as a subtraction from state income.

Gains or losses are reported on Schedule D, Part I, line 1a and Part II, line 8a. The capital transactions are treated as gains or losses for most state tax returns even though the interest is not generally considered income.

5) **Treasury Notes**: The interest is taxable on the federal tax return, but is usually tax–free on the state. Just as with T–Bills, it is taxable when received, but in this case, payments are usually received twice a year. If a premium was paid for the Note, a portion of it gets subtracted from interest each year (amortization). If the Note was purchased at a discount, a portion of the discount gets picked up as additional income each year. If a Treasury Note is sold before maturity, there could be a gain or loss on the disposition depending on the price paid and the amount of amortization taken to that point.

How To Report: The tax treatment of Treasury Notes is virtually the same as with T–Bills, the only difference being that the income is reported throughout the life of the Note as it is received. Interest is reported as federal interest on Schedule B (if total interest is over $400), or simply to line 8a (if total interest is $400 or less). On most state tax returns, you pick up the full amount of interest reported to the federal government and put down federal interest as a subtraction from state income, as done for T–Bill interest. Gains or losses are reported on Schedule D, Part I, line 1a and Part II, line 8a. The capital transactions are treated as gains or losses for most state tax returns even though the interest is not generally considered income.

6) **U.S. Savings Bonds**: The taxpayer has the choice of either declaring the interest for tax purposes at the time it is received, when

the Bond is redeemed, or amortizing it throughout the life of the Bond. There is also an exclusion for college tuition as was discussed previously (see Chapter 5). If the interest is taxable, it is taxable on the federal tax return, but is usually tax–free on the state, just as with T–Bills and Treasury Notes. If a savings bond is sold before maturity there could be a gain or loss on the disposition depending on the price paid.

How To Report: Interest is reported as federal interest on Schedule B (if total interest is over $400), or simply to line 8a (if total interest is $400 or less). On most state tax returns, you pick up the full amount of interest reported to the federal government and put down federal interest as a subtraction from state income. Gains or losses are reported on Schedule D, Part I, line 1a and Part II, line 8a. The capital transactions are treated as gains or losses for most state tax returns even though the interest is not generally considered income.

7) **Municipal Bonds**: The interest is usually exempt on the federal tax return (except for Private Activity Bonds which are subject to alternative minimum tax), exempt on the investor's state tax return if it is the state issuing them, and taxable on the tax return of a state which is not the investor's resident state. If a municipal bond is sold before maturity, there could be a gain or loss on the disposition depending on the price paid.

How To Report: Interest is reported as tax–exempt interest on Schedule B and not included in the total carried to line 8a (if total interest is over $400), or simply to line 8b (if total interest is $400 or less). On in–state tax returns, you pick up the full amount of interest reported to the federal government (without the amount of municipal interest in the total). You do not have to deal with any addback or subtraction, since it is also tax–free in the state of origin.

If it is an out–of–state issue, you must start with the federal income, and add back the out–of–state municipal interest.

Gains or losses are reported on Schedule D, Part I, line 1a and Part II, line 8a. If the bond is sold before maturity, the capital transactions are treated as gains or losses for federal tax purposes even though the interest is not generally considered income. If it is held to maturity, a gain can be recognized, due to a purchase at a discount. However, a loss can not be taken for bonds purchased at premium.

One final word: you can not deduct margin interest expense paid to carry tax–free notes. If an investor has paid margin interest to carry a mixed portfolio for any one tax year (a portfolio containing both taxable and non–taxable items), he must allocate the amount of margin interest as to deductible and non–deductible.

8) **Nikkei Put Warrants**: Treated as commodities and marked to market at year end for tax purposes. They are reported as are other commodities (see #3 above).

9) **Calls or Puts on the FTSE 100**: Treated as equity options to non–dealers and not marked to market. They are reported as are other equity options (see #2 above).

10) **Stock Dividends**: A stock dividend is a dividend paid to the stockholder in stock rather than cash.   This distribution may also be paid in warrants or other rights to acquire the stock.

Generally a stock dividend is not a taxable event, but rather the investor's tax basis of the lot of stock is reduced by some factor. For example, if an investor paid $100 per share for 50 shares of IBM, his basis for the entire purchase would be $5,000. If he sold any shares, the basis for each one would be $100 per share.

Assuming a non–taxable stock dividend of one share was paid for every one share held, the taxpayer would have 100 shares for which he paid the same $5,000. The basis per share, assuming he sold any of them would go down to $50 each (reduced by a factor of 1/2). In this way it will be reflected when the stock is sold.

Stock splits are treated essentially the same as stock dividends for tax purposes.

11) **Return of Capital**: If a corporation makes a distribution more than the accumulated profits of the company, it is considered to be a "return of capital." In this case, also, there is no taxable event. Rather, the investor's tax basis is reduced by the amount received. In this way it will also be reflected when the stock is sold.

Any return of capital above the original investment in the stock (the investor's tax basis) is usually treated as a capital gain and reported in the same manner as other capital gains on the Schedule D.

Appendix

12) **Dividend Reinvestment**: Although the dividend is reinvested, it is usually taxed as an ordinary dividend and reported on Schedule B (if over $400) or simply on the front page of the 1040, line 9. In this case, if a dividend is reinvested and taxed, the investor's basis for the stock would be **increased** to reflect such a taxable event. This would avoid paying taxes on the dividend when received and then paying taxes on it again as part of the sale. If an investor did not increase his tax basis, the proceeds from the additional stock or mutual fund shares reinvested would be considered an additional gain.

For example, if an investor owns a mutual fund where he reinvests dividends and the mutual fund pays a $401 dividend at year end, the taxpayer reports the dividend on his Schedule B. But, when it comes time to sell the mutual fund, his tax basis is increased by the dividend amount. In this way the tax paid on the dividend is reflected in the cost per shares of the fund. He will then have that much less of a gain or more of a loss on the sale of the mutual fund.

13) **Mutual Fund Switch From Equity to Cash**: Every time an equity fund is redeemed and put into cash, a taxable event takes place. That is, of course, unless the mutual fund is part of a retirement plan.

Thus, every time a switch is made from equity to cash, it translates into the sale of equities for tax purposes just as if the investor owned the stocks outright and sold them all. Every time a switch is made to equity from cash, it translates into the acquisition of tax basis as with the purchase of individual stocks.

Many investors who regularly switch between cash and equity in a non–retirement, no–load mutual funds are generating taxable transactions every time a switch is made. For this reason, detailed records must be maintained as all of these transactions must be reported on the tax return.

How To Report: Both gains and losses are reported on Schedule D. If they are short–term, they are listed on Part I, line 1a (if the transaction is reported to you on a 1099b, the most common way) or Part I, line 1d (if it is not reported to you on a 1099b).

If the gain or loss is long–term, it is reported on Part II, line 8a (if the transaction is reported to you on a 1099b, the most common way) or Part II, line 8d (if it is not reported to you on a 1099b).

266

14) **Short Sales of Stocks and Shorting against the Box**: A short stock sale occurs when an individual contracts to sell stock he does not own or does not wish to deliver at the time of the sale. A short sale seller usually borrows the stock for delivery to the buyer.

At a later date, the short seller will repay the borrowed shares by either purchasing those shares or relinquishing the shares he already holds but does not want to give up at the time the short sale is made. He will usually pay interest for the privilege of having borrowed the stock to sell short. This will be treated as an ordinary investment interest expense for tax purposes.

If a short seller "shorts against the box," he already owns the stock at the date he shorts it but chooses to short shares other than the ones he owns. A shorting against the box transaction is treated identical to that of simply shorting the stock.

The act of delivering the stock to the lender (repaying) and shorting against the box is called "closing the short sale." In both cases, this is the point that the taxable event occurs.

When a stock is sold short and the transaction is closed, a seller will realize a gain on the transaction if the price he pays for the borrowed shares are lower than the price he sold them for. If he covers at a higher price, he will realize a capital loss.

In other words, it is possible for an investor to short a stock even if he owns it at the time. This allows for the locking in of gains on a stock without actually selling that stock. In doing so, an investor would postpone the realization of capital gains which would then be incurred and reported by the outright relinquishing of the stock.

How To Report: Both gains and losses are reported on Schedule D. If it is short–term is it listed on Part I, line 1a. If the gain or loss is long–term, it is reported on Part II, line 8a.

The only distinction in the way a short sale is reported is when the sales date comes before the purchase date. Whether a gain or loss is long–term or short–term will generally be determined by how long the seller held the stock he uses to close the sale.

Let us look at an investor who shorts a stock against the box where he has owned the stock for more than a year. When he covers with his own stock, even a month later, the nature of the transaction will have been long–term (because he covered with stock he owned for more than a year). This is a general rule and there are certain exceptions to it which prevent investors from turning long–term gains or losses into short–term gains or losses, and vice versa.

15) **Incentive Stock Options**: An incentive stock option is an option granted to an individual in connection with his employment to purchase stock in the employer's corporation. No income is realized by the employee upon the granting of an incentive stock option if it is a qualifying transfer (certain conditions must be met by the employer). In addition, if it is a qualifying transfer, no income will be recognized when the option is exercised to obtain the stock.

How To Report: The income or loss will be recognized at the time of the sale of the stock and is determined by subtracting the tax basis from the proceeds realized. Both gains and losses are reported on Schedule D. If it is short–term, it is listed on Part I, line 1a. If the gain or loss is long–term, it is reported on Part II, line 8a.

Any reduced cost of the stock due to an incentive stock option will be reflected at that time as an additional gain (or reduced loss) on the sale of the stock because it will have resulted in a reduced tax basis of the stock.

ENDNOTES

[1] *Bartlett's Quotations*, 13th Edition, November 1991, Little Brown and Company. Boston, MA. Page 709A.

[2] For illustrative purposes, I use a flat tax rate instead of a graduated one in all the AMT calculation examples.

[3] For illustrative purposes, I use a flat tax rate of 31% as was the maximum in 1990.

[4] Very briefly, a **cash basis taxpayer** is one who declares income and deductions, "as the cash flows," either in or out (i.e., when salary is received, rather than earned). This is the opposite of an **accrual basis taxpayer** who recognizes income and expense as they are **incurred**. A **calendar year taxpayer** recognizes the tax year as being from Jan. 1 to Dec. 31, as opposed to any other 12–month period.

[5] U.S. Master Tax Guide, CCH, Inc., 1992, page 184, paragraph 710.

[6] U.S. Master Tax Guide, CCH, Inc., 1992, page 234, paragraph 920.

[7] U.S. Master Tax Guide, CCH, Inc. 1992, pages 247–248, paragraph 945-949.

[8] U.S. Master Tax Guide, CCH, Inc., 1992, page 305, paragraph 1195.

[9] U.S. Master Tax Guide, CCH, Inc., 1992, page 306, paragraph 1201.

[10] U.S. Master Tax Guide, CCH, Inc., 1992, page 308, paragraph 1208.

[11] Simon & Shuster, 1991.

[12] As a rule, Public Activity Munis are 100% tax–free, Private Activity Munis are tax–free to some degree (percentage can be obtained from a broker), and U.S. Treasuries are **100% taxable** for **federal** tax purposes.

[13] As a guide, most states do **not** tax income from U.S. Treasuries, do **not** tax income from **in-state** municipals, but **do** tax income from **out-of-state** municipals.

[14] Bond **pays** 9% per year, 9% multiplied by $10,000=$900.

[15] Ending principal less the $10,000 originally invested ($25,937 - $10,000 and $21,589 - $10,000, respectively).

[16] $15,937 - $7,690 actual return on investment using the 5.87% **true yield** ($17,690 - $10,000 original investment).

[17] $8,247 overstatement /$7,690 true return on investment.

[18] $7,690 return/$10,000 investment.

[19] U.S. Master Tax Guide, CCH, Inc., 1992, page 260, paragraph 972.

[20] *IRS Confidential*, Boardroom Reports, Inc., 1987, 1988, page 59.

[21] Publication No. 1 (6-89), Department of the Treasury, Internal Revenue Service, "Your Rights as a Taxpayer."

[22] Notice 746 (Revised 10/89), Department of the Treasury, Internal Revenue Service, "Information About Your Notice, Penalty and Interest."

[23] *Tax Avoidance Digest*, March 1992, Vol. II, No. 3, Agora Inc., 824 East Baltimore St., Baltimore, Md. 21202.

[24] *Ibid*, p.140

[25] *Ibid*, p.140

[26] Robert C. Carlson, J.D., CPA, *Tax Liberty*, Agora, Inc., 824 East Baltimore St., Baltimore, Md. 21202 1991.

[27] *More Wealth Without Risk*, Charles J. Givens, Simon & Schuster, 1991.

[28] *More Wealth Without Risk*, Charles J. Givens, Simon & Schuster, 1991.

ERRATA

The Serious Investor's Tax Survival Guide

ENDNOTES

Page 269, Endnote 11, should read:
More Wealth Without Risk, COPYRIGHT© 1988, 1991 by Charles Givens.
Reprinted by permission of Simon & Schuster, Inc.
Page 270, Endnote 20, should read:
Reprinted with permission of: Boardroom Classics
                               330 West 42nd St.
                               New York, NY 10036
Page 270, Endnote 27, 28 should read:
More Wealth Without Risk, COPYRIGHT© 1988, 1991 by Charles Givens.
Reprinted by permission of Simon & Schuster, Inc..
Page 271, Endnote 29, 39, should read:
More Wealth Without Risk, COPYRIGHT© 1988, 1991 by Charles Givens.
Reprinted by permission of Simon & Schuster, Inc..
Page 271, Endnote 30, 34, 36, should read:
Reprinted with permission of: Boardroom Classics
                               330 West 42nd St.
                               New York, NY 10036

[29] *More Wealth Without Risk*, Charles J. Givens, Simon & Schuster, 1991.

[30] *IRS Confidential*, Boardroom Reports, Inc., 1987, 1988, page 55.

[31] *Ibid.* p.153.

[32] *Tax Avoidance Digest*, February, 1992, Vol. 11, No. 2, Agora, Inc. 824 East Baltimore St., Baltimore, Md. 21202.

[33] *Ibid.* p.162

[34] Ms. X, Esq., *How To Beat The IRS*, Boardroom Books.

[35] Philip P. Storrer, *The 1981 Tax Fighter's Guide*, Harbor Publishing Co.

[36] *IRS Confidential*, Boardroom Books, Inc., 1987, 1988, page 58.

[37] Randy Bruce Blaustein, Esq., *How To Do Business With The IRS*, Prentice-Hall Books.

[38] *IRS Manual Transmittal*, 4200-471.

[39] Charles J. Givens, *More Wealth Without Risk* (Simon & Schuster, 1991).

[40] Robert C. Carlson, J.D., CPA, *Tax Liberty*, Agora, Inc., 824 East Baltimore St., Baltimore, Md. 21202 1991.

[41] U.S. Master Tax Guide, CCH, Inc., 1992, pages 27–28, paragraph 42.

[42] U.S. Master Tax Guide, CCH, Inc., 1992, page 445, paragraph 1903.

[43] *Ibid.* p.218.

[44] *Ibid.* p.219, page 426, par. 1760.

[45] Scott P. Murphy, CPA, *The Tax Advisor*, August 1992, pages. 517–518

[46] U.S. Tax Cases, 1989, CCH, paragraph 9633.

ENDNOTES

[47] *Ibid.* p.225

[48] *Ibid.* p.226

[49] *Ibid.* p.226

Glossary

Accrual Basis — An accounting method of reporting income when earned and expenses when incurred, as opposed to reporting income when received and expenses when paid. Ant: Cash Basis.

Accrued Interest — Interest that is added to the sales price of a bond when it is sold. This interest has accrued since the last interest payment up to but not including the settlement date.

Adjusted Basis — Cost adjusted by additions and subtractions to reflect changes that have occurred. Examples of adjustments would be dividends that are reinvested in a mutual fund, or futures contracts that have been marked to market at a previous year end. This adjusted basis is then used to calculate capital gains and losses upon disposition of the property.

Adjusted Gross Income — The basis on which an individual's taxable income is calculated. It is the gross taxable income before any itemized deductions are taken.

Alternate Documentation — In the audit process, an auditor will ask for specific forms of backup, and many times, when it is not possible to present the type asked for, another type will suffice.

Alternative Minimum Tax (AMT) — A tax calculation required in addition to your normal tax calculation. The Alternative Minimum Tax base is much larger, and although the AMT tax rate is less, many of the deductions allowed in the regular tax calculation are eliminated for AMT purposes. Therefore, many times the Alternative Minimum Tax is greater and must be paid instead of the lower regular tax calculation.

Amortization — The accounting process whereby the cost of an asset is spread out over its life. Certain intangible assets, such as the goodwill of a business are amortized instead of depreciated (the same process, but for tangible property).

Annuity — A form of insurance in which the insured pays a pre-determined sum either all at once or in installments to a life insurance company. After this time period, which is determined at the start, the purchaser receives a sum of money for a specific period. During the time of contribution, the interest accumulates tax–free until it is withdrawn, at a future date such as retirement. There are many different types of annuities available to the taxpayer including self–directed annuities which qualify for this tax deferred treatment.

Appreciation — An increase in property value for the purpose of tax assessment, resale, insurance, and so on.

Asset — Any property, physical or intangible, that has monetary value.

Auditor — One who inspects and makes a determination of accuracy and completeness of any set of books or records.

Balance Sheet — The section of a business's financial statement which lists the assets, liabilities, and owner's equity.

Basis — The tax cost of any property.

Bond — An evidence of debt issued whenever a corporation or government entity borrows money.

Broker Dealer — The legal designation of a market professional who has a regular place of business and trades for the purpose of market facilitation with the hopes of obtaining a profit. Treats any holdings of stocks and options as if they were inventory items. See *Dealer* and *Market Maker.*

Business Property — Any property used in the process of trying to generate income.

Business Expense — Any expense incurred in the process of trying to generate income.

Call — An option contract which gives the buyer the right to purchase something for a certain price within a specific period of time. In the case of calls on an index, such as the OEX which are settled in cash, it is the right to receive an amount of money based on the call level and the index closing price.

Capital — The sum of a company's long–term debt, capital stock, and surplus. Syn: Paid–in–Surplus.

Capital Appreciation — The increase in the market price of assets owned.

Capital Asset — An asset which is defined in the tax code as property which is **not** (1) an inventory asset, (2) held for sale to customers, (3) a note receivable in the ordinary course of business, (4) depreciable business property, (5) real property used in trade or business, (6) a copyright, or (7) a government publication received from the government.

      Capital Assets are stocks, bonds, securities, or any form of these. Taxpayers must pay the full tax on the capital appreciation, but are limited to a deduction of only $3,000 net loss for any year.

Capital Gain (Loss) — The gain (loss) realized on the sale of a capital asset. The selling price less cost basis.

Carry Forward Loss — Any portion of capital loss not utilized in the current year can be carried forward to future years. It will then be subject to the same $3,000 limitation as in the original year. Individuals can carry capital losses forward for an unlimited amount of time, but corporations will lose them if they are not utilized within five years.

Carryback (Carryforward) — The transfer of one year's tax deductions, losses, or credits backward (or forward) to another year.

Cash Basis — An accounting method of reporting income when received and expenses when paid as opposed to reporting income when earned and expenses when incurred. Ant: Accrual Basis.

Cash Flow — Money received by a business minus money paid out. Cash flow is also defined as net income plus depreciation and depletion which are non–cash expenses.

Certificate of Deposit (CD) — A certificate for a bank deposit which earns a specific interest rate for a given period of time ranging from several days to several years. CDs earn interest in two different ways which directly affect their tax treatment. In most cases, interest is added upon maturity and is taxed at that time. Income may be deferred into future years by investing in a CD to defer the receipt of interest until the maturity date. In some cases, however, interest is added to the CD periodically throughout its life, in which case it is taxed in the year it is received.

Charitable Contribution — A donation to a federally approved charity which is an allowable deduction from adjusted gross income.

Charitable Remainder Trust — A trust set up for the purpose of donating assets to a charity, and where the income stream goes to the donor. The "remainder" or the original property goes to a charity after a certain period of time, stipulated in the trust. This date can be set up as the date of death of the donor or any other date within 20 years of the establishment of the trust.

Charity — An organization whose primary intent is not to create or accumulate wealth for itself. Rather, its primary purpose is to assist others. An approved charity is exempt from federal taxation, and a donation to this type of charity can be deducted on a taxpayer's tax return.

Clifford Trust — A tax–saving device that calls for the return of capital to the grantor (donor) after ten years or more and the payment of income to a beneficiary during that time period. This type of trust was usually set up with a child or elderly parent as the beneficiary and put the income to be taxed for this period in a lower tax bracket. For the most part the Tax Reform Act of 1986 eliminated the tax benefit of this type of trust.

Cost Basis — Money on which tax has been paid. A return of cost basis is a return of capital and not subject to tax.

Compensation — Payment for the performance of services, including fees, salary, commissions, fringe benefits, and similar items.

Current Asset — Property that can be reasonably converted into cash, sold, or consumed during 12 months or less. Current assets include cash, U.S. Government bonds and other highly marketable securities, accounts receivable, and inventories.

Custodian of a Minor — One who manages a gift to a minor under the Uniform Gifts to Minors Act. Also, someone who takes charge of an incompetent's affairs is a custodian.

Dealer — An individual or firm that buys and sells for its own account. Both brokers and specialists may act as dealers, selling to customers from their own inventory, and act as agents who enter into transactions on behalf of their customers. See *Broker–Dealer* and *Market Maker*.

Deduction — An item subtracted from adjusted gross income to arrive at taxable income. Thus, deductions proportionately reduce the amount of tax which will be due.

Deferred Annuity — An annuity that guarantees payment of income, installment payments, or a lump sum to be made at a future date. This type of annuity has preferred tax treatment. The tax on any income earned on the principal is deferred until the money is taken out of the annuity. See *Annuity*.

Deflation — A persistent fall in the general level of prices.

Deferred Revenue — Income which has been received but not earned such as prepaid rent to a landlord. On the landlord's balance sheet it would be listed as a liability.

Depletion — An accounting allowance for the shrinkage or exhaustion of an asset, nearly always a natural asset such as gas or oil.

Depreciation — An amount charged against earnings to allow for the aging of plant and equipment owned by a firm, or any other decline in the value of physical assets. This method of spreading the expense of an asset out over its life although the money might have been paid up front is required. Since the amount is deducted directly from taxable income, the method of calculating depreciation is crucial. The major methods are straight line, double declining balance, and sum–of–the years digits.

Discriminant Function System — A point system the IRS uses to evaluate the taxpayer's return. The deductions are compared to what the IRS considers to be the "norm" for a person in his profession, his geographic area, and his income level. The greater the difference between your tax return and the "norm," the greater your chance is of being selected for an audit. This is only one of several different techniques that the IRS uses to determine who will be audited. See *Taxpayer Compliance Measurement Selection* and *Target Group Selection.*

Dividend — A portion of a corporation's earnings it distributes to its stockholders in proportion to the number of shares owned. Considered to be part of investment income for tax purposes by the stockholder.

Dividend Exclusion — Prior to 1986, there was a $200 per taxpayer, $400 per couple, exclusion on dividend income for individual taxpayers. This was eliminated with the Tax Reform Act of 1986.

Dividend Reinvest — The option to have the company reinvest an investor's dividends automatically when they are paid instead of receiving them; most commonly this is done in mutual funds. The tax treatment of reinvested dividends is the same as for dividends which are not. They are fully taxed, regardless of whether or not the taxpayer actually received them. When the fund is ultimately sold, the taxpayer then adds the amount of dividends on which he has paid tax to his cost basis to arrive at the tax basis of the investment. In doing this, the investor will not be taxed, once again, on a dividend he has already paid tax.

Double Declining Balance Method — An accounting method that charges more for depreciation in a fixed asset's early years and less later.

Dow Jones Industrial Average — The most widely used market indicator composed of 30 large and actively traded issues.

Earmarking Shares of Stock — The assigning of a purchase price to a specific stock. For example, let us assume that an investor had purchased a stock at two different prices. If he bought the first lot at $100 per share and the second lot at $110 per share, he would have the choice as to which lot would be sold first. Depending on his tax situation, an investor could choose to use either the higher or lower tax basis for the stock sold. This is called earmarking the stock. An alternative method for determining which tax basis to use would be the first–in first–out method whereby the first issues purchased become the first issues sold.

Earned Income — Income that is derived from work performed, products sold, and so forth, as opposed to income from investments.

Employee Stock Ownership Plan (ESOP) — The purchase by employees of stock in their own company, usually at less than market price. Prior to 1986 an employee could get preferred tax treatment of such a plan by not taking possession until after retirement; however, the benefit of such plans is now curtailed.

EE Savings Bonds — Treasury Bonds which mature at some later date, usually ten years. Interest is not paid until maturity, although they can be cashed in for less than full value at any time. These bonds have a preferred tax treatment in that you can choose not to declare any taxable income on them until they become due. Also, under certain circumstances, they can be cashed in tax–free if the proceeds are going to pay for a dependent's college tuition. See *Treasury Bonds.*

Equity — Ownership of a company which has value. A stock certificate represents such equity and is often referred to as being the equity.

Escrow — The placement of assets with a third party to ensure the performance of the terms of a contract or some other condition.

Estate Tax — The tax due when an individual dies. The tax is calculated on the taxable estate to which various credits are applied. There is free passage between husband and wife of items in the estate.

Exclusions — An amount of income which is allowed to bypass the taxation process. Such would be the case in the dividend exclusion prior to 1986. Exclusions were significantly limited in the Tax Reform Act.

Exercise — To implement the rights of an option or warrant. For example, a call holder exercises a call or put by buying or selling 100 shares of the underlying stock at the agreed upon price (exercise price).

Fiduciary — A person legally appointed and authorized to represent and act on another's behalf.

Financial Statement — A formal statement of the financial condition of an individual or business rendered by accountants at a particular point in time. For a business, the principal forms of financial statements are the balance sheet and the income statement.

First–in First–out (FIFO) — A method of assessing inventory in which it is assumed that the first items acquired (in) are the first to be sold.

Fiscal Year — Any 12–month period used for a tax or accounting year other than January 1st to December 31st. A calendar year, on the other hand, is specifically the 12–month period from January 1st through December 31st.

Fixed Assets — Tangible physical property owned by a business that is used in the production of income.

Fraud — The act of intentionally misstating income, usually presumed to be such if there is a misstatement of more than 25% of total income, although that number is not fixed. It is more a determination of circumstance and intent rather than of fact.

FTSE 100 — The British equivalent to the Dow Jones Industrial Average.

Futures Contract — A contract calling for the delivery of a commodity or financial instrument at a specific future time for a specified price. Futures contracts, for the most part, are marked to market at year end and treated as if sold, for tax purposes, even if they are not.

General Ledger — The main accounting book for a business. Financial statements are taken directly from this book.

Generation Skipping Transfer Tax — A surtax above and beyond the normal Gift and Estate Tax. This tax is levied upon any transfers made between skipped generations, such as from grandparent to grandchild.

Gift Tax — A tax levied upon the transfer of wealth between two people who are not married. There are levels below which no tax is paid due to the Unified Credit.

Gifting — The process of annually utilizing your maximum exemption so that you pass as much wealth down to future generations, tax–free, as is possible. If you don't use your annual gift tax exclusion, you lose it. It can not be carried forward to the next year.

Grandfathering — The concept of linking an investment to the tax law under which it was purchased. For example, if municipal bonds were tax free one year and then became taxable the next a grandfathering clause in the tax law would allow those people who purchased municipal bonds when they were tax–free to continue to treat them that way as long as they owned the investment.

Hassle Audit — If the audit of one section of a taxpayer's tax return produces no change or very little change, the IRS should not audit the same sections again for at least three years.

Hedging — Reducing risk of loss by taking a position in futures opposite to the position one holds in the current market. The tax treatment of hedges is complex and depends on the type of hedge and the specific business of the hedger.

Hobby Loss — A business which produces a loss on a taxpayer's return for any three out of five years is presumed by the IRS to no longer be a business, but rather a hobby which is not deductible. This is not to say that its decision is final, and you may have the opportunity to prove otherwise. Prior to tax reform the period was a bit more liberal; it was for any two out of five years. There are exceptions to this presumption and the IRS will allow a loss for a longer period of time (such as in thoroughbred horse raising, or in the case of an artist).

Home–In–Office — A deduction allowed for part of the expense of your house or apartment used for business. This can only be deducted now if there is income to deduct it from; you can not use it to create a loss. In most cases, it must be a part of the house which is used **exclusively** for business, and generally must be your only place of business, although there are exceptions to this rule.

Illiquid — The description of an asset which can not be readily turned into cash without paying a penalty for haste.

Income Statement — A financial statement which summarizes business or personal revenues and expenses for a specific fiscal period of time.

Index — A measure of relative value compared with a base quantity for the same series. Stock indexes, such as the OEX, are frequently weighted to reflect the prices and number of shares outstanding. The Dow Jones Industrial Average is another example of an index.

Index Option — An option contract traded on an index most commonly settled for cash. The tax treatment for most index options, such as OEX Index Options, is identical to futures contracts, i.e., marked–to–market at year end.

Individual Retirement Plan (IRA) — A tax sheltered investment plan which allows an investor to accumulate funds for retirement by making tax–deferred contributions to the account. The extent of the immediate tax benefit, through deduction of the contribution, though, depends on the tax circumstances of the taxpayer.

IRA Rollover — The reinvestment of retirement assets to avoid payment of tax on a sum received when terminating a plan, terminating a job, or simply moving retirement assets to another plan.

Installment Sale — The sale of an asset whereby the buyer pays the seller the sales price over a period of time. The gain is recognized in proportion to money received over that same period of time. Can not be done with stocks and several other asset classes.

Intangible Asset — An asset that does not exist physically but has value to an individual or a firm because it can generate income. Such assets are goodwill, franchises, and patents.

Interest — A price paid for the use of money. Interest income is taxed as investment income when received for cash basis taxpayers. Interest expense is deducted when paid by cash basis taxpayers, subject to limitations.

Inventory — General term for the products owned by a business which will be sold in some way. For a Broker–Dealer the term refers to any stock or option he carries for sale to others in the course of his business. Because of this treatment, the Broker–Dealer is not limited to a $3,000 per year loss on these items as is the individual investor or trader.

Investment Interest Expense — The cost of money borrowed in order to carry an investment. Syn: Margin Interest.

Investment Income — Essentially dividends, interest, and capital gains.

Investment Tax Credit — The deduction of a percentage of the cost of new business equipment allowed by the federal government prior to tax reform. It appears as if President Clinton will try to reinstate this credit during his administration.

Junk Bond — A bond with a low quality rating and a high interest rate due to the higher percentage of defaults on these issues.

KEOGH — A tax–deferred retirement savings plan for the self–employed.

Kiddie Tax — The nickname for a surtax charged to children under 14 years of age who have over $1,000 of investment income. This was created under the Tax Reform Act to limit the transfer of income to younger taxpayers in lower tax brackets.

Essentially, anyone in this category pays a tax on unearned income above $1,000 at the parents' higher rate.

GLOSSARY

Last–In First–Out (LIFO) — The accounting method in which items acquired last are counted as those sold first.

Leverage — The use of borrowed capital to increase earnings.

Liabilities — Debts owed by an individual or business entity.

Limited Partnership — A form of business in which one or more partner is liable only to the extent of the amount of dollars they have invested. Limited partners are passive partners and can not participate in management decisions.

Liquidity — The ability to turn an investment into cash without it losing any significant value as a penalty for haste.

Long–Term Capital Gain (Loss) — The taxable gain (loss) that an investor has held over a certain period of time, currently one year. Long–term gains get preferred tax treatment and now are taxed at a maximum 28% rate.

Loophole — A gray area of the tax law which Congress probably would have ruled against if they had seen it. Loopholes are not the way to formulate a strategic tax plan and are used by desperate taxpayers who did not have the foresight to plan properly.

Margin — The amount of equity as a percent of current market value required to be maintained in a margin account.

Margin Interest — The amount of interest charged to an account for maintaining the margin position with less than full amounts of cash in the account. Syn: Investment Interest.

Marked to Market — The adjustment in a brokerage account to make it conform to a new market price. The convention of computing, for tax purposes, a gain or loss on futures positions at the year end closing value, regardless of whether or not the position is sold at that point.

Market Maker — A dealer willing to take the risk of holding a security or option position in order to facilitate trading in that security or option. Syn: Broker–Dealer and Dealer.

Miscellaneous Deductions — The general category of itemized deductions within which certain expenses fall. Examples of this are investment expenses, accounting fees, etc. The Tax Reform Act put strict limitations on the deduction of these expenses.

Mitigating Circumstance — A factor under which the IRS may waive penalties such as underpayment of tax and late filing of a tax return. They are subjective to a certain extent and vary in interpretation from agent to agent.

Monetary Policy — The policy of the Federal Reserve Board that determines the growth and size of the money supply which, in turn, effects interest rates.

Money Market — Collective name for short–term credit instruments which are relatively safe, offer low yield, and are very liquid.

Municipal Bond ("Municipal") — A debt security issued by a state, municipality, or other political subdivision (such as school, park, etc.) to raise money to finance expenditures. Bonds such as these are usually given some degree of tax preference on federal and state tax returns.

Mutual Fund — A type of investment which offers for sale outstanding securities redeemable upon demand for current net asset value. The fund invests in a portfolio of assets and is collectively owned by the owners of shares in the fund. All owners of the fund also share in gains or losses of the fund. Syn: Open–End Investment Company.

National Association of Securities Dealers (NASD) — The self–regulatory agency for the over–the–counter market.

National Association of Security Dealers Automated Quotation Systems (NASDAQ) — The computerized service which provides its subscribers with information on over–the–counter securities. Commonly used as a reference for the OTC market itself.

Nikkei — The Japanese equivalent of the Dow Jones Industrial Average.

Net Worth — Assets minus liabilities of an individual or firm. For a corporation it is shareholder equity.

No–Load — A mutual fund which does not charge a sales commission, usually because it does not employ a sales staff. Shares may be purchased directly through the fund. In the newspaper, the price it is offered at is equal to the net asset value (NAV).

OEX — A market index composed of 100 well–known stocks similar to the Dow Jones Industrial Average: however, somewhat broader based. OEX options are traded on this index are settled monthly for cash. These options are treated as futures contracts for tax purposes.

Option — A contract for the right to buy (or call away from the owner) or the right to sell (or put to the buyer) a certain quantity of a commodity, security, or futures contract at a set price (strike price) by a set time (expiration date). Index options are settled for cash on expiration, and for tax purposes are generally treated as futures contracts.

Ordinary Income — A common nomenclature for income which is not passive or investment in nature.

Original Issue Discount (OID) — A bond issued at a discount from face value. The bond receives no interest, but the discount is taxed as if received annually as ordinary income.

Out–Of–The–Money — Description of a call whose strike price is higher than the market price of the underlying instrument, or a put whose strike price is lower than the market price of the underlying instrument.

Over–the–Counter (OTC) — The market for securities that are not traded on any organized stock exchange.

Partnership — A form of business organization in which two or more individuals enter into a business, pool their resources, and share the profits. The profits flow through to the partners and are taxed on their individual tax returns.

Passive Activity Loss (PAL) — Loss from activities such as limited partnerships where the investors do not materially participate in the management of the business. These losses are only deductible against passive income for tax purposes. Prior to 1986 they were deductible against ordinary income as well and were therefore used extensively as tax shelters.

Passive Income — Income from activities such as limited partnerships where the investors do not materially participate in the management of the business.

Passive Income Generator (PIG) — A profitable passive investment purchased with the expressed purpose of generating income against which PALs can be taken.

Penalty — A fine imposed by a government agency which is not deductible on the tax return.

Pension — A form of investment in which regular contributions are made over a period of time with the earnings reinvested and paid out after retirement.

Portfolio — The total holdings of an individual including stocks, bonds, etc.

Portfolio Income — Income generated from interest, dividends, and capital gains held as investments which are not classified as passive investments. Syn: Investment Income.

Position — The number of shares owned (long position) or number of shares owed (short position) by an individual.

Premium — The amount by which the selling price exceeds the value of the investment.

Prime Rate — The rate of interest charged by commercial banks for short–term loans to its best ("prime") corporate customers.

Private Activity Bonds — Municipal bonds sold by a municipality or subdivision and taxable in varying degrees under the alternative minimum tax.

Problems Resolution Officer — An IRS official who facilitates solutions to problems which may arise between a taxpayer and the IRS.

Proceeds — The actual amount received by the seller of an investment. Gross proceeds is the amount before deducting expenses incurred in the sale. *Net proceeds* is the amount after such expenses are subtracted.

Profit — The excess of income over the cost of obtaining it. For investors, it is difference between the security's cost basis and its sales price.

Proprietorship — A business that has a single owner who is personally liable for all claims against it and solely responsible for raising capital to expand it. No separate income tax return must be filed for such an entity, as the income or loss is reported on the individual's income tax return (Schedule C).

Put — An option contract which gives the buyer the right to sell (or "put to the buyer") a certain quantity of a commodity, security, or futures contract at a set price (strike price) by a set time (expiration date). Index puts, such as those on the OEX, are settled for cash upon expiration and for tax purposes are treated as futures contracts.

Put Warrants — Puts on warrants. See *Warrant*.

Random Selection — Another method of selecting tax returns for audit by the IRS. This selection process has nothing to do with the data on the return, but rather is part of a certain percentage of returns selected at random.

Real Property — Any real estate, including land. The taxation of real property was drastically altered by the Tax Reform Act of 1986 and now provides much less opportunity for use as a tax shelter.

Recession — A slowdown in the business cycle of a nation's economy.

Retained Earnings — The amount of business net income after all dividends have been paid to shareholders.

Retirement Plan — An investment specifically set up as a vehicle to provide for one's retirement. These plans are often set up with a deferral of tax on all earnings within the plan until the money is withdrawn for use after retirement.

Return of Capital — A non–taxable return of investment money to the investor. This has no tax consequence whatsoever.

Rollover — See *IRA Rollover.*

Sales Load — The commission fee charged for the purchase of a mutual fund. Front loads are charged upon purchase and back loads are charged upon sale of the fund.

Self–Directed — Term describing an IRA or KEOGH account actively managed by the owner.

Settlement Date — The date on which a transaction must be settled with cash.

Short Against the Box — The sale of a security the seller owns but prefers not to deliver. This is sometimes done for tax purposes to postpone the recognition of a gain on a security owned while still locking in profit on that security.

Short Sale — The sale of a security the seller does not own but rather borrows to sell. This sale is consummated for tax purposes when the security is either purchased back or delivered out of portfolio by the seller.

Short–Term Capital Gain (Loss) — A capital transaction completed in one year or less.

Simplified Employee Pension Plan (SEP) — A retirement plan in which an employer contributes to an IRA and the employee also makes contributions. This plan is often used by sole proprietors who are the employees as well as the employers.

Small Capitalization Stocks — Stocks with less outstanding shares than the larger "Blue Chip" companies.

Sole Proprietorship — See *Proprietorship.*

Standard and Poors 500 (S&P 500) — A market index composed of 400 industrial stocks, 20 transportation stocks, 40 financial stocks, and 40 utility stocks. Similar to the Dow Jones Industrial Average but broader based. Futures contracts, settled for cash, are traded based upon this average.

Stock — A share of ownership in a corporation which represents a claim on its assets and earnings. For tax purposes, stock is considered to be a capital asset and is subject to the rules on capital gains and capital losses.

Stock Dividend — A dividend in the form of stock rather than cash. In most cases, there is no tax consequence at the time of the dividend, but rather when the stock is sold.

Stock Index — A statistical grouping of prices of selected stocks that tracks the changes in their value for purposes of analysis, investing, and hedging. The construction of such groupings varies. Some are weighted differently than others to reflect imbalances in shares outstanding as well as share price differences. The S&P 500 Index is an example of a stock index.

Stock Index Futures — Futures contracts on various stock indexes which began trading on the commodity exchanges in 1982. One example of these are the S&P futures contracts based on the S&P 500 Index. These are typically settled in cash.

Stock Split — The division of a company's outstanding shares of stock into a larger number of shares without any change in the total value of shares outstanding. As a result, the price of each share falls proportionally. For example, a 2 for 1 stock split of a $100 stock would result in each stockholder having twice as many shares of a stock now worth $50 per share. There is no direct tax consequence to a stock split.

Substantial Element of Pleasure — A subjective determination the IRS occasionally makes in disallowing any number of business deductions or charitable contributions. The IRS will sometimes argue that the taxpayer derived significant enjoyment from an activity that effectively negates the business or charitable nature of these expenses.

Supply Side Economics — A school of economic thought promoted under the Reagan Administration which subscribed to the theory that in order to raise tax revenues the government must lower the tax rates.

Tax Shelter — An investment whereby one can not only earn a return, but also avoid or postpone paying taxes on the income within the structure of the tax law. These have been severely limited in recent years.

Treasury Bill (T–Bill) — A marketable short–term U.S. Government debt security with an expiration date between 30 days and one year from issuance. The T–Bill is taxable upon redemption if held to maturity, and the interest is taxable on the federal return, but tax–free on the state tax return.

Treasury Bond — A marketable long–term U.S. Government debt security with an expiration date between 10 and 30 years from its issuance. It has a fixed rate of interest. A Treasury Bond is also taxable upon redemption if held to maturity, and the interest is taxable on the federal return, although tax–free on the state tax return. There is a provision for paying interest as it is earned, if the taxpayer prefers, instead of waiting until maturity. If the interest is used to pay for a dependent's higher education, in many situations, the interest will be tax–free.

Treasury Note — A marketable medium–term U.S. Government debt security with an expiration date between one and 10 years from issuance. A Treasury note pays interest semi–annually and the interest is taxable upon receipt, on the federal return, although tax–free on the state tax return.

Target Group Selection — Certain professions which have a higher probability of being selected for audit are considered to be "targeted" for the selection process. Doctors and other high income professionals are thought of as some of the targeted groups.

Tax Deferred — A characteristic of certain types of investments which can earn and accrue income for a period of time without tax being paid on the income at that time. The tax will become due at some future point, usually the time the income is withdrawn from the investment.

Tax Simplification — A catchy phrase to describe the process whereby Congress tries to revise and simplify the tax laws at the same time.

Taxpayer Compliance Measurement Program — The official government program of randomly selecting tax returns for audit to determine the public's general level of compliance with the tax laws. This dreaded audit will often inspect every item on the tax return, from the birth certificates of dependents to the validity of the signatures on the tax return.

Total Return Investment Planning (TRIP) — The process of factoring tax liability into the calculation of investment yield to arrive at "true yield."

Trader — A specific classification of investor who tries to capture very short–term trading moves. The designation of "trader" is a somewhat subjective one and the law is ambiguous. The tax advantages the trader enjoys over the investor are significant. He can deduct 100% of his investment interest and other trading expenses instead of being limited to many new restrictions passed under the Tax Reform Act. There are several cases which establish legal precedent for this designation. However, due to the higher stakes now involved, many cases will probably be challenged in the near future.

   Factors weighed by the courts include the level of trading activity, the basis for making a trade, and the profit objectives of the trader. This is not an easy area of the tax law and the determination can have significant ramifications for the taxpayer involved. Get professional help with this if you have any doubts as to how to set it up.

Trust — The legal transfer of property to one person, called the trustee, who holds it for the benefit of another person, called the beneficiary. The trustee is usually expected to invest the property so that it yields income, and generally has the power to sell, mortgage, or lease it as the need arises. The trustee has a fiduciary responsibility to the beneficiary, which simply means that the trustee must put the benefit of the beneficiary above all other factors.

Unearned Income — Income derived from investments that is not related to any kind of service. It includes both investment income and passive income.

Unified Credit — A lifetime exemption from gift or estate taxes of the first $600,000 of property. This is above and beyond the annual exclusions for gifts and the marital exemption for estates.

Unified Gift To Minors Act (UGMA) — The act that permits gifts of money and securities to be given to minors while allowing adults to act as custodians.

Venture Capital — Money earmarked for a high risk and potentially high rate of return investment. Often the capital is lost on many endeavors before a profitable one is found. It is anticipated that at some point a large enough profit will be made on at least one of the investments so as to offset and produce overall profit for the investor.

Warrant — A security giving the holder the right to purchase securities at a stipulated price. This is usually a long–term instrument, affording the investor the option of buying shares at a later date at the subscription price, subject to the warrant's exercise.

Wash Sale—A sale is considered to be a wash sale if it resulted in a loss and the item is purchased again within 30 days of the time it was sold. Wash sale losses can not be taken as tax losses as they are deemed to be tax–motivated transactions. There are no restrictions, however, on selling an item for a gain and then repurchasing it within 30 days.

Write Off — The act of deducting an expenditure on your tax return.

Index

Index

298